EUROPEAN LABOUR PROTEST 1848-1939

European Labour
Protest 1848-1939

Dick Geary

ST. MARTIN'S PRESS NEW YORK

Library of Congress Cataloging in Publication Data

Geary, Dick.
    European labor protest, 1848-1939.
    Bibliography: p.182
    Includes index.
    1. Labor and laboring classes—Europe—History.
2. Labor disputes—Europe—History. I. Title.
HD8376.G4 1981   331.89'294   81-4474

ISBN 0-312-26974-9   AACR2

CONTENTS

PREFACE

This book does not attempt to provide a chronological history of the various labour movements which came into existence on the European continent in the period after 1848. Rather it seeks to examine some of the major issues involved in the study of European labour protest against the evidence of several countries, of France, Germany and Britain in the main, though also of Austria, Italy, Spain and Russia to a lesser extent. It will ask what kinds of workers initiated different types of protest at different points in time and why; how the shape of labour protest developed from place to place and over time; whether it is meaningful to talk of the 'embourgeoisement' of European labour in the period before 1914; and why the inter-war years were characterised by revolution and intense social conflict in some countries and not in others. In all of these cases more questions will be raised than answered; an outcome which is perhaps inevitable in an area of such complexity and unavoidable given the infant state of labour history in most European countries, with the definite exception of Britain and the possible exception of France. Of principal concern will be the protests of ordinary working men, of the rank and file of the labour movement, rather than the ideologies and concerns of their ostensible leaders. Indeed, this distinction will loom large in the following pages.

In attempting to cover such a vast area, what follows is necessarily dependent upon a synthesis of the work of others, excepting some sections on Germany; however, it is written from a standpoint which is often far removed from that of the original authors. It has also benefited from the advice and help of countless colleagues and students at the universities of Cambridge and Lancaster. In particular I would like to express my gratitude to my original research supervisors, Dr Jonathan Steinberg and Dr E.H. Carr, and to Martin Blinkhorn, Geoff Crossick, Ralph Gibson and Gordon Phillips. Much that is valuable was suggested by them. The errors and eccentricities of what follows are my own.

ABBREVIATIONS

ADGB:	General Confederation of German Free Trade Unions
ASE:	British Amalgamated Society of Engineers
CGL:	Italian Trade Union Confederation
CGT:	French Trade Union Confederation (Anarcho-syndicalist to 1914, socialist 1921 to early 1936, socialist and Communist 1936 onwards)
CGTU:	French Communist Trade Union Federation (1921 to early 1936)
CNT:	Spanish anarcho-syndicalist Union Federation
DMV:	German Metalworkers' Union
KAPD:	German Communist Workers' Party (broke away from KPD, 1920)
KPD:	German Communist Party
PCF:	French Communist Party
PCI:	Italian Communist Party
PSI:	Italian Socialist Party
PSOE:	Spanish Socialist Party
SFIO:	United French Socialist Party (1905 onwards)
SPD:	German Social Democratic Party
SPÖ:	Austrian Social Democratic Party
THES:	*Times Higher Education Supplement*
UGT:	Spanish Trade Union Federation (socialist)
USPD:	Independent German Social Democratic Party (broke away from SPD in 1917 and rejoined in 1922)

1 INTRODUCTION

In nineteenth- and early-twentieth-century Europe government authorities and the traditional ruling strata viewed various forms of lower-class protest almost always as the work of 'agitators', 'conspirators' or preferably 'outsiders'. Thus the British government of 1842 attempted to portray the confused strikes and riots of that bitter year as a coherent and concerted conspiracy, the so-called 'Plug Plot'. Thus King Frederick William IV of Prussia chose to believe that the revolution of 1848 had been 'systematically prepared' by unsavoury characters dwelling in foreign parts; and thus many European governments mistook the insurrection of the Paris Commune in 1871 for the work of an international organisation of conspirators, Karl Marx's International Working Men's Association (the First International). As late as 1918 many German aristocrats, and not only they, could believe quite firmly that the November Revolution of that year was brought about by the machinations of Slavs and Jews.

That the upper crust should see the mechanics of protest in such a blinkered fashion is hardly surprising. To lay the blame for disruption on a small minority of ungrateful misfits, 'alien scum' or even 'politically motivated' trade union leaders was and in some quarters still is good propaganda. The limited horizons of an entrenched but fearful elite are further and easily explained in terms of the isolation or limited social intercourse of such a group. What is more difficult to explain and certainly less excusable is that historians of the socialist and labour movements have themselves so often resorted to a modified version of the conspiracy theory. In this context British labour historiography is the exception rather than the rule. The relative absence and insignificance of inspiring ideological controversy or institutional socialism in Britain before the turn of the century in a sense obliged historians to turn their attention to the 'grass-roots' activity of ordinary working men (and more rarely women) in the absence of anything more exciting. On the Continent, however, things were different. The early appearance of revolutionary socialism in France and Germany and the subsequent emergence of mass Communist movements there and elsewhere, the Civil War in Spain and even more the Bolshevik Revolution in Russia immediately and understandably excited interest and have since held the attention of laymen and scholars. An unfortunate consequence of

13

this, however, has been that at least until recently what passed as the history of working-class movements in the various countries of Europe was in reality nothing of the sort. Only a few years ago what purported to be a course on 'European Labour Movements' in an English university consisted primarily of an examination of a series of intellectual and ideological debates — Marx *v*. Bakunin, Kautsky *v*. Bernstein, Russian populism, French anarcho-syndicalism — rather than a study of the activities of labouring men and women.[1] Such areas of enquiry are perfectly legitimate, of course; and it is hardly surprising that academics should be interested in matters intellectual. But the relationship of these ideologies to the concrete historical development of the labour and socialist movements is at best tangential. Even at the level of the leadership of what has often been regarded as the most doctrinaire of all European socialist parties before 1914, the German Social Democratic Party (SPD), there is overwhelming evidence of at best misunderstanding and more often of ignorance of or indifference towards Marxist theory.[2] If this was true of labour's ostensible leaders, then how much more problematical it is to assess what Marxism meant to the rank and file of the party. We do know, however, that when they did borrow books from trade union or party libraries — and most did not — they normally took away works of escapist fiction.[3] For France we know that the industrial behaviour of supposed anarcho-syndicalists differed little from that of their non-anarchist colleagues; whilst one eminent leader of the French anarcho-syndicalist trade union organisation, the Confédération Générale du Travail (CGT), on being asked his opinion of the theories of Georges Sorel, replied that he only read Alexandre Dumas![4] Much of what follows will provide further evidence of ideological ignorance or confusion on the part of the membership of various socialist parties and radical groups.

Obviously there have been innumerable studies of the non-ideological history of European labour; but most of these have been institutional histories of political parties and trade unions. Such work needs to be done; but most of it has been written from the top downwards: divisions within the labour movement have been seen through the eyes of union and party leaders rather than through the ordinary experience of the working-class rank and file. Most arguments to the effect that the German labour movement became less radical in the period before the First World War, for example, are based on an analysis of the behaviour and attitudes of the party leadership of the SPD; whilst the Russian Revolution has usually been analysed in terms of the history of the Bolshevik and Menshevik parties and the personality of Lenin rather than the work experience of ordinary Russians, despite recent attempts to correct the balance.[5]

There are several reasons why the institutional and leadership approach fails to do justice to the history of the European socialist movement. In the first place, most of the socialist parties which came into existence in the nineteenth century and some of their Communist successors were mass political movements, involving thousands, even hundreds of thousands, of members: on the eve of the First World War the SPD had a membership of over a million, for example. In addition these organisations, at least in their early days, were democratic and their rank and file had some, albeit a declining, influence on the decision-making process. There were also occasions on which rank and file opposition to official leadership became manifest, as we shall see. Hence any adequate attempt to grapple with the history of the SPD, of the French Socialist Party, the SFIO (Section Française de l'Internationale Ouvrière), or of the Italian Socialist Party (PSI), will have to take into account the attitudes and activities of the working-class rank and file.

At this point, however, further difficulties arise. Even if we were able to construct an adequate history of the organised socialist move-ment, vast areas of labour protest would remain unexplored. Many workers joined trade unions and the ranks of industrial protest – strikes, for example – and yet refused or did not consider extending their support to organised socialism, most obviously in Britain. Perhaps even more significantly, most workers belonged to no organisation at all before 1914, even in the advanced industrial nations of Europe: on the eve of the First World War no more than 9 per cent of the French, 25 per cent of the German and slightly more of the British labour force had been recruited into economic or political organisations. Not only that, but many workers who had never been organised previously often participated in strikes and even more radical forms of activity. The 'unorganised', for example, played a major role in the strike waves of 1905 in Germany and Russia, in the revolutionary events in the latter country in 1917 and in the former in 1918, as they also did in the French upheavals of 1936. Any study of labour protest, therefore, cannot restrict its concerns solely to ideologies, institutions or leaders.

It is true that a great deal of time and effort has recently been expen-ded in the analysis of strikes and in particular of strike demands.[6] The argument goes that these will tell us exactly what mattered to ordinary workers, far more so than the reflections and statements of their would-be leaders. However, it is not clear to me that strike demands will indicate the whole range of working-class grievances and ambitions:

strikers will often ask for what they think they can get, rather than for everything they desire. More importantly, failure to strike by no means necessarily indicates satisfaction with the existing economic, social and political order. As we will see, there are circumstances in which to strike is either impossible, dangerous or simply counter-productive; yet at the same time these non-striking workers could protest in a variety of ways: by lowering productivity, absenteeism, the *threat* of going on strike.

This last point raises yet further problems. This book is primarily concerned with collective protest; but what of individual protests against industrialism or the capitalist system? Is increased alcoholism a form of protest? Might not the most effective form of protest to the new industrial order in mid- and late-nineteenth century Europe have been emigration to the New World? Is absenteeism a continuation of 'pre-industrial' behaviour in a novel setting or a genuine objection to prevailing economic reality? The answer might vary from case to case, from individual to individual; but what the present work is concerned with is collective responses to the problems of industrial society and primarily those that have taken some organised form, even if only for a short period of time. In particular, it is concerned with *why* certain groups of workers did join together to combat exploitation and oppression.

When the emphasis is shifted from political and trade union leaders to the experience of ordinary working people, then attention must move away from ideological considerations towards the real grievances of the worker, both in the factory and at home. Most obviously there is a connection between raw economic data and labour protest. Inflation, for example, provided the stimulus to strike activity in several European countries between 1910 and 1914, as it did to the massive post-war upheaval in Central Europe. Yet it would be extremely dangerous to assume that poverty or impoverishment are the direct causes of radical labour protest. In fact, the relationship between living standards and labour protest is highly complex: the first groups of industrial workers to participate in organised protest, form trade unions and join socialist political parties were almost invariably recruited from the relatively well paid sections of the work-force. This would suggest that the simple explanation of industrial and political militancy in terms of poverty will not do, despite the fact that the theory is far from dead.[7] It is true that economic insecurity has favoured radicalism in certain circumstances: the background to Luddism, 'physical force' Chartism and the riots of 1842 in England was acute unemployment. This also provided the mainstay of support for the German Communist Party (KPD) between the wars. Yet unemployment could also militate against trade union organisation and reduced the temptation to strike throughout most of this period: in times of high unemployment the militant worker could be replaced relatively easily and his bargaining power was thus significantly reduced. Again it was the more secure workers who first organised and participated in strikes most frequently. The relationship between skill, high wages and job security is equally clear; and it is of the utmost significance that it was such skilled workers who formed the rank and file of trade unions and political parties of labour in Britain, France and Germany before the First World War. The unskilled, on the other hand, both before and after 1914 were to prove much more difficult to mobilise for any length of time, although they were to prove especially volatile at times of economic and political crisis, as we will see.

In addition to wage rates, levels of unemployment and skill differentials, factory size appears to have had some, albeit a disputed, influence on the structure of industrial and political protest. In some places, for example in Russia between 1910 and 1918[8] and in Germany in the course of a virtual civil war after 1918,[9] there seems to have been a connection between political radicalism and employment in large-scale concerns. However, in Germany before the First World War the largest concerns tended to possess the most quiescent labour force, in the sense that few employees joined unions — other than the 'yellow' unions of the bosses — and strike rates were relatively low.[10] On the other hand, it might again be argued that such quiescence was the temporary consequence of the strong bargaining power of employers and that when social upheaval undermined that power, these workers were to prove themselves extremely volatile once more.[11] In addition to the mere size of economic units, however, the organisation of the work processes and the structure of authority therein could generate a host of grievances against increasing discipline,[12] harsh foremen — a perennial complaint[13] — and the like. On the other hand, potential protesters might easily be deterred where the employer monopolised the local labour market, tied pension schemes to good behaviour (= abstinence from industrial disputes), and perhaps also, as was the case in the rapidly expanding industrial towns of the Ruhr before 1914, provided company housing.

This last point leads us into another set of variables which had a profound influence on the class consciousness and actions of the industrial proletariat: the home environment of the worker. Where his house was owned by the employer, there the risks involved in strike activity were huge and manifest, as the bosses never tired of pointing out: for involvement in strike or union activities might entail almost immediate eviction. Where workers lived in socially homogeneous communities, it has been argued, they were much more likely to develop some form of solidaristic working-class consciousness: so David Crew has attempted to explain the frequent resort to collective industrial action on the part of coal-miners in Bochum.[14] Metalworkers in mixed residential communities, on the other hand, displayed less solidarity and less militancy; and studies of working-class attitudes in Britain as late as the 1960s suggest the same importance for residential segregation.[15] Joan Scott has argued that the transition from passivity to industrial and political action on the part of glassworkers in the French town of Carmaux was at least partly related to their increasing contact in the home environment with miners with prior traditions of organisation;[16] whilst Erhard Lucas has argued that the violence which accompanied industrial and political conflict in the Ruhr town of Hamborn in the course of the German Revolution was to a certain extent a reflection of a social environment that was more generally drunken and violent.[17]

The worker, then, found himself in a situation at home and at work in which he — forgive the masculine shorthand, for the pressures to which the female worker was subject were at least as great and normally infinitely more oppressive — was subjected to multiple pressures; but the way in which he experienced and reacted to these pressures was not a simple consequence of purely material concerns but also a consequence of inherited values and expectations. One possible explanation for the superficially paradoxical fact that many of the early trade union and socialist militants were in fact relatively skilled and highly paid is that they were people with high and perhaps even rising expectations; whilst some of the most radical workers came from groups who had known better days and who were reacting to a threat not only to their livelihood but also to their skills, independence and status (English handloom weavers in the first half of the nineteenth century, for example). This last theme also recurs in later stages of industrialisation with the introduction of new technology and the radicalisation of those workers affected by deskilling (Carmaux glassworkers, skilled engineers on 'Red Clydeside' at the end of the First World War). Equally, as we shall see in the case of Spain later,[18] peasants from areas which possessed traditions of rural radicalism carried their hostility to authority into the factories of Catalonia, whilst those with a conservative rural background behaved differently. In fact, groups with traditionally low expectations (Irish immigrants in England, Polish workers in Germany, peasants from East Elbia or the impoverished French countryside, women workers almost everywhere) entered the ranks of organised protest — strikes, trade union and party political membership — relatively late in the day.

To say they did not 'protest' might be inaccurate in so far as individual acts of violence, the seeking of solace through the bottle or even the confessional box, were by no means uncommon. But it does seem clear, as Shorter and the Tillys have argued,[19] that the dislocation theory of protest — the alienation of rural men and women in a new and hostile urban environment — does not work, at least for organised collective action. There seems to be something of a time-lag between the uprooting and participation in what might be described as new forms of protest adapted to the industrial order: thus lengthy residence in a particular town was often a characteristic of those skilled workers throughout Europe who first formed trade unions.[20]

An analysis of these different variables across what are in certain respects artificial national boundaries reveals an astonishing similarity of behaviour on the part of certain occupational groups which defies any supposed 'national characteristic'. Printers, engineering workers and their like formed the rank and file of stable union organisation in Britain, France, Germany and elsewhere from an early date. The unskilled were almost invariably the most volatile in their behaviour. Almost everywhere strike waves corresponded to times of low unemployment. Hence the activities of labour protesters in the industrial sphere do seem to follow a pattern amenable to considerable and significant generalisation.

Sadly — for those who prefer history in some kind of schematic strait-jacket — this picture of tidiness disintegrates when we turn to the question of *political* action. It may be possible to produce some general formulae which govern the transition from industrial to political militancy — that is, why workers engage in conflicts not only with their employers through strikes and unionisation but also either with the state (attempting to overthrow the existing political order) or in struggles for a share in political decision-making within the existing political framework. Indeed, the first chapter of this book is concerned with the provision of precisely such formulae.[21] However, it remains true that the political identity of European labour movements has registered huge temporal and national variations; and it seems to me that further non-economic variables here intrude, in particular the attitudes of other sections of society and principally of the state towards labour itself.

Most obviously, a repressive state apparatus can transform economic into revolutionary struggles through direct military intervention, as happened in Russia in 1905. The brutality of the Guardia Civilia in Spain bred working-class violence in response. The prohibition of legal channels of protest could lead protest over wages and working conditions into violent insurrection, as it did in France in the 1830s on more than one occasion, and in Britain too in the early nineteenth century. On the other hand, the *relatively* liberal institutions of late-nineteenth century Britain obviously bear some of the responsibility for working-class reformism; whilst the semi-autocratic constitutional system of Germany's Second Reich, something of a half-way house between 'democratic' England and 'autocratic' Russia, bred a labour movement which could never really decide whether it wished to be reformist or revolutionary. No such choice existed for Lenin and his colleagues. Conversely, of course, working-class radicalism could breed state repression; whilst the liberal character of the British state was at least in part the result of the absence of a genuinely revolutionary labour movement. Chicken and egg.

The same could be said of the relationship between the consciousness of working men and the attitudes adopted towards them by other social groups. Where liberal values survived in the middle class — perhaps even where there simply was a middle class — and in particular where collective bargaining did not encounter the intransigent hostility of employers — as it did in France and Germany in the main before 1914 — there industrial relations did not produce any automatic road to political agitation or socialism, as the history of the English working class and the laments of Engels so readily testify. (Hence also the Leninist theory, still with us in, for example, East German historiography and John Foster's controversial study of mid-nineteenth century Oldham, which basically argues that the working class remains doomed to a purely 'economistic' consciousness without the intervention of the party or at least a radical intelligentsia.[22]) On the other hand, the very rapidity with which at least some sections of the German bourgeoisie forsook liberal values and the autocratic management which confronted German workers in their factories clearly contributed to the formation of a labour movement with its own independent political institutions in the 1860s. Often, in fact, it becomes difficult to disentangle economic and political struggles, as Rosa Luxemburg pointed out in the case of the 1905 revolution in Russia.[23] There are also cases in which the same group of workers seems to have fluctuated between industrial and political protest, depending upon the economic conjuncture.[24]

Finally, some words of explanation and some of warning. In explanation of the terminology which is doubtless employed in far too cavalier a fashion in both the preceding and the following pages, I have used industrial action to refer to forms of protest directed against the employer and working conditions in an immediate sense rather than against the whole of the prevailing social and political reality. This action has consisted chiefly in go-slows, strikes and various forms of trade union activity. Political action I have taken to refer to action through political institutions – parties, revolutionary societies – or that is concerned with the overthrow of existing political institutions. This distinction, as has already been pointed out, is more than a little forced. Strikes for higher wages can lead to the fall of governments. Complaints about the structure of authority in the factory could easily be defined as 'political'. However, the distinction retains some validity, as certain groups of workers were economically militant but never politically radical.

'Militancy' is a term I have normally used to describe frequent *industrial* protest (unless the term has been preceded by the qualifying adjective *political*). 'Radical' I have tried to reserve for those people and their actions which have demanded more than a short-term improvement in living standards and some kind of structural reordering of the economy and of politics (socialisation, rule by workers' councils, replacement of the prevailing economic, social and political elites). 'Revolutionary' covers much the same ground; whilst 'reformist' implies a belief in and concentration on improvements in the condition of labour by piecemeal reform within the prevailing economic and social order. Again these categories are far from watertight. Some 'reformists' believed that piecemeal reform would eventually lead to the overthrow of capitalist property relations. Some of those who demanded socialisation did so simply to protect their jobs, rather than through any millenarian mission. But again I hope these terms will help to delineate what were also real differences in outlook and activity between different groups of workers.

This leads me to my words of warning. At the level of theory it may be possible to distinguish between a 'revolutionary' labour movement in, say, Russia or Catalonia, and a 'reformist' working class in Britain and southern Germany; but to manipulate these distinctions in this – by no means uncommon – way may be to play slave to an inappropriate terminology that says more about the attitude of intellectuals than about workers themselves. It could – and will – be argued, in fact, that the basic motivation of both Russian and English workers was identical and nothing more than the desire to fill their bellies; but the rectification of these immediate material grievances entailed different strategies because of the surrounding circumstances which differed so greatly from country to country. In particular, the rectification of those grievances in Russia in 1917 involved the ending of the war, which in turn involved the overthrow of first the Tsarist and then the Provisional government. It was the framework, not different 'levels of consciousness', which made the difference.

The following chapters are organised into three principal sections, to a certain extent chronologically, although some specific themes and arguments are illustrated with data from more than one chronological period. Chapter 2, 'The Emergence of Organised Protest', is concerned with the differences between industrial and preindustrial protest, with why an organised labour movement had emerged in several parts of Europe by the 1860s; and with the social composition of the rank and file of that movement. To treat these themes, data has been drawn from an earlier time span in Britain, as industrialisation occurred there in advance of the Continent. Equally obviously, some valuable comparative data can be taken from the later experiences of Russia and to a lesser extent Spain and Italy, where the major impact of industry was felt later. Chapter 3, 'Maturation and Organisation 1890-1914' − with maturation here used in a sense which is in no way intended to be normative − deals with the massive growth and institutionalisation of labour protest in the period before the First World War and attempts to answer the question as to whether any process of deradicalisation took place at this time. Chapter 4, 'War, Revolution and Emergence of Communism', attempts to explain the emergence of mass radical and Communist movements and yet at the same time to do justice to the absence of a real revolutionary impulse on any significant scale in inter-war Britain. It also confronts the central problem of labour's failure to conquer power almost everywhere and even to survive the Fascist onslaught in some places. In many ways the experiences of Fascism, the Second World War and then the Cold War changed the face of labour protest; but that is another story.

Notes

1.   This was true of a course of the University of Lancaster in 1973. The course has changed radically since then.
2.   Hans-Josef Steinberg, *Sozialismus und Sozialdemokratie* (Hanover, 1969).
3.   Ibid., Ch. 6.
4.   Peter N. Stearns, *Revolutionary Syndicalism and French Labour* (New Brunswick, 1971). For the quotation see Edouard Dolléans, *Histoire du Mouvement Ouvrier*, vol. 2, *1871-1936* (Paris, 1946), p. 130.
5.   J.M.L. Keep, *The Russian Revolution: a Study in Mass Mobilization* (Westfield, 1976).
6.   Such a concern plays a large role in Stearns's analysis of French syndicalism

and also in his *Lives of Labour. Work in a Maturing Industrial Society* (London, 1975), Ch. 9. Also Edward Shorter and Charles Tilly, *Strikes in France 1830-1968* (Cambridge, 1974); David Crew, *Town in the Ruhr. A Social History of Bochum, 1860-1914* (New York, 1979); Albin Gladen, 'Die Streiks der Bergarbeiter' in Jürgen Reulecke (ed.), *Arbeiterbewegung an Rhein und Ruhr* (Wuppertal,1974), pp. 113-67.

7.   Such a 'poverty' explanation of protest appears in Stefano Merlo, *Proletario di fabbrica e capitalismo industriale* (Milan, 1978); and in Jürgen Tampke, *The Ruhr and Revolution in the Rhenish-Westphalian Industrial Region 1912-1919* (London, 1979) in an attempt to explain different levels of radicalism amongst the Ruhr communities.

8.   Leopold Haimson, 'The Problem of Social Stability in Urban Russia, 1905-1917' in Clive Emsley (ed.), *Conflict and Stability in Europe* (London, 1979), pp. 235-46.

9.   Peter von Oertzen, *Betriebsräte in der Novemberrevolution* (Düsseldorf, 1963), p. 275; Richard Comfort, *Revolutionary Hamburg* (Stanford, California, 1966), Ch. 8; Dick Geary, 'Radicalism and the German Worker: Metalworkers and Revolution 1914-1923' in Richard J. Evans (ed.), *Society and Politics in Wilhelmine Germany* (London, 1978), p. 278; Gerald D. Feldman, 'Socio-economic Structures in the Industrial Sector and Revolutionary Potentialities, 1917-22' in Charles L. Bertrand (ed.), *Revolutionary Situations in Europe, 1917-1922: Germany, Italy, Austria-Hungary* (Montreal, 1977), pp. 159-68.

10.   Harvey Mitchell and Peter N. Stearns, *Workers and Protest. The European Labour Movement, the Working Classes and the Origins of Social Democracy 1890-1914* (Itasca, Illinois, 1971), p. 172.

11.   See below, pp. 125f. and p. 143f.

12.   This was the case at Siemens, for example. See Jurgen Kocka, *Unternehmerverwaltung und Angestelltenschaft* (Stuttgart, 1969), p. 65.

13.   Stearns, *Lives of Labour*, p. 168.

14.   Crew, *Bochum*, pp. 186-94.

15.   Ibid., p. 191f.

16.   Joan Wallach Scott, *The Glassworkers of Carmaux* (Cambridge, Mass., 1974), pp. 117f.

17.   Erhard Lucas, *Arbeiterradikalismus:Zwei Formen von Radikalismus in der deutschen Arbeiterbewegung* (Frankfurt am Main, 1976).

18.   See below, p. 79f.

19.   Shorter and Tilly, *Strikes in France 1830-1968*, pp. 5-9.

20.   This would at least explain to some extent why unskilled workers, who in certain places moved around regularly, were less amenable to organisation. See Stephen Thernstrom, *Poverty and Progress. Social Mobility in a Nineteenth Century City* (Cambridge, Mass., 1964); Robert J. Bezucha, 'The "Pre-Industrial" Worker Movement: the *Canuts* of Lyon' in Emsley, *Conflict*, p. 49; Charles Tilly, 'How Protest Modernised in France, 1845-1855' in William O. Aydelotte, Allen G. Borgue and Robert Vogel (eds.), *The Dimensions of Quantitative Research in History* (Oxford, 1972), p. 204f.; and Richard Tilly, 'Popular Disorders in Nineteenth Century Germany', *Journal of Social History*, no. 1 (1970), vol. IV, pp. 25-30. However, there are problems with this contention. The prologue to the foundation of unions covering more than a single locality has often been a degree of mobility within a relatively broad area *where* the workers involved were moving from identical job to identical job. This is the contention of David Crew, 'Regionale Mobilität und Arbeiterklasse. Das Beispiel Bochum' in *Geschichte und Gesellschaft* (1975), pp. 99-120; and of Heilwig Schomerus, *Die Arbeiter der Maschinenfabrik Esslingen* (Stuttgart, 1977), p. 77.

21.   See below, pp. 47-70.

22.   For the East German view see the *Geschichte der deutschen Arbeiter-bewegung* published by the Central Committee of the East German Communist Party in many volumes in Berlin in 1966; and John Foster, *Class Conflict in the Industrial Revolution* (London, 1974).

23.   See the relevant selections from Rosa Luxemburg's writings in Robert Looker (ed.), *Rosa Luxemburg. Selected Political Writings* (London, 1972), pp. 117-34.

24.   As in the case of some British Chartists. See Malcolm I. Thomis and Peter Holt, *Threats of Revolution in Britain 1789-1848* (London, 1977), p. 119; and David Jones, *Chartism and the Chartists* (London, 1975), p. 140. Also Asa Briggs, *Chartist Studies* (London, 1977), pp. 5ff.

THE EMERGENCE OF ORGANISED PROTEST

Introduction

Modern forms of protest, characterised by the struggle between employers and employees over wages and working conditions, by the use of the strike as a major weapon, by organisation locally and nationally over time, has clearly been related to the growth of industrial society; but, of course, the onset of what we know as the Industrial Revolution has varied enormously from place to place, as has the rapidity of its development. By 1848, the ostensible starting-point of this study, Britain had undergone almost a century of rapid economic development, employing new technology and large-scale production in some sectors, in particular textiles, although factory workers still constituted a numerical minority of the total labour force and in some sections of industry domestic and artisanal manufacture not only survived but even continued to grow. What this entailed was that by 1848 innumerable forms of working-class protest had already developed in Britain: Luddism, strikes, trade union organisation, even labour involvement in politics in the shape of Chartism. On the Continent things were different. In France the first major burst of economic modernisation came between 1830 and 1848 under the July monarchy: textile industries developed around Lille, Rouen and Mülhouse (Alsace), this last area being almost as technologically advanced as Lancashire, whilst coal and metallurgical industries found a home in the Loire basin around St Etienne. Further and more profound growth followed in the Second Empire (1852-70) with the extension of the rail network and the opening of a more modern mining and metallurgical sector in the north-east. However, throughout the nineteenth century and to some extent even into the twentieth France possessed a large and backward artisanal sector, with significant implications for the nature and scale of labour protest, as we will see. With industrial growth in France from the 1830s, none the less, came the formation of working-class friendly societies, co-operatives, trade unions and even revolutionary secret societies. In Germany the working class only began to engage in such activities on a significant scale after 1848; and this, of course, reflected the relatively late point of industrial take-off. However, from the 1850s Germany experienced a spectacularly rapid process of industrialisation, above all in coal, iron and steel. This produced gigantic concerns in heavy industry with a concentrated labour force, side by side with small-scale manufacture in other areas; and as we will see, this was again a fact of some significance for the rapid emergence and large scale of labour protest, but also for its fragmented nature. Spain possessed a textile industry which had formed as early as the eighteenth century in Catalonia, but witnessed a subsequent decline; and a heavy industrial sector in the northern Basque provinces, which was formed much later and with the help of foreign capital. Not surprisingly, labour protest assumed different forms in these two distinct areas. Italy remained economically backward really until after the turn of the century but then witnessed massive and rapid heavy industrial growth in the Turin-Genoa-Milan triangle. Russia began to modernise only in the 1860s and 1870s; but up to the First World War the overwhelming mass of the population remained untouched by the faltering attempts to create an industrial state. However, the industry that existed was heavily dependent upon either the Tsarist bureaucracy or foreign investment. This had enormous implications for social conflict, above all in terms of the relative absence of an independent bourgeoisie, as we shall see. Furthermore, what industry there was used highly modern technology and entailed a huge concentration of the industrial labour force in a few giant concerns, the most famous of which was the Putilov works in St Petersburg.

With the development of industry came a development in the structure of labour protest which can be crudely — qualifications will be made subsequently — classified in the following way.

Preindustrial Protest

The classic example of this type of protest was the food riot, extremely common in virtually all European countries in the eighteenth century, which began to decline in importance after 1850 in the more industrialised states but which was far from extinct at a much later date. Riots against conscription, increases in taxation and the like also fall into this category. In most cases this kind of protest was typified by direct and often violent action. It tended to be sporadic and lacked a stable organisational framework. Normally it was highly localised and often it had a mixed social basis. In a sense, therefore, preindustrial protest was the 'spontaneous reaction' of a socially amorphous crowd to immediate pressures. However, as we shall see, such protest was far from 'irrational', was predicated upon a prevalent set of social values, often involved certain kinds of elementary organisation and was sometimes successful, at least temporarily. In short, preindustrial protest, although far removed from more modern conflicts between employer and employee over working conditions, was equally distinct from 'mindless violence', as prejudiced contemporaries and latter-day commentators have sometimes maintained.

Early Industrial Protest

In this category I would include Luddism in early-nineteenth-century Britain and the machine breaking which was endemic in France and Germany in the 1830s and 1840s. This type of protest exhibited many of the characteristics of earlier protest: in the main it was localised, sporadic, lacking in formal organisation over time, and it was often violent. Once again, however, we will see that such action was far from mindless, that it often involved elementary forms of organisation, at least at a local level, and that it was also often successful in achieving certain short-term goals. It is perhaps best regarded as 'bargaining by riot'. There were ways, however, in which early industrial protest looked to the future, as well as to the past; for although it was often directed against the new values of *laissez-faire* industrialism and was initiated by groups whom economic modernisation rendered marginal, it was also clearly engendered by the process of industrialisation and in many cases constituted a bitter conflict between the owners of capital and their employees. It might be argued that this type of violent protest represented problems of adjustment during the early stages of industrialisation and hence may not be irrelevant to an understanding of, say, the militancy of Russian workers in the early twentieth century. The category could also comprehend certain types of struggle in rural areas, most obviously, perhaps, the Swing riots in Britain in 1830: for here too was a movement of rural wage-earners concerned to protect their living standards and which engaged in certain kinds of machine breaking.[1]

Modern Industrial Protest

This last category is typified less by the use or threat of physical violence, or rioting, although both remained common in industrialised nations in the twentieth century, but rather by the use of industrial muscle, in particular the use of the strike as the dominant tactic, together with the creation of formal organisations, trade unions and political parties of labour, which have a relatively stable and continuous existence. What we are dealing with here is a clear confrontation between the employer and his employees; although the degree of militancy exhibited by this confrontation has registered huge temporal and geographical variations. The struggle of labour no longer takes the form of warfare against the industrial order as such but rather against specific conditions within it:

wages, length of the working day, distribution of the national product, property relations.

Before examining these various types of protest in more detail, it should be made clear that I do not regard these categories of protest as 'stages' through which labour is bound to register its grievances in any chronological sequence. In the first place, some groups of workers never engaged in such activities as machine smashing. In the second place, it is possible to discover the simultaneous existence of all three types of protest in the same historical situation, in England in the 1830s and 1840s, for example, and in the Continental revolutions of 1848. Sometimes the same groups of workers could vacillate between industrial and political struggle, between violence and strikes, depending on the economic conjuncture: violence in years of depression and weak bargaining power, peaceful strikes in a more favourable economic context (witness the ups and downs of British Chartism in the 1830s and 1840s). Furthermore, violent protest, intimidation, threats of violence, were never a mere reflex of working-class immaturity or adolescence. Factory managers were threatened with violence in twentieth-century France. Strikers sometimes intimidated their colleagues to join them – although nothing like as often as the employers liked to maintain. Civil war and unprecedented violence characterised large parts of industrial Germany in the aftermath of the First World War. Unorganised protest was far from dead after 1900, playing a major role in wildcat strikes in several European countries immediately before 1914 and also in the revolutions that swept through Russia, Austria, Germany and Hungary in 1917/19. There were even cases, admittedly uncommon, of a kind of Luddism in several parts of Europe in the early twentieth century, as a second wave of technological modernisation and work reorganisation threatened the economic existence and status of certain groups of workers, both skilled and unskilled, as we will see.

Finally, I do not regard 'modern industrial protest' as in any sense 'more rational' than earlier forms of struggle. In early, as in later, times, protesters were rarely ignorant and malevolent thugs, but people with a clear set of values and expectations that had been affronted in some way. The manner in which they set about redressing their grievances depended upon a terrain which was more often than not determined by their enemies, be they employers or governments, rather than by themselves. The resort to violence could be as rational in certain circumstances as could the decision to make collective agreements with employers in others.

Preindustrial Protest

We are here principally concerned with protest by industrial workers in industrial society; but some discussion of preindustrial protest is necessary in order to ascertain what was novel and what was not about modern protest movements. Riots against conscription and taxation, which also overlapped with food riots at times of harvest failure, were endemic in eighteenth-century Europe. There were, for example, large-scale peasant disturbances in both Russia and the Habsburg Empire in the 1770s and 1780s, as there were most famously in France both prior to and during the great French Revolution. As late as 1830 and again in 1841 there were riots against taxation in France, especially in the south-west. It is perhaps the food riot, however, which provides the classic case of this type of protest. It formed an integral part of the revolutions of 1789, 1830 and 1848 in France and was common in Germany in the hungry 1840s. Nor was it absent from Britain, where, for example, many riots were provoked by the high price of grain in 1795. In some places the rioting urban 'mob' had far from disappeared much later: many large towns in Italy experienced riots in 1868, there were food riots in several German cities in the course of the First World War and also, of course, in St Petersburg as a prelude to the February Revolution of 1917.[2]

This type of protest took a direct and very often violent form on the part of crowds of a heterogeneous social composition:[3] masters and their journeymen might have different interests when it came to wages but were obviously united in their desire to keep bread prices low. The riots tended to be localised, lacked formal organisation over time, were sporadic and could disappear from the face of the earth as rapidly as they had arisen.

It would be quite wrong, however, to see in the riot and 'preindustrial protest' an unchanging example of mindless violence of little or no potential. The nature of food riots, for example, changed over time.[4] Hence the 'preindustrial' label obscures perhaps more than it reveals. Furthermore, the use or threat of violence in food riots was quite often successful in fixing the price of grain; and this 'taxation populaire' was as common a form of action as was the more primitive looting of grain stores.[5] The participants would requisition the merchant's stocks, auction them at what they considered to be a fair price and hand over the takings to the merchant at the end of the day. It should also be noticed that the rioting crowds were not indiscriminate in their choice of targets: they selected only those merchants who were especially wealthy or who were suspected of profiteering and did not attack the property of those who either acceded to their demands or were above suspicion.[6] This further reveals some minimal form of organisation — the distribution of handbills, for example[7] — and that it was not hunger as such which generated protest, but rather 'artificial scarcity'.[8] The rioters protested either against the actions of hoarders and speculators, or against the failure of government to engage in the regulation of the grain trade, an activity which it was traditionally expected to perform in both France and England.[9] No automatic chain of causation led from economic distress to rioting. Rather there existed a conflict between the expectations, values and attitudes of the rioters, between a 'legitimizing notion' (E.P. Thompson) and contemporary government practice.

It may also prove difficult to distinguish between 'preindustrial' and later forms of protest for other reasons. The violence associated with early protest was often present at later stages of industrial development as well. In Britain in 1866 some Sheffield cutlers violently attacked those of their colleagues who refused to join their unions in the infamous 'Sheffield Outrages';[10] whilst strikers in France in the late nineteenth century retained a predilection for threatening their employers with hanging.[11] Furthermore, many of the later practices of labour in industrial society seem to be rooted in a distant past. The humiliation of blacklegs harks back to the preindustrial rituals of popular justice,[12] as do some of the songs and ceremonial of organised labour in the late nineteenth century.[13] Gareth Stedman Jones's study of the urban poor in nineteenth-century London also sees continuity between many examples of unrest late in that century and the urban riots of the preindustrial era.[14] Even the tidy distinction between the riot and the strike begins to break down upon closer examination. First, food riots were by no means exclusively rural and regularly involved industrial workers;[15] whilst Reddy has shown that what at first sight appears like a strike in Rouen in 1830 was nothing of the sort: it was not really a case of workers downing their tools to bring economic pressure to bear on their employers, for they quickly returned to work. Rather the workers left their places of employment to form crowds which would then take action in the traditional way.[16] In fact the crowds moved from mill to mill in exactly the same way as the grain rioters had done in 1768.[17] It is also true that the same group of workers could both strike and organise, and yet participate in riots and insurrections at much the same time. Such seems to have been the case in Britain in the 1840s, for example.[18]

Finally, it would be wrong to imagine that the preindustrial riot was exclusively economic in its aims or motivation. Crowds with economic grievances could be moved by urban liberals to participate in movements for political reform, as occurred in France, Germany, Italy and Spain on many occasions. Rudé has shown how in the French Revolution of 1789 politics and bread prices often became inextricably intertwined.[19] Riots against taxation, tolls and conscription were obviously political, in so far as they were directed against the exactions of the state; whilst even the primitive bread riot had political connotations in so far as it was often opposed to the failure of government to regulate the grain trade.[20]

Having said this, however, there remain significant differences between a society in which protest is *predominantly* direct and violent on the one hand, and industrial society in which the principal weapon of labouring man becomes the strike and organisation. Indeed, Charles Tilly has attempted to locate this transition in the case of France quite specifically in the 1850s.[21] Organisation over time as the basis for protest was relatively uncommon in the preindustrial period, with the admitted exceptions of *sans-culotte* organisation in the revolutionary committees of 1792-4 in Paris and the various Jacobin clubs of London and other artisans in Britain. What industrial society has produced, however, is a conflict organised on an unprecedented scale and a conflict between clearly identified antagonists within the industrial order: employer and employee. Such was not the case with the food riot. Furthermore, the food riot was not a reaction to the industrial order as such, although it was often against capitalist agriculture and the free grain market. Therefore, even if some aspects of preindustrial protest were carried into a new society, the shape of protest had quite dramatically changed in the industrial states of Europe. The strike did replace the riot; and above all labour organised.

Industrialisation and Protest

The transition from the early forms of protest discussed above to more modern conflicts was obviously predicated upon that major economic and social upheaval which has come to be known as the Industrial Revolution. However, the precise relationship between industrialisation and the emergence of modern labour protest is nothing like as clear as was once imagined. The most ancient and perhaps still the most popular explanation in lay circles of working-class opposition to the new industrial order begins with a recitation of the horrors that confronted the early industrial labourer both at home and in the factory: and such impoverishment theories of protest are still given credence by some academics today.[22] There can be no doubt that for a great many people the early days of the Industrial Revolution brought innumerable forms of misery and distress. The rapid growth of industrial towns such as Manchester brought with it appalling housing conditions, as Engels stated so eloquently in 1844;[23] whilst the expansion of Paris, which more or less doubled in size between 1800 and 1850, and other French industrial towns such as Lille and St Etienne, led to a breakdown of municipal services, sewerage and health facilities, a high incidence of disease (cholera and typhus) and increases in rates of insanity, infanticide, suicide, beggary, crime and prostitution.[24] In Germany the combination of a high rate of natural population growth and massive emigration from the rural east to the industrial west, especially the Ruhr, produced a spectacular urban explosion in some places: Gelsenkirchen tripled in size between 1868 and 1871 with the development of mining and Thyssen's industrial empire.[25] The consequence was spiralling rents, crowded and unhygienic living conditions and in some towns the appearance of *Mietskasernen* (rental barracks) to house the new working class.

Conditions away from the factory were far from idyllic, therefore; at the factory, where working men and women, even children, spent most of their waking hours, conditions were equally deplorable. In the factory the worker was prey to high accident rates, a host of industrial diseases and also the increasing discipline imposed by management. Indeed, the loss of independence may well have been resented as much as anything else: in some places restrictions on the freedom of factory workers, especially on that of formerly independent artisans, provoked resistance,[26] whilst in others the attempts of employers to control the lives of their employees reached extraordinary proportions.[27]

Having said this, few economic historians will today accept the old view that the Industrial Revolution entailed universal working-class impoverishment, although the question of living standards has been the subject of heated debate, especially as far as Britain is concerned.[28] What does seem quite clear, however, is that different groups of workers fared differently. Many artisanal trades which remained unaffected by new technology and reorganisation were able to exploit both their skills and their organisational strength to maintain high wage levels. This appears to have been true of traditional metalworkers in small concerns. Some factory workers may also have benefited from industrial expansion, which provided them with jobs and good wages, especially if they were skilled. This appears to have been the case with engineers, printers and the mechanics of Birmingham.[29] On the other hand, aggregate statistics suggesting improved living standards are most misleading: for they omit to mention the increasing use of female and child labour, which might improve total family income but hardly register improved living standards, and above all the regularity of unemployment.[30] In fact several recent studies of working-class living standards in a country as prosperous as late-nineteenth-century Germany continue to stress the insecurity of working-class existence, problems of accident and unemployment, and the declining wages that came with advancing years.[31]

There can be no doubt that certain groups of workers suffered great hardship in the early days of the Industrial Revolution. This appears to have been especially true of agricultural labourers, for whom a year's work would have been the exception rather than the rule, and the domestic workers, threatened by both competition from advanced machinery and the simple fact that too many people were employed in their industries for them to be viable, even without this competition. For these groups the 1830s and especially the 1840s were times of declining earnings. In England wages for handloom weavers had dropped from 30s a week in 1800 to 5s in the early 1830s.[32] Aggregate calculations of real wages on the Continent suggest an even more general decline in living standards. In Germany one calculation suggests that average real wages declined by about 26 per cent between 1800 and 1848, whilst average real wages in France also fell significantly between 1817 and 1848.[33]

A further problem which confronted most workers in the industrialising states of Europe, but again most particularly domestic workers in this period, was that of unemployment generated by seasonal and cyclical unemployment, engendered by traditional harvest failure in some cases, by foreign or factory competition and the business cycle in others. The combination of these various economic ills meant that in the German textile town of Krefeld in 1847 three out of every eight looms were idle. In Cologne at the same time something like a third of the total population was dependent on some form of public assistance for survival.

It would be mistaken, however, to attribute either poverty or artisan and domestic worker discontent solely to the impact of new technology and the competition of mechanised factories. On the Continent a major problem was that population growth was *not* matched by industrial expansion, which might have provided jobs to absorb the increase. Significantly, the two European countries which were missing from the revolutionary ranks of 1848 were Britain and Belgium, the two most industrialised nations. Artisans were further faced by a whole set of problems which had little or nothing to do with the introduction of new technology: this is suggested by the fact that many of the artisans on the barricades in Paris and Berlin in 1848 belonged to trades which had so far experienced no major technological innovations.[34] Rather they faced competition from sweat-shops (as in the case of French tailors undercut by off-the-peg clothing under the July monarchy), with the influx of cheap and not necessarily unskilled labour from the countryside. There is evidence that shoemaking and tailoring were becoming sweated trades in Marseilles by the 1840s, that workers in textiles were increasingly dominated by merchant capitalists, who supplied both the raw material and owned the finished product, and that in Germany cabinet-makers were becoming *de facto* employees of large furniture manufacturers and that tailors were increasingly dependent sweated labourers.[35] In short, the reorganisation of industry by masters or merchants and the simple fact that there were too many handloom weavers except in years of exceptional boom conditions caused considerable problems, as did the abolition of laws protecting entry into a trade and apprenticeship.[36] It should also be said that the handloom weaver, depressed artisan and unemployed domestic worker did not see their difficulties as purely economic but were equally incensed by the loss of the dignity and status that had previously come with independence.[37] In the case of downwardly mobile artisans and outworkers it does seem reasonable to claim that the poverty engendered at least in part by the Industrial Revolution is relevant to any understanding of their protests. The same cannot be said, however, for the new factory workers. As we will see, organised protest remained the almost exclusive preserve of skilled and relatively well paid workers in small and medium-sized concerns well into the twentieth century. The most impoverished factory workers were normally the last to join the ranks of collective labour protest.[38] A further piece of evidence which hardly fits the impoverishment theory of protest is that strike activity and rates of unionisation tended to increase in times of economic expansion rather than depression. Thus the connection between protest and poverty is far from direct and simple. Nor should it be imagined that workers were invariably opposed to the introduction of new machinery. Some workers who had entered factories *before* mechanisation and who were in possession of skills and organisational resources were able to maintain their relatively privileged position by restricting entry to the trade, as in the case of printers;[39] whilst others were liberated from the necessity of an often harsh, unremunerative and long apprenticeship by the introduction of new technology. In the earliest stages of industrialisation, in fact, it might be suggested that labour protest assumed two quite distinct forms: the desperation of the really impoverished and downwardly mobile on the one hand, and the relatively prosperous organisation of the skilled, who were not confronted by immediate misery and whose activities more properly belong to a later section of this chapter.[40]

Early Industrial Protest

Protest of this second type could be regarded as transitional, part of a long road that leads from outright hostility to the new industrial order to an acceptance of industrialism, although this last in no way implies any necessary acceptance of particular conditions within the new society or of its specific organisation. Hostility to the new industrial order and the poverty it engendered could assume many forms, some of which might or might not be described as protest: alcoholism, desertion of factories by former peasants in Russia, common absenteeism on the part of miners in south Wales, in Carmaux in France and the Ruhr and Silesia in Germany, even the flight to a land of promise in the New World – over a million people emigrated from Central Europe in 1847 alone, whilst between 1880 and 1893 a further 1.3 million left Germany's Second Reich, although this last wave is perhaps more correctly explained by rural over-population and agricultural depression rather than problems specific to industry.[41]

The form of anti-industrial – a term soon to be qualified – protest which has received the most attention from historians, however, has been that of explicit antagonism to the introduction of industrial machinery, of shearing machines, power looms, etc., which deprived framework knitters, handloom weavers and others of their skills and their livelihood. In Lille workers petitioned their government for legislation against the introduction of machinery in 1817, and Silesian weavers later followed their example. One slogan heard in the French Revolution of 1830 was 'down with the machines', whilst anti-industrial demands also came from the organisations of German artisans in the 1848 Revolution. Most famously of all, workers sometimes turned on the new machines and their owners with violence. Between 1811 and

1817 framework knitters in Leicestershire and Nottinghamshire destroyed shearing machines, West Yorkshire croppers attacked gig-mills and cotton weavers in south Lancashire also participated in Luddite violence. Violent machine breaking was not restricted to the British Isles, however. Incidents of machine smashing were common in France in the first half of the nineteenth century: in Vienne in 1819, in St Etienne in 1830, on which occasion over 2,000 workers are said to have been involved, in Paris, Bordeaux, Toulouse and St Etienne again in the following year. As late as 1848 several factories were fired by insurgents. In Germany rioters broke machines at Solingen in 1826, as did Krefeld silk weavers two years later. Saxon weavers followed suit in the 1830s and, most famously of all, there was an uprising of Silesian linen weavers in 1844, a rising celebrated in Gerhardt Hauptmann's classic drama, *Die Weber*.[42] It is also worth noting that this kind of violence against machinery and employers was far from exclusively urban: the Captain Swing riots in eastern England in 1830 involved the destruction of agricultural machinery to safeguard jobs and wages, as did innumerable examples of incendiarism in the same area in the 1840s.[43]

At first sight this kind of protest had much in common with its predecessor. It was usually localised in nature, sporadic, and obviously involved direct action and often physical violence. Sometimes it overlapped with the traditional food riot, as in the Middleton-Overton area of north Lancashire in 1812,[44] and generally it lacked formal organisational structures. However, we must once again resist the temptation of describing Luddism as irrational and mindless violence. Where the introduction of new machinery did not entail declining living standards and status it was not resisted. The targets of the rioters were specifically selected and the Luddites often displayed a considerable degree of organisational planning: in England what was sometimes involved was the disciplined movement of disguised men over considerable distances and armed attacks on carefully selected targets. Rural violence and machine breaking also displayed similar discipline.[45] Often the resort to violence only came *after* the aggrieved had petitioned governments for redress of their grievances unsuccessfully, as in the case of the Silesian weavers and most English domestic workers who participated in the Luddite risings. Sometimes, in fact, the resort to violence was even successful in safeguarding jobs or protecting wages, at least in the short term.[46] What we are dealing with again is 'bargaining by riot'.

This last point raises a further problem. It seems that in certain circumstances the destruction of machinery or the threat of such destruction was generated less by hostility to machinery as such — what might be described as the classic form of Luddism and anti-industrial violence — but was rather simply part of a tactic to bring pressure to bear on employers to improve wages and working conditions.[47] That is, it performed much the same function that the strike was to do later. In a further sense, too, the machine smashing that was endemic in Europe was forward-looking: it was predicated upon advancing industrialisation and in many cases constituted a bitter struggle between the two great protagonists of the new class conflict, employer and employee.

It is even true that certain kinds of Luddism re-emerged at the turn of the century with a new wave of technological innovation: construction workers at Dortmund threw sand in a crane in 1900, whilst the dockers of Le Havre pushed cranes into the sea on two occasions. Another such incident was the destruction of mechanised grain elevators by Belgian grain loaders in 1907.[48] It is true, of course, that these later examples of Luddism were rare; yet it remains equally true that much modern labour protest of a very different kind was also generated by the deskilling of formerly skilled workers. Some of the first groups of workers to organise used their organisational strength to protect their interests against unskilled competition and to restrict entry into their trade.[49] In England the New Model Unions of the 1850s and 1860s pursued a variety of restrictive practices. Carmaux glassworkers first organised when their skills and status were threatened by technological innovation in the 1880s, as miners there had done in a similar situation thirty years earlier.[50] The increasing militancy of skilled metalworkers and miners in Germany from about 1910 onwards and the revolutionary movements on 'Red Clydeside' and in Central Europe at the end of the First World War have been explained in a similar way.[51] The solution that these workers now proposed to alleviate their condition, however, was no longer the abandonment of advanced machinery as such, but rather a change in the organisation of industrial society and in particular of the structure of authority in the factory ('workers' control').

Modern Industrial Protest

As has been suggested already, the transition from violent direct action to the employment of the strike as a weapon and the creation of formal organisations cannot be equated with any simple chronological progression. In some contexts violence played the role of the strike, whilst many early strikes were violent. Furthermore, violence remained endemic in twentieth-century industrial nations and did not simply disappear from the face of conflict. Attacks on blacklegs were common. In France, Germany, Italy, Spain and Russia troops were still used against strikers after 1900, whilst the inter-war years in Central Europe witnessed a bloody civil war. Some workers who did more normally strike and join labour organisations might also engage in Luddite violence, as we have seen. However, modern industrial protest did come to predominate over earlier forms of conflict and distinguished itself therefrom in a number of ways. It was no longer directed against industrial society as such but against either conditions of work within it or against the structure of authority and ownership. In short, it ceased to be backward-looking. It also sought to solve the unpleasantness of working-class existence less through the use of naked force than through the exploitation of industrial muscle (strikes, trade union organisation), although the use of violence was by no means necessarily ruled out of court by those organisations. The extent to which formal organisation itself served to reduce social antagonisms and radical feelings will be discussed in the next chapter. What characterised this modern conflict above all, however, was that the antagonists were employer and employee. For example, in 1789, 1830 and in the early days of 1848 in France masters and their journeyman had mounted the barricades together, united by common interest over bread prices and similar political ambition. In the June Days of 1848, however, their paths separated and they now confronted one another over questions of wages, working conditions and the ownership of property. A similar division can be detected in Germany later in the same year.[52]

The Strike

Obviously the strike, the withdrawal of labour by employees to pressurise their employers to rectify their economic grievances, was not new to the first half of the nineteenth century, as many examples in Britain and several in France testify.[53] It was precisely in this period, however, that it became a common, if not the most common, form of labour protest in the more economically advanced countries. In England it replaced the riot as the dominant instrument of working-class struggle in the 1830s. In France there were virtual strike waves in 1833/4 and 1840, especially in Paris; and in both France and Germany in the course of the revolutions of 1848 after the relaxation of laws against combination and association. Most of these Continental strikes lasted but a short period of time — normally just a few hours — and involved a minute percentage of the labour force. They were also almost exclusively restricted to demands of an economic nature. In England, on the other hand, strikes often involved relatively large numbers of workers and were sometimes tied to the demands of the Chartists for democratic political reform.[54] After the 1848 revolutions in Continental Europe governmental repression and legal prohibition put an end to any widespread strike activity in most states; but such activity re-emerged in both France and the various states of Germany in the 1860s and was especially pronounced in the early 1870s, suffering a further decline for most of the late 1870s and the 1880s.

The timing of strikes seems to depend primarily upon the fluctuations of the business cycle. In times of relatively high unemployment, as in the so-called Great Depression of 1873-96,[55] strike rates were low in most European countries, whereas the economic boom of the early 1870s produced an unprecedented wave of strikes in Germany.[56] This would seem to be because boom conditions produce a high demand for labour, thus strengthening the worker's bargaining power and protecting him against dismissal, at the same time as generating inflation, which acts as the stimulus to strike. Times of depression, conversely, weakened the job security of the employee, thus making it riskier to strike, and were often accompanied by an increase in living standards for those who remained in work on account of price deflation. Strikes also and predictably were concentrated in periods of political relaxation and circumstances of legality for obvious reasons. The effective legalisation of strikes in Britain in 1824 was followed by a dramatic increase in the number of strikes, as was the temporary political relaxation in France and Germany in the initial stages of the revolutions of 1848. It is also possible that these revolutions raised working-class expectations of government support in their struggle against their employers and hence provided a further stimulus to strike activity. Similarly the resurgence of strikes in France in the 1860s followed a liberalisation of the laws against combination in 1864 and in particular in 1868; and the same thing happened in Germany, for similar reasons, in 1863 and the late 1860s.[57]

That workers went on strike from a position of strength rather than weakness and that rising or frustrated expectations rather than simple poverty provided a major stimulus to their actions is further evidenced by the fact that those who went on strike up to the late 1880s were primarily skilled workers, who were relatively well paid, had served apprenticeships, had traditions of organisation upon which they could rely, and also traditionally high expectations. In England those who formed the earliest and most stable trade union organisations, in France those who went on strike under the July monarchy (1830-48), in

Germany those who joined strike movements in the 1860s were printers, tailors, carpenters, masons and the like and not the unskilled factory proletariat. Those factory workers who did engage in frequent industrial disputes were the new 'labour aristocracy', engineering workers, machine builders, etc. In Germany the workers in the large plants of heavy industry remained relatively inactive until the first great miners' strike of 1889, although there had been some activity in the mines before that date and although the iron and steel industries of the Ruhr were blessed with industrial peace until relatively late in the day. In France the factory workers in the newer industries only really became involved in strike activity on a significant scale in 1869/70 and from then on their involvement was merely sporadic. In England it was the great dock strike of 1889 which first heralded the way to the new struggles of the unskilled worker.[58] The reasons for this will be examined below.[59]

As Peter Stearns has argued,[60] strikes assume an especial significance in the early days of the Industrial Revolution. In the first place, they provide a far more direct introduction to the aims and aspirations of the ordinary working man and woman than do the remarks of his or her ostensible leaders. This is particularly true of this period in so far as going on strike involved invariable economic hardship – unless workers had access to subsistence farming as well, which might also strengthen their proclivity to strike, as seems to have been the case in some parts of France[61] – the possible loss of one's job, confrontation with the police and even troops, which sometimes, as in several parts of the Loire mining basis in 1869 and in Germany as late as 1912, led to bloodshed and death.[62] The demands made by workers prepared to risk these hazards were overwhelmingly concerned with wages before the 1890s and sometimes with the length of the working day, though complaints about harsh foremen and factory discipline were not uncommon.[63] Strikes had a further significance: they often formed the prologue to formal organisation. For in the course of a strike or in the wake of defeat workers came to recognise the need for some kind of organisation to protect their interests over time and sustain solidarity during strikes, as happened, for example, during the 1864 dock strike in Hamburg.[64] Furthermore, state legislation to prevent combination could channel economic grievances in the direction of politics, as appears to have happened in Britain in the early nineteenth century, in France in the 1830s and 1840s and Germany in the 1880s.[65] Most obviously, the physical repression of a strike by government troops could have the same effect: Waldenburg miners went over to German Social Democracy after the suppression of a strike in 1869, for example.[66]

Perhaps the most striking example of this road from economic to political protest, however, is provided by the incidents of 'Bloody Sunday' during the Russian Revolution of 1905, when an attack on loyalist trade unionists led by an Orthodox priest and carrying a petition to the Tsar led to the erection of barricades and the beginnings of a real revolution.[67]

This does not mean, of course, that there is any necessary connection between industrial militancy and political radicalism. Engels was bemused by the way in which England had experienced countless labour disputes and seen the rise of a strong trade union organisation and yet at the same time remained immune to working-class political radicalism.[68] In Germany workers with considerable economic grievances often petitioned the Kaiser for help against their employers, as did metalworkers in Solingen, Silesian weavers and miners in the Ruhr; i.e. their hostility towards their conditions and the employers they held to be responsible for those conditions was not translated into any form of opposition to the political *status quo*.[69] In France some workers who did believe in quite radical social change (the overthrow of capitalist property relations) none the less eschewed the world of formal politics, which they saw as understandably bourgeois and necessarily corrupt after the great betrayal of the June Days of 1848, when a bourgeois national guard fiercely repressed lower-class insurrection. For these workers the way to escape the constraints of capitalism was initially through Proudhonist co-operatives and subsequently through anarcho-syndicalist trade unions and the general strike.[70]

Finally, as far as strikes are concerned, the fact that certain groups of workers were absent from the ranks of strikers should not be interpreted as evidence of satisfaction with the prevailing political, social or economic circumstances. It might just as easily reflect repression on the part of the state or employers, the weak bargaining power of the workers in question or any number of other things which will be discussed below.[71]

Organisation

In the course of the Industrial Revolution workers not only began to strike more frequently; they also developed an extremely rich organisational life, especially in the old artisanal centres such as London, Paris, Berlin and Leipzig, where traditions of organisation went back to the guilds. Throughout the nineteenth century skilled workers formed smoking and discussion clubs, educational associations, consumer and producer co-operatives, trade unions and political parties. Now it may be objected that some of these types of association have little or nothing to do with protest, in the sense that we normally understand the word: what of educational associations and friendly societies, for example? We will see, however, that this objection has only a qualified validity; for such organisations were often the prologue to more militant enterprises or even a respectable façade for them.

One of the earliest and certainly most common forms of working-class organisation in the nineteenth century was the mutual aid or friendly society. There were over a million such societies in England by 1815 and throughout the century their membership remained more numerous than that of the trade unions. In France friendly societies proliferated in the 1830s and there were approximately 2,000 of them by the 1840s. Many others were formed in Spain in the 1840s and in Russia in the 1870s. It is hardly surprising that such societies tended to recruit overwhelmingly from the skilled and relatively prosperous sections of the working class: the ability to make regular payments into society funds was not vouchsafed to the more impoverished who lived on the margins of survival. These friendly societies were primarily concerned with the provision of insurance against those misfortunes which would otherwise have doomed the worker to dependence upon charity (accident, sickness and old age) in the days before the state made any significant intervention in this area. They also often placed great emphasis on traditional artisan values such as moderation in drink, respectability, sexual propriety, even where bourgeois philanthropy was utterly absent from their foundation. Quite often such societies expressly forbade any involvement in politics or even political debate amongst members. However, the attitude of the state to such apparently innocuous organisations and the hostility of employers as well suggests a slightly different picture: in Britain and France in the early nineteenth century and in Germany in the years of the anti-socialist law between 1878 and 1890 governments often suppressed such working-class associations. There were a number of reasons for this. The possession of funds on the part of some groups of workers obviously enhanced the potential for strike activity and was sometimes used to support it. In France and Britain at times when trade unions were illegal the distinction between the friendly society and the trade union became blurred to say the least; and in France mutual aid societies could easily develop into what were called 'sociétés de résistance'. In England the 'no politics' rule was often ignored; whilst in Germany during the persecution of the anti-socialist law friendly societies, even choral and smoking clubs, were front organisations for opposition to the prevailing political system.

(This is not to say, however, that this was their sole function or even why they had initially come into existence. On the contary, they were part and parcel of traditional artisan society; which was also why the proscription of more formal organisations such as political parties and trade unions failed to break the back of working-class resistance to the authoritarian Wilhelmine state.[72])

Many of these observations can be applied with equal force to working-class educational societies. Many of these also possessed 'no politics' rules. Some in England even forbade the discussion of economic issues or attempted to prescribe the kind of political economy, normally of the Manchester *laissez-faire* school, which might be reasonably debated. Once again these associations were the preserve of the labour aristocracy, the outcrop of artisan values of independence and respectability, and were meant to provide the worker with access to classical culture and its values. In Breslau the artisans believed that a process of education and enlightenment should precede any extension of political rights to the working class. Such was also the position of August Bebel, subsequently to emerge as one of the founders and leaders of an independent working-class and socialist movement in Germany. It is also true that many working men's educational associations were actually founded by middle-class reformers and liberal philanthropists, such as those established by Sonnemann in the Germany of the 1860s. To some extent their foundation can be attributed to genuine philanthropical concern. In others the aim was expressly to mobilise working-class support behind the liberal movement (as in the case of Sonnemann); and in many the intention was to instil the values of self-help and anti-socialism into the ranks of labour. Thrifty, sober and respectable workers made better employees.

Once again, however, educational associations could form the basis for other kinds of more radical working-class activities. Even the skilled worker who initially desired nothing more than some veneer of culture to establish his respectability and acceptability with members of the higher social orders, a type whose initial motivation, therefore, could hardly be described as radical, could be radicalised by his treatment at the hands of his middle-class superiors if they refused to recognise his standing. In England workers did demand the discussion of heterodox economic theories, leading to frequent controversy with the middle-class founders and leaders of educational associations; whilst in Germany Lassalle's General Union of German Workers (ADAV) and the Eisenach party of August Bebel and Wilhelm Liebknecht, the first two working-class political parties to emerge in that country in the

1860s, both arose, at least in part, from pre-existing workers' educational associations in which there had been conflicts between bourgeois and working-class members. It would be mistaken, of course, to imagine that all workers' educational associations followed this road to political radicalism: in Württemberg, for example, liberal educational societies with a working-class membership survived side by side with Social Democratic organisations well into the 1870s, whilst Catholic and Evangelical (Lutheran) workers' associations had far from disappeared from Nuremberg at the same time.[73]

One form of working-class organisation which more clearly connected with some kind of dissatisfaction with the prevailing economic order, however, was the co-operative movement, at least in its early days. Wholesale co-operatives of the kind which emerged in Britain in the 1820s intended not only to provide cheap goods for workers but also to use their funds to create communities of co-operative production which would bypass employer control of the labour process; and some such communities were established in the 1830s. In France the movement towards co-operative association has been described as *the* principal form of working-class activity in the 1830s and 1840s, and again in the 1860s; and in both countries co-operative associations were often closely connected with other forms of labour activity, including trade unions, as they were also in Württemberg in Germany in the 1860s. In all of these places the co-operative movement recruited overwhelmingly from the skilled sections of the work-force and expressed traditional values of independence. However, the orientation of the co-operative movement towards other forms of economic and political activity varied enormously. The Owenites in Britain began with a radical critique of the economics of *laissez-faire* capitalism centred on the labour theory of value and yet refused to become embroiled in political conflict; and the same was true of some workers' organisations in France under the Second Empire (1852-70), which despaired of middle-class politics after the great betrayal of June 1848 and ceased to expect anything of an unsympathetic state. In Germany many of the co-operatives founded by Schulze-Delitzsch in the 1860s subscribed to the values of self-help, albeit collective self-help, and were close to the liberal political movement. On the other hand, Louis Blanc, who was to enjoy a short pre-eminence in the French Provisional government of 1848, looked to the state to support his 'national workshops', whilst Ferdinand Lassalle, extraordinary adventurer and one of the inspirers of an independent labour movement in the Germany of the 1860s, demanded democratic reform precisely so that a newly constituted workers' state would fund the producers' co-operatives which, in turn, he saw as the only solution to the 'iron law of wages' that operated under normal conditions of capitalist production. There were also Chartist co-operatives in Britain in the 1830s and 1840s, which, as the name implies, did not restrict their attention simply to the economic field.[74]

The classic form of labour organisation, however, the one which dominates contemporary concerns and which was to have the greatest long-term significance, was the trade union, the organisation created to improve the economic situation of the worker or at least to defend it against the attacks of rapacious employers and the ravages of inflation. In Britain some skilled groups of workers – woolcombers, cordwainers, shoemakers, hatters, shipwrights, tailors – had an organisational history which went way back into the eighteenth century and which was by no means fully curtailed in the repression of the early years of the following century. However, the legalisation of union activity in 1824 led to a proliferation of trade societies capable of organising strikes. To the 1820s the most common form of union in Britain was that of a single trade in a single town, a union which in fact often acted as a friendly society as well and which often attempted to control apprenticeship and entry into the trade in a highly exclusive fashion: English cotton-spinners, for example, attempted to exclude handloom weavers from their organisation. In the 1830s most unions remained exclusive in their membership, despite some justifiably famous and abortive attempts to found general national unions, such as Robert Owen's ill-fated Grand National Consolidated Trades Union (GNCT). Increasingly the workers organised in craft unions came to rely on peaceful collective bargaining rather than direct action, although by no means exclusively, as we have seen. It was only with the formation of the so-called 'New Model Unions', however, and in particular with the foundation of the Amalgamated Society of Engineers (ASE) in 1851 that effective national federations of trades unions came into existence. Yet it should again be noted that these new organisations were no less exclusive in their practices than their predecessors, demanded high subscriptions and recruited from skilled factory workers, such as the engineers themselves. What was new about them was their centralised direction, stability and success. It cannot be denied that such exclusive and cautious unionism was not to the liking of all sections of the British labour movement and there were some acrimonious debates on the subject in the 1860s. There were, furthermore, some attempts to unionise the less skilled sections of British labour in the following decade; but such attempts achieved only a short-lived success and the unskilled thus remained outside the ranks of organised protest until the 'new unionism' of the late 1880s and 1890s. As late as 1883 the ASE had succeeded in mobilising only 10 per cent of the work-force in the British engineering industry.[75]

A similar pattern can be detected elsewhere. In France in the face of governmental repression masons, carpenters, tailors, printers, hatters, shoemakers and engineering workers organised under the July monarchy (1830-48) and even more overtly in the course of the revolution of 1848 following the relaxation of the laws of association and combination. After further legalised repression in the 1850s the French trade union movement resurfaced in the 1860s amongst precisely the same groups of workers, whilst miners and workers in the relatively new textile factories took much longer to form their own independent organisations. Skilled workers in Russia also formed unions in the 1860s and 1870s, when that country first embarked upon its slow, staccato and painful process of economic modernisation, whilst their less skilled colleagues engaged in very different forms of activity, as we will see. In Italy it was workers in long-established, small-scale industrial establishments who formed the backbone of organised protest up to the turn of the century. Again textile and metalworkers in the larger factories only organised successfully late in the day.[76]

It has sometimes been claimed that Germany differs from the above pattern of economic mobilisation in so far as the trade union movement there emerged only after and as an adjunct to the political organisation of labour. Modern research has shown this contention to be a nonsense. In the Rhineland and in Wuppertal craft associations were formed in the 1840s. In the revolution of 1848 German workers not only made democratic demands on occasion, but sometimes formed embryonic unions, as in the case of skilled cigar-makers, printers and machine-builders. As in France in the 1860s, so in Germany at the same time the relaxation of the laws against combination and association saw a further revival of union organisation on the part of these workers, as well as of masons, carpenters, tailors, shoemakers, leather workers and the like.[77]

Often these trade unions of the 'labour aristocracy' refused to become involved in any form of political activity. Unionised miners in Britain, for example, did not wish to be associated with the Chartists and their political agitation. Printers in Britain, France and Germany, although amongst the first to establish strong and stable unions, often turned their backs on political matters quite deliberately, as did German cigar-makers. It has further been argued for the German case in the 1840s that workers' associations only became involved in political action where a sympathetic lead was given by local bourgeois radicals.[78] Furthermore, the timing of waves of unionisation, as well as the fact that it was primarily the better-off workers who were involved, once again suggests that the unions gained their support not through the weakness and impoverishment of the unskilled factory proletariat but rather from the powerful bargaining position of skilled labour. The British labour movement turned from direct action to industrial organisation in the years of economic prosperity between 1848 and 1880; whilst the formation of craft associations in Germany followed a sustained improvement in the living standards of skilled workers.[79] In such circumstances, of course, skilled labour enjoyed not only the strong bargaining power confirmed by a tight labour market but also rising expectations rather than impoverishment.

It would be mistaken, however, to conclude from the above that union organisation and political radicalism were mutually exclusive. The frustration of attempts to form economic unions by either the state or intransigent employers could force 'moderate' unionists into the ranks of radical political protest. Such was to a certain extent the case in Britain in the early years of the nineteenth century. In France too the repression of working-class industrial action in the 1830s and 1840s led to insurrections in Lyons and in Paris on more than one occasion, as well as to the formation of revolutionary secret societies with both a middle-class intellectual and a working-class membership, as in Blanqui's famous Société des Saisons.[80] Equally, the suppression of many trade unions and other forms of working-class organisational life in Germany under the anti-socialist law (1878-90) led some workers to look to the SPD and political action as the solution to their problems.[81]

Politics

In terms of the development of strike activity and industrial organisation we have seen that considerable similarities existed across national boundaries in terms of the social composition and structure of labour protest. It is in the realm of politics that things become far more problematic. In some countries workers, or at least those of them that were enfranchised, seem to have remained loyal to traditional, socially heterogeneous political parties, such as the Tory and Liberal parties in Britain: there the emergence of an independent political party of labour of any significant scale only came after 1900. In Germany, on the other hand, independent working-class political parties came into existence as early as the 1860s and both Lassalle's General Union of German Workers (ADAV) and the so-called Eisenach party of August Bebel and Wilhelm Liebknecht subscribed to some kind of socialist doctrine by the end of the decade. In fact by 1875, when the two groups merged to found the Social Democratic Workers' Party (SdAP, subsequently SPD) at Gotha, there was a single, united socialist party in existence in Germany's Second Reich. In France, although the political wing of labour remained fragmented in a number of different organisations until the formation of the SFIO in 1905, the move towards working-class independent political activity had begun in earnest at the national workers' congresses of 1876, 1878 and 1879. Some French trade unions had also been affiliated to what is mistakenly regarded as Marx's First International in the late 1860s, although their precise political affiliation is none too easy to determine.

In addition to the problem of explaining the emergence of independent labour politics in some countries and not in others there is, of course, the further question as to why the political organisations of labour that did come into existence assumed different ideological forms in different places. Amongst some groups of French and Catalonian workers anarcho-syndicalism gained a hold; amongst others socialism was to provide the ostensible ideology of their leaders, as in Germany and in some sections of the French, Italian, Spanish and Russian labour movements. But that socialism had a more radical tinge in, for example, Russia and parts of Italy than in Germany. Innumerable attempts have been made to explain this diversity; and some of these explanations are examined below.

The Role of Ideology and Ideologists. Lenin argued, following Kautsky and in the light of Engels' remarks concerning the failure of the British working class to translate its industrial militancy into political radicalism, that workers would not get beyond the level of economistic demands and what he described as 'trade union consciousness' if left solely to their own devices. It required the intervention of a radical bourgeois intelligentsia to instil revolutionary socialism into the ranks of the proletariat.[82] Of course, this theory or variants of it are still with us in, for example, John Foster's controversial study of class conflict in nineteenth-century Oldham and East German studies of the labour movement in industrial Germany.[83] Clearly there can be no doubt that gifted agitators and intellectuals have helped to politicise if not necessarily to radicalise labour protest on many occasions. The revolutionary stance of the Russian working class in 1905 and 1917 (and certainly the radicalism of the Bolsheviks) has to be seen against the background of a revolutionary bourgeois intelligentsia, which included Lenin in its ranks. The emergence of an independent labour movement in Germany in the

1860s was certainly furthered by the propagandistic activity of Ferdinand Lassalle and subsequently by the existence of a Marxist intellectual tradition. France saw the birth of modern working-class protest coincide with the development of the socialist theories of Fourier, Blanqui, Blanc and many others. Conversely, the absence of a revolutionary intelligentsia in Britain, apart, perhaps, from the early nineteenth century, when it could in fact be argued that labour protest was more radical, may well have had something to do with working-class reformism.

The fate of radical ideologies, however, depended upon far more than the persuasive powers of intellectuals. That radical ideas found a more favourable reception amongst some sections of the British working class in the 1830s and 1840s than at a later date suggests that changing circumstances — affluence, a more liberal state — rather than ideological activity itself determined the perceptions of labour. Marxism was adopted as the official theory of German Social Democracy in the 1880s in circumstances of capital concentration, economic depression and governmental repression, i.e. in circumstances which the new orthodoxy seemed to explain. In France and Spain, as we will see, it was workers in particular industrial structures and with distinctive backgrounds who found the message of anarcho-syndicalism appealing. As few would deny, therefore, the impact of theory depended upon far more than the ability of the individual agitator or the mere existence of an 'intellectual tradition'. It is possible, however, to go even further than this in disputing the mobilising power of imported ideology: it can even be demonstrated that the various ideologies ostensibly adopted by the labour movement had a very limited significance indeed. Many of the Russian workers who participated in the revolutionary events of 1905 appear to have been incapable of recognising the differences between Mensheviks and Bolsheviks, whilst in the July rising of 1917 some workers who were actually members of the Menshevik party carried placards bearing Bolshevik slogans! Given that many of the revolutionary leaders had been forced into exile and that domestic repression restricted their access to the ordinary factory worker in Tsarist Russia, this is hardly surprising. However, the social cleavage between the bourgeois intellectual leadership of *both* the Menshevik and Bolshevik wings of Russian Social Democracy and the proletarian rank and file must have made problems of communications even greater, as is testified by the lamentations of several party activists. Martov, for example, expressed his disquiet over his early contacts with the working class in the following way:

> In my circle I twice delivered talks on the aims and methods of socialism, but real life kept on interfering ... Either the members of the circle would themselves raise the question of some event that had occurred in the factory ... or someone from another workshop would appear, and we would have to spend the time discussing conditions there.

On the other hand skilled workers in Russia at the turn of the century often seem to have resented the attempts of bourgeois intellectuals to teach them anything. One of the members of the St Petersburg League of Struggle, a parent organisation of what became the Russian Social Democratic Party, attacked those who saw in the movement 'merely a means of consoling the stricken consciences of repentant intellectuals'; whilst Abram Gordon, a self-taught engraver from Vilno, told intellectuals to beware of treating workers like himself as 'the cannon-fodder of the revolution'. It might also be suggested that the radicalisation of Russian workers in 1917 had little to do, at least initially, with Bolshevik propaganda or Lenin's arrival at the Finland station. There was, as it were, an inbuilt structure of radicalisation which existed independent of revolutionary leadership and which was exemplified by the disquiet of factory committees with political caution even before Lenin's return to his homeland, by the fact that the July rising of 1917 happened almost in spite of the Bolsheviks – as Lenin himself admitted: the masses were more Bolshevik than the Bolsheviks. The rectification of material grievances in Russia in 1917 required primarily the ending of the war. This further necessitated the removal firstly of the Tsarist and then of Kerensky's Provisional government. Hence the radicalisation of workers in Moscow and St Petersburg. This is not to say that the activities of the Bolshevik party were not responsible for the actual seizure of power in 1917; simply that the occurrence of a second revolution stemmed directly from the immediate needs of the Russian proletariat and was likely without Bolshevik ideology.[84]

The significance of official ideology for the activities of the working-class rank and file was equally dubious in the case of another supposed bastion of labour radicalism before the First World War, namely the French anarcho-syndicalist movement. As stated in the opening chapter, one leader of the CGT, which regularly proclaimed its commitment to the revolutionary general strike at trade union congresses, disclaimed any knowledge of the writings of radical theorists. More importantly, the patterns of industrial militancy and the strike demands developed by anarcho-syndicalist workers in France differed in no important respect from those displayed by workers with no attachment to anarcho-syndicalist theory or organisation.[85] The muted significance of ideology for the behaviour of ordinary working men and women is further demonstrated by an analysis of the history of the German labour movement. Hans-Josef Steinberg has shown, for example, that even the leadership of the SPD in the three decades before the First World War had only a limited understanding of Marxism, even in its vulgar Kautskyite form, despite the fact that it was the official ideology of the party from the Erfurt congress of 1891; that many of these leaders subscribed to a more general evolutionary view of social development; and that the party rank and file rarely read even the popularisations of Marx provided by Kautsky and Bebel, preferring escapist fiction.[86] Other studies of various SPD cultural activities also reveal a relative absence of radicalism.[87] In the early days of German working-class politics in the 1860s attempts to delineate clear ideological divisions between the Lassallean and Eisenach parties have been shown to be misleading: both were really umbrella organisations of pre-existing workers' associations with an ideological identity that was extremely confused and neither were the mere creations of talented individual ideologists like Lassalle.[88] Later, in the case of the revolutionary upheavals in Germany at the end of the First World War, the membership of a particular political organisation with a particular supposed ideology in no way guaranteed that the rank and file party members of the various socialist factions understood the precise nature of the ideological divisions between the various left-wing groups, as I have attempted to show in some detail elsewhere.[89] There were even miners in the Ruhr in 1919 who belonged to both the German Communist Party and anarcho-syndicalist organisations!

What this means, first of all, is that it is no easy matter to identify the specific ideological persuasion of any particular group of workers, even when they can be shown to have been card-carrying members of certain political organisations. In the second place, this suggests that ideological influence was far from the determining factor in patterns of political radicalism; a point given further weight by the fact that many of the workers who participated in revolutionary struggles at the end of the First World War in Moscow, St Petersburg, Berlin, the Ruhr, Milan and Turin were precisely those who had not been mobilised by labour organisations, their leaders or their ideologies before 1914. Third, what one can see here is the volatility of working-class political action: some workers could be mobilised for industrial and even radical political activity very rapidly and yet just as rapidly disappear from the ranks of protest, as in France in 1919/20 and again in 1936/8, and in Germany between 1918 and 1923. This again suggests that explanations of the fortunes of working-class radicalism have perhaps more to do with specific economic conjunctures or other concrete historical experiences, such as the failure of strikes and insurrections, than with the implantation of radical ideology 'from without'.

This should not be interpreted as a statement to the effect that workers were never 'revolutionary' or 'radical': indeed, I will attempt to demonstrate in the following chapter that certain specific sections of the European working class both before and after the holocaust of 1914-18 were committed to revolutionary goals. Nor is it to deny that ideology in a more general sense of a set of received ideas and values, as distinct from an imported political theory, was completely irrelevant to the forms of behaviour displayed by certain groups of workers. In particular, this more general conception of ideology obviously has a central role in explaining differential patterns of both radicalism and violence and a much greater one than the theories transmitted by intellectuals. It can hardly be accidental that socialism appealed to some sections of the Spanish labour force, for example, and anarchism to others, depending not only on factory structure but differing rural backgrounds and expectations. Violence in industrial relations and even the paramilitary activities of Nazis and Communists in Weimar Germany during the depression could also mirror a more generally violent society, as has been argued in the case of Hamborn in the German Revolution of 1918 and that of youth gangs in Berlin in the early 1930s.[90] Equally clearly, artisanal values of independence, self-respect and dignity played a part in the generation of protest in early-nineteenth-century England.[91] However, this kind of 'ideology' is manifestly not the same as an intellectual system imported into working-class ranks by an outside intelligentsia, is not what Lenin is talking about in his references to 'consciousness from without'; it is rather a set of perceptions and values into which individual workers are socialised through inumerable agencies, through their backgrounds, work and home environment.

Living Standards and Political Radicalism. It has often been argued that poverty breeds not only discontent but working-class radicalism; and that conversely there is a clear connection between proletarian affluence and reformist labour politics. The relatively high wages enjoyed by British workers in the second half of the nineteenth century have been seen as one possible explanation of the failure of revolutionary socialism to attract a mass following in Britain; whilst the violence and insurrectionary activities of certain sections of British labour in the earlier part of the century tended to disappear thereafter as real wages rose by about 84 per cent between 1850 and 1900. Similarly in Germany there was a sustained rise in working-class living standards from the early 1870s until at least 1900 and this again has been seen as one of the factors which diminished revolutionary initiative within the SPD.[92] On the other hand, the relatively low wages of the Russian and Spanish working class might well have had something to do with their apparently radical politics.

There is a further and rather more sophisticated connection posited between political reformism and working-class prosperity: the theory of the 'labour aristocracy'. Lenin, following remarks made much earlier by Engels in the face of the political quiescence of the English working class, argued that certain groups of skilled workers and in fact precisely those who came to dominate the European labour movement before the First World War benefited disproportionately from the boom conditions of capitalism and in countries like Britain which exploited cheap labour in her colonies. In a sense a small and wealthy working-class elite lived off the back of exploited colonial labour and was bought off by the benefits of Empire. This theory has been taken up with some enthusiasm subsequently.[93] The argument says not only that the relative affluence of skilled labour made it less interested in talk of revolution and the overthrow of the capitalist system; but also that it led to an internal differentiation of the labour force and militated against the formation of a solidaristic working-class consciousness. Hence, so the argument goes, the trade unions in Britain, which before 1914 recruited overwhelmingly from skilled labour, had little interest in revolutionary arguments. Hence, also, the growth of reformism within pre-war German Social Democracy has been attributed to the dominance of a similar labour aristocracy in its ranks in a country in which significant wage differentials between skilled and unskilled labour remained. Conversely, the relatively low wage differentials between different sections of the French working class in the nineteenth century have been adduced as an explanation of the emergence of a revolutionary and solidaristic consciousness.[94]

The connection between earnings and the presence or absence of radical sentiments amongst European labour will be pursued at some length in a later discussion of various theories of embourgeoisement;[95] but certain points should be raised here which cast some doubts upon the efficacy of 'labour aristocracy' theories. In the first place, the emergence of a labour aristocracy in nineteenth-century Britain predated the turn to reformism. As Musson has pointed out, the labour aristocrats were there all the time, including the period of intense social conflict in the early years of that century.[96] Nor is there any clear connection between poverty and radicalism on the one hand and affluence and reformism on the other. It is true that appalling living conditions formed the background to the militancy of downwardly mobile domestic workers in Britain and on the Continent in the 1830s and 1840s; but the poverty of the most depressed sections of the factory labour force in the late nineteenth century did not necessarily lead to such a conclusion. Female textile workers in Germany, for example, had a host of grievances but did not translate these into industrial or political action on any significant scale before the First World War, with a few isolated, albeit notable, exceptions. Conversely, the revolutionary Marxism of the SPD and the revolutionary anarcho-syndicalism of the CGT were embraced not by the unskilled and utterly downtrodden but precisely by sections of this so-called 'labour aristocracy' in France and Germany before 1914. Both organisations recruited from the skilled and relatively prosperous sections of the work-force. Indeed, their very prosperity gave them not only the financial resources to organise and act but also a set of expectations, the frustration of which was the usual signal for hostility to the prevailing order. Above all, the fact that similar types of labour aristocrats embraced different political perspectives in Britain and Germany, despite their roughly analogous economic situation, suggests that the connection between affluence and political reformism is at best problematical. In fact it was not immediate material deprivation which generated political radicalism in addition to industrial militancy, but rather the extent to which the rectification of economic grievances was or was not possible through that process which is jokingly known today as free collective bargaining between the employer and his employees.

Industrial Impotence and Political Action. The changing fortunes of British Chartism in the 1830s and 1840s suggest that it was workers who had tried various methods of industrial struggle which had failed who turned to politics as a remedy for their economic grievances; and that they did so in circumstances of economic depression, when high unemployment had drastically reduced their bargaining powers and consequent industrial muscle. In a sense insurrection and other forms of direct and often violent action reflected the desperation of the handloom weaver.[97] On the other hand, boom conditions and the stronger bargaining position which resulted from a tight labour market led to a concentration on forms of industrial struggle and organisation, namely strikes and trade union membership, on the part of a significant group of workers.

Later French experience also suggests a connection between industrial weakness and direct action. The activities of anarcho-syndicalist strikers, for example, which sometimes entailed violence and even industrial sabotage, can be explained by the very weakness of the French trade union movement before 1914: at the turn of the century the average *syndicat* had a very small membership (often no more than 200 persons) and a weak financial structure, not only because of its diminutive size but also because a significant minority of unionists did not pay their dues. Under such circumstances unions hardly possessed the industrial muscle to bring employers to their knees simply through the withdrawal of their members' labour. As a result French workers were obliged to turn to more direct, even spectacular, forms of protest than the peaceful strike. This same weakness also helps to explain a further phenomenon which is central to the account of strike activity in France provided by Shorter and Tilly, namely the way in which French strike waves tended to peak at times of *political* crisis. Precisely because the industrial effect of strikes was limited by the numerical and financial weakness of the *syndicats*, French strikers directed their attention not simply to the industrial arena but to the state. To a certain extent strikes became demonstrations, the prime intent of which was to influence both the government and the rest of the community to bring their pressure to bear on the side of the working class in the struggle against an uncompromising *patronat* for improved wages and living conditions.[98] This was likely to be especially true at times when certain political changes suggested that government could be expected to show a more sympathetic attitude to the problems of labour, as with Millerand's entry into the French Cabinet in 1899 and the election of the Front Populaire in 1936; and in the wake of the 1918 revolution in Germany which had installed an all-socialist government. All of these events clearly led to a raising of working-class expectations on the industrial as well as on the political front.

A further factor which could channel industrial grievances into the field of politics was the attitudes and strategies adopted by employers towards labour protest. Where employers showed some willingness to recognise trade unions as the legitimate representative of employee interests or at least to engage in some form of open negotiation with their work-force, as was the case, for example, in the British iron and steel industry where arbitration boards were in operation from the 1860s, there was no necessary reason why dissatisfaction with material conditions should spill over into the political arena. Indeed, a major reason why British workers espoused non-radical politics and failed to break with the existing middle-class political parties before the turn of the century was the ease with which employers concluded collective wage agreements with their workers' representatives. Obviously it will not do to exaggerate the liberalism of the British managerial class: there were many employers who refused to recognise trade unions and something resembling an employers' offensive was launched against the British labour movement after 1900. Yet the contrast with the situation on the other side of the English Channel remains striking: nothing like as many French workers were covered by collective agreements as their English counterparts and the hostility of the *patronat* in France to such collective bargaining may again explain the resort to politics on the part of the French working class.[99]

This last point does raise a serious problem of definition, however. A struggle for trade union recognition is obviously an economic struggle in so far as workers desire the more effective representation of their interests to guarantee at least the defence of and sometimes improvements in their living standards. However, the question of trade union recognition is also a political question in so far as it raises the issue of employer authority within the factory, control of the situation on the shop floor, i.e. an issue of power, if only in the workplace. A great many trade union struggles in the nineteenth and twentieth centuries were about precisely such questions; and this applies as much to Britain as to Continental Europe. If we accept this for the moment, however, this still leaves us with the question of why the economic struggles of labour have led in some places at certain points in time to more overtly political struggles at a national level, struggles for political power and control over the state apparatus or at least for an effective and independent voice within existing political institutions.

To return to the connection between industrial impotence and political action on the part of the European labour movement, it may seem odd at first sight to talk of the industrial weakness of the German proletariat before the outbreak of the First World War, given the massive support enjoyed by the SPD, the largest socialist party in Europe, and some impressive unions, such as the giant Metalworkers' Union (DMV). It is further true that much the same percentage of the work-force (25 per cent approximately) had been mobilised by the trade union movement in Wilhelmine Germany, as in Edwardian Britain, on the eve of the First World War. However, German employers and especially those in the heavy industrial sector revealed an almost total hostility to independent working-class organisation (although many were prepared to establish dependent company unions, the so-called 'yellow' unions) until the political pressures of government in the course of the First World War and above all in the wake of the revolution of 1918. This is clear if one compares the figures concerning the number of workers covered by collective agreements in Britain and Germany before 1914. In Britain in 1910 no fewer than 900,000 miners, 500,000 railway workers, 460,000 textile workers and 230,000 metalworkers benefited from such agreements; whereas in Germany three years later the equivalent figures related to only 16,000 textile operatives, 1,376 metalworkers and a miserly 82 miners! Furthermore, the high degree of capital concentration in the increasingly important German heavy industrial sector enabled employers to operate very effective blacklists of potential trouble-makers from either Social Democratic or Free (i.e. SPD-associated) Trade Union ranks. Thus industrial magnates like Krupp of Essen and the Saarland coal baron Stumm-Halberg were able to dismiss or refuse to hire workers who belonged to the SPD or the Free Trade Unions, or who read Social Democratic literature, attended SPD meetings or even frequented public houses which were known as Social Democratic meeting places. Their power to engage in such autocratic behaviour was not based upon the survival of 'preindustrial' attitudes on either their part or that of their employees but was rather a function of the very modernity of the industrial structure and their monopoly of the labour market; and upon the fact that the spectacularly rapid urbanisation of the Second Reich's industrial heartland required the provision of company housing. This further tied the employee to his boss; for participation in industrial action would almost certainly be followed by eviction. Thus protest became a risky business for a working class which in any case had to suffer the vicissitudes of the business cycle and recurrent unemployment. Even those German workers who did join trade unions or engaged in strike activity in the decade before the First World War found themselves faced by an increasingly powerful federation of employers, prepared to adopt lock-out tactics to defeat strikes. In short, the prospects of successful industrial action actually receded and an increasing number of strikes ended in defeat.[100] Under these circumstances the only mechanism for the effective representation of working-class economic interests became the semi-democratic institutions of the Wilhelmine Empire and in particular that party which expressly stood for the industrial proletariat, the SPD. Thus one reason why more workers in Germany voted socialist than in any other European country in this period relates at least in part to industrial impotence on the part of labour and the opposing strength of the capitalist enemy. This connection was clearly recognised by a German worker who had the good fortune, as he saw it, to spend some time in Britain and who wrote:

> Trades Unionism and politics are kept distinct in this country [Britain]. It would be to the disadvantage of the working classes themselves to sever themselves in the matter of politics from the middle classes, since the attitude of the latter towards the workman has been friendly.[101]

A final contribution to the theory that political action on the part of workers can be the consequence of industrial weakness comes from the experience of the British labour movement in the ten or so years immediately before the outbreak of war in 1914. A series of unfavourable decisions in the law courts and above all in the House of Lords, together with the adoption of increasingly repressive anti-union tactics by employers, led several unions, such as that of the mine-workers, which had previously stood aloof from the campaign for separate labour representation in Parliament, to turn to politics in an attempt to remove restrictions on their activity. Thus the emergence of independent labour politics in Britain was a consequence of a weakening of industrial muscle; and thus the origins of the British Labour Party were primarily defensive in character.[102] A further point to emerge from this salutary experience for the British working class was that the most effective road to the politicisation of industrial protest was built by the interference of the state.

The State and Political Radicalism. There were many ways in which the activities of various European governments forced workers to engage in political as well as industrial protest. Most obviously the repression of strikes by armed police or troops could transform relatively peaceful action for limited ends into a full-scale and violent confrontation with the state; and such experience obviously served to sharpen working-class perceptions of the role of the state in maintaining the industrial as well as the political *stătus quo*. The classic demonstration of this was perhaps 'Bloody Sunday' 1905 in Tsarist Russia. On that day a group of workers in St Petersburg belonging to the Gaponite trade union organisation, an organisation led by an orthodox priest and loyal to the Tsar, carried a petition to one of the imperial palaces asking for the redress of certain immediate economic grievances. For their troubles they encountered violence at the hands of government troops and almost immediately barricades went up. Strikers now demanded political change as well as improved living standards. In short, a real revolution ensued in which, as Rosa Luxemburg demonstrated so forcefully, it became impossible to distinguish between economic and political strikes.[103] In fact it becomes virtually impossible to make such a distinction in authoritarian states. Under repressive regimes which forbid strikes and working-class organisation through laws against combination and association the simple desire to protect immediate material interests led of necessity to political action; for such laws prevented even pure forms of industrial action and organisation and yet they were laws made and changed not by particular interests in civil society but by the state, by governments. Thus it was to a certain extent the repressive apparatus of successive British governments in the early nineteenth century – the Combination Acts, the use of spies and *agents provocateurs*, the deportation of unionists, as in the notorious case of the Tolpuddle martyrs, the employment of troops to quash peaceful demonstrations, as in the Peterloo massacre – which in certain cases transformed economic discontent into violent insurrection and in others led the protesters to demand a change in the governmental system. As E. P. Thompson has remarked: 'In the end, it is the political context as much as the steam engine, which had the most influence upon the shaping of the consciousness and institutions of the working class'.[104] On the other hand, one of the reasons for the relatively reformist position adopted by most of the representatives of British labour in the second half of the nineteenth century must lie in a surrounding political atmosphere which was relatively unoppressive, in a situation in which the vote was gradually extended, although certainly not to the whole of the working class, in which the state interfered in industrial conflicts relatively rarely and in which the major repressive laws of the earlier part of the century were revoked.

Before going on to look at the way in which governmental action served to shape labour protest in Continental Europe, however, some qualifications must be made to the picture painted above. In the first place, of course, governmental action is not utterly discrete from other variables. The adoption of a radical ideology by certain labour leaders, for example, might provoke repression on the part of a state which had not necessarily been illiberal previously. Second, once a situation had arisen in which working-class organisations did adopt a particular ideological orientation in politics, then obviously that to a certain extent developed its own momentum. Having embraced politics for whatever reason, as it were, those politics might then determine subsequent forms of working-class activity rather than being a mere reflex of external constraints. Such is the case, for example, with German Social Democracy prior to 1914: to a certain extent the passivity of the SPD, its refusal to engage seriously in attempts to mobilise the peasantry of the Second Reich and its hostility to bourgeois liberalism were a consequence of the peculiar brand of Marxism it espoused. It is also true that some workers came to particular political conclusions through their contact with revolutionary literature, as among certain sections of the Parisian artisanate under the July monarchy. It cannot be doubted, moreover, that demands for political representation on the part of skilled workers were not exclusively prompted by a desire to have particular economic interests represented, but were also a consequence of ideas of self-respect and a worthiness that should be recognised by equal treatment. Finally, the actual measures adopted by governments towards labour also related to the nature of governments themselves, to the manner of their selection, their social composition and their historical traditions. Hence, for example, the much more liberal reactions to socialism of the southern German states compared to that of autocratic Prussia.

Having said all this, however, it does seem to me that the major determinant of the forms of political action adopted by the different national labour movements was the role of the state and of the social groups it claimed to represent; for at the level of industrial action clear similarities existed between similar occupations in different countries. Furthermore, it remains true that certain kinds of governmental interference in industrial relations did transform what began as economic protest into political action.

In part the more radical face of working-class politics in Continental Europe can be linked without too much difficulty to the more repressive nature of the political regimes to be found there. In France the law against association, the *loi le Chapelier*, was passed by the National Assembly in 1791; and from that date until the revolution of 1848, and with additions which made it all the more repressive in the 1830s, it effectively prevented peaceful protest on the part of French workers, who turned either to full-scale insurrection, as in Lyons in 1831 and 1834 and Paris in 1832 and 1834, or to revolutionary secret societies, such as August Blanqui's Société des Saisons.[105] The June rising of 1848 was followed by brutal repression at the hands of Cavaignac's bourgeois troops, some of the strikes of the 1860s often resulted in bloodshed, as in the Loire mining industry in 1869, and the defeat of the Paris Commune two years later witnessed the slaughter of over

20,000 Communards.[106] Even after the turn of the century French Republican governments, some with initially radical credentials, were prepared to use troops to undermine the strikes of miners in 1906, dockers and electrical workers in 1907 and postmen in both 1907 and 1909. Striking postmen and railway workers, who participated in major industrial militancy in 1910, were often dismissed from their jobs; and on occasion strikers were actually drafted into the army. Against this background it is hardly surprising that both the political and the trade union wings of the French labour movement before the First World War subscribed to revolutionary ideologies, to Marxism or to anarcho-syndicalism, at least in theory.

Having recounted this chronicle of repressive state action to explain the radicalism of the French working class, however, it could be fairly objected that any description of the French working class as a whole as 'revolutionary' or 'radical' before 1914 is misleading. Peter Stearns has shown that revolutionary ideas had little significance even for those workers who joined anarcho-syndicalist trade unions; whilst the united French Socialist Party, the SFIO, which finally emerged in 1905, was an unholy fusion of Marxist and non-Marxist elements, of the ideologically committed and the non-sectarian, of reformists and revolutionaries. When it came to the crunch, when the Third Republic was threatened by external enemies, as in 1914, or by internal enemies, as in the Dreyfus Affair of the 1880s or by the Fascists in the 1930s, the French working class rallied to its defence. That this should be the case is hardly surprising; for, although the French working class experienced much greater governmental repression than its English counterpart, that repression was far from total. Even in the Second Empire (1852-70) there were circumstances in which the state, in the shape of the local prefect, intervened on the side of labour in industrial disputes, especially in areas such as Alsace where the *patronat* was anti-Napoleonic. If the reforming autocracy of Louis Napoleon could not simply be described as the tool of capitalist interests, as Marx himself admitted, this was even truer of the Third Republic (1871-1940). After the initial suppression of left-wing initiatives in the wake of the Commune, the new Republic legalised trade union and strike activity in 1884. The existence of universal manhood suffrage and parliamentary sovereignty obviously helped to render the state more sympathetic to the demands of an emergent working class than it had been in the first half of the nineteenth century when the landed aristocracy and then the *grande bourgeoisie* held sway. The combination of the vote and parliamentary sovereignty enabled the organisation of the French working class to play a significant role in political life: by 1914 the SFIO not only had a membership of 91,000 but was winning around one and a half million votes in elections to the Chambre des Députés, where it was strongly represented. In short, one possible explanation of the ambivalence of labour politics in France in the nineteenth and early twentieth century can be located in the complex nature and behaviour of the French state.[107]

The emergence of a mass socialist movement alienated from the Wilhelmine state and ostensibly embracing revolutionary Marxism as its official ideology also obviously related to governmental actions. For most of the 1850s and the early 1860s all forms of labour organisation in Germany were viewed with suspicion by the authorities and many were suppressed. A ruling agrarian elite, horrified by the revolutionary upheaval of 1848, had no understanding of or sympathy for working-class aspirations. The semi-autocratic Wilhelmine Empire (1871-1918) continued this repressive tradition. The exceptional law against socialists, which was in operation from 1878 to 1890 and under the terms of which socialist literature was banned and many labour leaders were imprisoned or exiled, further served to turn the Social Democratic movement away from the state-socialist theories of Lassalle, and Dühring and to the Marxism of Karl Kautsky, which proclaimed that the state was an instrument of class rule and that the problems of capitalist society could only be overcome through its destruction. Even after the termination of the exceptional law in 1890 the state still harassed the representatives of the German working class. Several forms of anti-socialist censorship survived, SPD newspaper editors were often imprisoned for 'insulting the Kaiser', Social Democrats were debarred from state employment, a ruling which related not only to white-collar civil servants but equally to postmen and railway workers, and perhaps most importantly of all, no socialists were ever taken into government, despite the fact that the SPD became the largest political party in the Second Reich. This was so not only because of the reactionary mentality of Germany's governing elite; it was possible because Germany was not a parliamentary state before the revolution of 1918. There was a Reichstag, of course, elected by universal manhood suffrage; but there was no parliamentary sovereignty: decisions were taken by the Kaiser and his entourage, whilst the Chancellor and his Ministers were responsible not to the Reichstag but to the Kaiser, who had the exclusive right to appoint and dismiss them. What this meant was that, despite its massive electoral support of four and a quarter million votes in the national elections of 1912, the SPD was still no nearer political power. The constitutional system of Imperial Germany meant that socialism could not come to power through the ballot box alone; and this was precisely why the revisionist theories of Eduard Bernstein and his supporters, who advocated the gradualist road to socialism, amongst other things, were rejected again and again by SPD party conferences. Once again, therefore, the radicalism of labour, its commitment to a total rejection of the existing social and political order, derived some of its strength from the activities of a repressive state apparatus.[108]

Once again, however, we are confronted with the complex reality of a style of labour politics which was not unambiguously revolutionary: no one would claim that the German working class before the First World War was uniformly committed to the complete overthrow of existing economic, social and political reality. In the ranks of the Free Trade Unions, in the states of south Germany and even in the national leadership of the SPD, reformists were easy to find.[109] This failure on the part of German labour to adopt a maximalist revolutionary stance, unlike, for example, the Russian Bolsheviks, obviously requires explanation; and part of that explanation at least, as in the case of France, lies in the fact that the German state was never as totally repressive as its Tsarist counterpart. The governments of Germany, having to survive amidst massive industrial and demographic growth, did make some concessions to bourgeois ideals, not only in the field of economic policy but also in terms of political rights (universal suffrage, civil liberties). From 1890 German Social Democracy was allowed to exist as a legal organisation and to develop a massive bureaucratic apparatus which gave it something of a stake in existing society. Competition at the polls also led to a dilution of official revolutionary ideology, especially in parts of south Germany where the party had to make some attempt to win over a large non-proletarian electorate. Thus differing degrees of governmental repression do seem to correlate with levels of working-class radicalism: autocratic Russia produced an unambiguously revolutionary movement, liberal England witnessed strongly reformist labour politics, whilst semi-autocratic Germany gave birth to a working class which was neither uniformly revolutionary nor reformist. Even at the level of local developments in Germany this proposition is amenable to demonstration: in the states of south Germany which possessed relatively strong liberal traditions and in which there was direct, equal universal manhood suffrage to the Landtag (provincial Parliament), as well as a relatively relaxed acquiesence in the existence of organised labour, there the SPD was predominantly reformist. On the other hand, in states such as Saxony and Prussia, which exercised relatively harsh laws of association and had complex and unequal electoral systems,

German Social Democracy was much more straightforwardly radical.[110]

The association of working-class radicalism and political violence finds further demonstration in Italy, where universal manhood suffrage was only introduced in 1912 and where troops were regularly deployed against strikers in the late nineteenth century; and in Spain, where the brutality of the Guardia Civilia produced a working-class mentality that was prepared to risk death, storm machine-gun posts with only the most primitive arms and institute what was perhaps the most total transformation of social relations ever in Barcelona and Saragossa in the course of a bloody Civil War.[111] Most obviously of all, Imperial Russia offers the clearest example of the way in which unlimited autocracy and unmitigated repression transformed the economic grievances of the working class into the political revolutions of 1905 and 1917.[112]

Political repression was obviously the most direct mechanism whereby the state impinged on the structure and aims of labour protest; but it was not the only one. Political crisis combined with a change in government, as when the socialist Millerand entered the French Cabinet in 1899 or when the Social Democrats came to power in Germany in the aftermath of the First World War or when the Popular Front took over the reins of government in France in 1936, could serve to raise the expectations of workers and lead to massive strike waves. On the other hand, the adoption of specific economic policies by various European governments also helped to radicalise some sections of the working class. In Germany the high protective agricultural tariffs, which were in existence from the late 1870s onwards and which enabled the ruling landowning classes to survive economically, were clearly detrimental to the living standards of the industrial working class and made manifest that government was biased towards particular class interests. The economic policies of English governments in the early nineteenth century had a similar effect. The abolition of much paternalist legislation left workers without the protection they had traditionally come to expect from the state in times of acute economic hardship; whilst the fact that it was the *reformed* Parliament which introduced the hated New Poor Law in 1834 led some workers to see the need for further political change, as, in fact, did the Corn Laws, which kept bread prices artificially high.[113]

A further road which led from economic to political discontent and which was also built by the activities of the state was the prosecution of war. The war against France in the early nineteenth century caused English governments to raise taxes; and opposition to taxes embraced both economic and political discontent. In Russia in February 1917 and during the months that followed the improvement of wages and living conditions required the ending of the war; and this in turn entailed the removal first of the Tsarist autocracy and then of Kerensky's government a few months later. Conversely, the relative improvement in working-class experience as a result of social insurance legislation, such as that introduced by British governments, might serve to explain the strength of reformist tendencies, whilst the absence of such legislation in France, combined with the manifestly corrupt nature of bourgeois politics in the Third Republic, may have contributed to the disgust felt by some French workers for their state.

In these numerous ways, through economic policies and wars which hurt working-class living standards and above all through direct and violent intervention in labour disputes, the state could act as a radicalising agent upon labour protest. The actions of the state, however, often reflected more general upper-class attitudes towards a troublesome proletariat; and it is to these that we must now turn.

The Attitude of Other Classes and Working-class Politics. We have already seen that the attitudes adopted by employers towards trade union organisation and other labour activity could force some workers into political action. At a much more general level, however, the attitudes of other social groups helped to shape working-class consciousness. In states in which preindustrial elites still played a predominant political role, as in Tsarist Russia and, with certain reservations, Imperial Germany, it is perhaps not surprising that attitudes towards labour were non-comprehending and overtly repressive. The rising labour movement constituted a threat to existing authority: it was not amenable to either the direct economic or indirect ideological controls which pervaded rural society, whilst its secular and democratic values, let alone its socialist attack upon private property, conflicted with all that traditional conservatives held most dear. More problematic, however, and perhaps more significant in transforming labour politics into independent and sometimes radical channels, was the attitude adopted by the increasingly numerous and powerful middle class in the states of Europe.

The Industrial Revolution, the expanding activities of the modern state and the servicing of civil needs by professional strata, saw a middle-class develop on an unprecedented scale in the nineteenth century. For many it seemed natural that this new social group, whose strength rested upon the possession of skills and capital rather than land or title, would produce a challenge to the old aristocratic order and power structure; and this is precisely what happened in the states of

Western Europe in the first half of the nineteenth century. The various revolutions in France in 1789, 1830 and 1848 reflected this demand for representation and equality of opportunity, as did the Reform Act of 1832 in Britain, which to a certain extent sought to recognise the industrial lobby. Even in Germany in the 1830s and 1840s, especially in the Rhineland and the south, an urban middle-class liberalism sought changes in the political structure and finally attempted to implement them in the revolutions of 1848. In some of these initiatives to extend citizenship rights the bourgeoisie could rely upon certain skilled sections of the labour force; in fact those who gave their lives on the barricades in Berlin and Paris in 1848 were recruited precisely from these latter groups.

This anti-aristocratic alliance did not survive for long in most European states. In Germany the 1860s did see a revival of middle-class attempts to mobilise support through liberal co-operatives, educational societies and the like; but this had rather paradoxical results. Most of the skilled workers who joined these liberal organisations did so for reasons which could hardly be described as revolutionary: their sense of status, independence, respectability and desire for recognition by higher social groups. But once in the associations these values came into conflict with middle-class attitudes. The bourgeois liberals refused to recognise the working man's equality within the clubs and would rarely allow him to participate in the running of such organisations; and the frustration of his desire for recognition and respectability led the worker to embrace independent and sometimes radical politics. Indeed, the emergence of an independent labour organisation in Germany in the 1860s was a consequence of precisely such conflicts within organisations originally founded by middle-class liberals.[114] As the German industrial working class exploded in size with rapid industrialisation in the second half of the century, in a situation in which there was universal manhood suffrage to the Reichstag, so the bourgeoisie moved increasingly to the right, especially as it became clear that the old style of liberal politics based upon small cliques of local notables could no longer control or manipulate a mass and increasingly self-conscious electorate. With the massive expansion of a political party committed to revolutionary Marxism, the German bourgeoisie developed what can only be described as a neurosis about the 'red peril'. At the same time certain sections of the industrial middle class were bought off by the Wilhelmine state through national unification, economic concessions and the distribution of titles. Hence the emergence of a 'feudalised' bourgeoisie so brilliantly satirised in Heinrich Mann's novel *Der Untertan*. Increasingly certain dominant sections of industry co-operated with the traditional ruling Junker class, which finally culminated in 1913 with the formation of the 'Cartel of Productive Estates'.[115] Now it has to be admitted that this model of a feudalised bourgeoisie does not have the universal currency that some historians have imagined.[116] Not all industrialists had common interests in economic policies of protection and some were distinctly unhappy about co-operation with the Junkers. Furthermore, there were frequent rifts between industrial and landowning interests over a variety of issues, especially taxation. However, as even the most thorough antagonist of the feudalisation argument will admit,[117] none of these divisions sufficed to obliterate what virtually all sections of the German aristocracy and bourgeoisie identified as their most important and common aim: the fight against socialism. In a sense, therefore, the abandonment of liberal values by a significant section of the German middle class in the second half of the nineteenth century (an abandonment, incidentally, shared to some extent by the *Mittelstand* of peasants, independent artisans and the like) forced the working class into isolation and independent politics.

To a lesser extent the same thing happened in France, though far from completely; for significant sections of the bourgeoisie remained committed to the liberal politics of the Third Republic and some even joined forces with the socialist movement. However, by their own testimony, French workers did feel increasingly betrayed and it was that betrayal which led them to identify the need for an independent political party of labour. As Victor Prost, a Dijon clockmaker and one of the most popular speakers at the first national congress of labour organisations in France in October 1876, stated: 'Citizens, our bourgeoisie is no longer in the path of progress. It is petrified in place like the wife of Lot ... has completely lost all the ties that once attached it to the people'.[118]

Conversely, the English middle class after the mid-century regularly made overtures to attract working-class support and certainly never displayed the same neurosis about lower-class activity as its Continental counterparts. Admittedly this image of a thoroughly liberal English middle class is somewhat misleading: certain sections of it also moved to the right in the later nineteenth century; but again this did not take place to anything like the same extent as it did in Germany and it happened within the context of democratic politics and parliamentary sovereignty. (As we have already seen, in fact, contemporaries commented on the difference.[119]) Furthermore, the French bourgeoisie never reneged on democratic values on anything like the same scale as its counterpart across the Rhine and some intellectuals actually committed themselves to the SFIO. In consequence the French labour movement was never as isolated as its German equivalent.

It is by no means easy to explain the differential behaviour of the European bourgeoisie. To a certain extent it corresponds to the degree of radicalism of the various indigenous labour organisations: it is hardly surprising that German liberals should be more frightened of labour politics that embraced revolutionary Marxism than the British were of a reformist working class. However, to say this is in a certain sense simply to restate the problem; for we have already seen that at least in part working-class radicalism was itself a consequence of bourgeois hostility. In a sense one finds a vicious circle in which middle-class attitudes radicalise labour and labour radicalism drives the middle class further to the right. Why, then, the differences in the initial response to labour protest? In part the answer perhaps relates to the presence or absence of universal suffrage when industrialisation is in its relatively early phases. Paradoxically the British bourgeoisie had least to fear from an alienated working class because most of that class was disenfranchised until after the First World War. In France from 1871, however, and in Germany from the same year the parties of the liberal middle class had to compete with working-class representatives in elections held under universal manhood suffrage. There was a real danger, increasingly realised in Germany, that democracy would lead to the triumph of non-bourgeois political groups.

A further explanation of different middle-class attitudes to labour, however, may also relate both to social attitudes in existence *before* industrialisation and the speed with which that process transformed social relations. In Britain a *relatively* large middle class with independent values was already in existence before the Industrial Revolution which more or less began in the middle of the eighteenth century. The relatively lengthy process of industrialisation, which dragged on for another hundred years or so, then enabled the middle class some time to draw a working class, whose formation was taking place only slowly, into the prevailing political culture. In Germany, on the other hand, there existed no strong or numerous middle class before the Industrial Revolution. To a certain extent the German bourgeoisie and the industrial proletariat were formed simultaneously and came to self-consciousness simultaneously. What is more, this process happened extremely rapidly; in the second half of the nineteenth century Germany was transformed from an agrarian society into an urbanised industrial giant. The result was that the German middle class, with only a weak and relatively recent sense of its own independent identity, was forced to look over its shoulder at a potential enemy from the very start. It was squeezed between the threat of lower-class disorder of the kind that had terrified it in 1848 and the even greater threat of socialism on the one hand, and a self-confident aristocratic ruling class on the other. Not surprisingly it opted for compromise with the latter. Similarly, the fact that the French working class never became as socially isolated as its German counterpart and that the French bourgeoisie retained traces of liberalism may also relate to its existence and possession of independent values before industrialisation, which only began in earnest under the July monarchy and which was still far from completed by 1914. In fact France remained a predominantly rural society until the inter-war period; and again the relatively slow formation of an industrial proletariat gave the middle class a breathing space it lacked in Imperial Germany. On the other hand, the fact that there was greater bourgeois neurosis about the working-class left in France than Britain related not only to the existence of universal suffrage but also to a history of past and violent conflicts, as in the June Days of 1848 and the Commune of 1871. In a sense a collective memory of past struggles shaped not only working-class but also middle-class consciousness.

At another level it has been argued that the existence of revolutionary attitudes and their ultimate success in Russia had a great deal to do with the relative absence of a liberal middle class, owing to the peculiar dependence of industrialisation there on either the state or foreign capital. Indeed, this was precisely what Trotsky argued and why he believed that Russia could be transformed into socialism without passing through a capitalist phase.[120]

This section has tried to explain various ways in which labour protest found its way into political as distinct from purely industrial channels, apart from the direct impact of political literature and the activities of individual politicians, whose role has often been grossly exaggerated, as has the role of simple material deprivation. Far more important was labour's treatment at the hands of the state and employers; and the sympathy with which other social groups viewed its aspirations. To a large extent labour protest remained purely industrial where it could satisfy its needs through the application of industrial muscle. The absence of such muscle, however, or its thwarting by laws and the intransigence of employers, transformed attitudes and the arena of conflict.

We have seen so far, therefore, that in the wake of the Industrial Revolution some groups of workers went on strike and formed economic organisations. Some also participated in political actions of various kinds for a variety of reasons. We must now examine in greater detail the kinds of workers who participated in these various types of labour protest.

The Social Composition of Labour Protest

The kinds of workers who formed the rank and file of organised protest in the early days of the Industrial Revolution were almost invariably skilled and rarely worked in large factories. Sometimes they were artisans at work in small shops. Sometimes they were a newer kind of skilled worker employed in modern factories or industries. However, it may be misleading to exaggerate the difference between these two groups, as is suggested by the experience of Italian labour organisation in the third quarter of the nineteenth century: rather than associating with their unskilled colleagues in the factory, skilled industrial workers participated in the same social and political organisations as the local artisans.[121] In fact artisans and skilled factory workers were often recruited from groups with the same training and expectations. In Britain certain groups of skilled workers moved into the factories and organised themselves before the introduction of new technology;[122] whilst in Germany some of the artisans who gained factory employment in the 1850s and 1860s continued to do much the same job as before, often sought redress for their grievances in a traditional way – for example, simply by asking to be transferred from one task to another that they deemed more satisfying – and resented above all attempts to impose a new discipline and routine upon them.[123]

The predominance of skilled workers in the formation of stable economic and political organisations is indisputable. In Britain the numerous friendly societies that sprang to life in the late eighteenth and early nineteenth century were the preserve of skilled artisans, who also formed the backbone of stable Chartist commitment – unlike depressed domestic workers, their membership of Chartist bodies did not fluctuate with the trade cycle. The first groups to form embryonic trade unions in Britain in the early days of the Industrial Revolution were likewise tailors, woolcombers, shipwrights, cordwainers and members of similar crafts, whilst the so-called 'New Model Unions' of the British working class in the 1850s and 1860s also recruited overwhelmingly from the skilled sections of the labour force, such as engineering workers. In the iron and steel industries as well it was the well paid and highly skilled who first unionised in the 1860s.[124]

In Continental Europe the picture was no different. In the 1830s and 1840s French joiners, carpenters, tailors, masons, hatters and shoe-makers were the people who formed friendly societies and trade unions, as they did again under the Second Empire in the next two decades. In Marseilles under the July monarchy (1830-48) artisan trades almost invariably possessed some form of labour organisation, whereas there is no evidence of such amongst the more 'proletarian' trades. In the Allier in central France socialist organisation first penetrated small mining villages rather than the larger mining centres. Most French unionists of the 1870s were also skilled; anarchists found their strongest support amongst Parisian artisans and the Parti Ouvrier, which emerged in the 1880s, was principally composed of skilled urban workers.[125] In Germany in the course of the 1848 revolution it was skilled printers, cigar-makers and machine-builders who organised, as they did again in the 1860s together with masons, shoemakers, tailors, carpenters and those in similar trades. In Ludwigshafen the organised labour movement remained restricted to the skilled sections of the work-force until after the turn of the century; and the same was true of the socialist move-ment. In Hamburg in 1868 Lassalle's General Union of German Workers was composed in the following way: seven out of every nine members of the branch were either cigar-makers, cobblers, joiners or tailors. There is further evidence that it was itinerant artisans who helped to spread the socialist gospel in Baden and that a similar informal network of communication between skilled craftsmen kept the Social Democratic movement alive during the persecution of the 1870s and 1880s.[126] In Austria it was typesetters, watchmakers and certain other skilled trades who succeeded in establishing successful craft associations by 1867;[127] whilst the Spanish Socialist Party drew its first support from printers in Madrid.[128] In Italy a pre-factory artisan culture was central to the formation of working-class organisation and consciousness, as Procacci has demonstrated. Artisans provided the backbone of worker activity in Milan and Turin in the 1870s; and it was skilled workers in printing, metalwork and clothing who took a lead in the formation of the Partito Operaio Italo (POI), a forerunner of the PSI. In fact, until the great Italian industrial boom of the early twentieth century the socialist movement recruited from urban craftsmen in small-scale concerns, often in small manufacturing towns.[129] Similarly in Russia, it was skilled workers, like tailors and locksmiths, in the 1860s and 1870s who first formed friendly societies, educational associations and more ambitious organisations such as the South Russian Union of Workers, formed at Odessa in 1873, and the National Union of Russian Workers, established in St Petersburg five years later.[130]

For some artisans and skilled workers what was involved was a desperate struggle to preserve their skills against machinery and their status and differentials against their less skilled and less fortunate colleagues. In many cases, as we have seen, the unions of the skilled were very restrictive in their practices. However, it was rare for the desperate and downwardly mobile to be involved in those organisations that were really successful in terms of their survival over time. They engaged in rather different styles of actions, as will be seen below. The success of the skilled in organisational terms was predicated upon strength, not weakness, as was clearly the case in trades untouched by technological modernisation, as in metalworking until the 1890s and as in new and expanding industries with a skilled work-force, such as engineering. The organisation of these groups followed improved rather than declining wages and was especially marked in times of economic boom. These were workers who had the time to engage in trade union and political activity, as the hours they worked were *relatively* few; and their relatively high wages gave them the financial resources to invest in the funds of trade unions and friendly societies. For example, the British Amalgamated Society of Engineers demanded a high subscription and was in a sufficiently strong financial position to donate no less than £3,000 to striking bricklayers in the winter of 1859/60.[131] Skilled craftsmen also enjoyed a relatively strong bargaining position *vis-à-vis* their employers, having skills to trade. Residential stability also seems to have furthered the prospects of organisation, generating informal networks of communication outside as well as inside the factory and helping to form a solidaristic consciousness. Thus strikes in France under the July monarchy took place in the older centres of manufacture, rather than in the big new cities or industries; protest came from groups well integrated into their communities.[132]

Finally, these relatively well paid and skilled sections of the working class possessed a culture which in a sense prepared them for organisation and action in a way that was not true for some of the most impoverished and unskilled factory workers. It was not only their strong position in the market that generated the ability to protest. First, artisans and skilled workers had expectations of a good wage, regular employment and decent treatment. It was such inherited expectations which made them so sensitive to a change in their circumstances. However, apart from such material considerations, they also possessed a sense of their own dignity, worth, independence and status which not only harked back to the guild privileges of the past but was reinforced by the whole system of apprenticeship; for apprenticeship was not simply about the transmission of technical skills but also involved the inculcation of values concerning status and tradition, pride not just in one's craft but one's personal worth. Hence the loss of independence or the absence of what passed for 'decent' treatment at the hands of new employers constituted a direct affront to these very values and guaranteed resistance. The skilled also possessed traditions of organisation going back to the guilds. Their lives were organised around long-standing associations peculiar to their crafts and they were used to and thought in terms of communal action. Hence it is perhaps not surprising that labour organisations in Germany appeared less in the exploding new industries of the Ruhr than in towns with strong guild traditions, such as Berlin and Leipzig.

Many of these points also apply to a group of workers who resorted to very different forms of action, namely direct action, violence and sometimes politics: the downwardly mobile artisans and domestic workers. These suffered a drastic decline in their living standards in the course of the Industrial Revolution, through a combination of falling wages and regular unemployment, as we have seen. As we have also seen, there were many different reasons for their plight. In some cases it was competition from mechanised factories, whether at home or abroad, that caused the problem, although this factor has often been exaggerated. Mechanisation also facilitated the exploitation of cheap female, child and unskilled labour. On other occasions the distress was a consequence of overmanning of a drastic kind in domestic weaving, both in the British and the Continental textile industry, of the increasing power of larger-scale merchants and manufacturers, of competition from the sweat-shops producing off-the-peg clothing, seasonal and cyclical unemployment, and a host of related phenomena. What made the reaction of the artisan and domestic worker to such hardship so much more pronounced than that of, say, unskilled factory textile employees was that the people affected had often been brought up in an environment of artisan values, with ideas of independence and expectations of some degree of financial security and social mobility. Indeed, in Britain handloom weavers even spoke of a former 'golden age' which was far from distant: for their industry had witnessed quite spectacular growth and an equally dramatic decline in a very short space of time.[133] Hence Luddism recruited from the ranks of framework knitters, handloom weavers and the like. Hence violent insurrection and other forms of direct action on the part of Chartists came from such groups of workers, whose commitment to this last cause was more sporadic and much more dependent upon economic fluctuations than that of the relatively secure artisans of London and Birmingham. In France many of the people who fought on the barricades in the June Days of 1848 came from trades experiencing high levels of unemployment and some kind of internal reorganisation, as was also the case in the Berlin upheavals of the same year. Later in the century French anarcho-syndicalism drew support from the depressed textile industries of Roubaix, Rheims, Roanne and Lyons, whilst the leading Social Democrats in Baden in the 1860s were displaced handworkers. The SPD in Halle also recruited predominantly from threatened artisans and August Bebel, the charismatic leader of German Social Democracy from the mid-1860s until his death in 1913, was elected to the Parliament of the North German Confederation in 1867 not by votes from the large industrial centre of Chemnitz, the 'German Manchester', but by the depressed domestic weavers of Gleichau-Meerane.[134] Obviously the long-term consequence of industrialisation was the demise of such groups and their volatile behaviour, although the process was a long and painful one and in the course of further industrial advance new skilled groups emerged which in their turn were subsequently threatened by deskilling.

For most of this early period before the emergence of really large-scale labour organisation in Britain after 1890, and in France, Germany and elsewhere subsequently, the unskilled factory proletariat employed in large firms was greatly underrepresented in the ranks of the organised. It was only after the 1880s that the Marxist party of Jules Guesde made headway amongst textile workers in the factories of northern France; and it has been suggested that whereas the Parisian artisanate was capable of devising spontaneous forms of organisation and ideology, these unskilled factory workers required external pressure for their mobilisation.[135] In Germany the trade union and socialist movements continued to be dominated by the skilled until after the turn of the century;[136] whilst English attempts to form strong national unions of the unskilled first came to nothing and only really took off with the 'new unionism' of the late 1880s.[137]

There are various factors which help to explain the absence of the unskilled factory proletariat, of manual labourers in various industries, of female machine operatives in textile factories and of groups like them, groups with no craft skills or training, from the ranks of organised protest. First, the unskilled by definition lacked bargaining assets in conflicts with their employers: they were easily replaced and thus weak in industrial muscle. Hence striking or joining a union could be an extremely risky enterprise, especially in times of economic depression and significant unemployment. This is one of the reasons why miners in villages in the Allier organised before their counterparts in the large urban centres: for their close contact with rural life and possession of agricultural resources made them less amenable to employer intimidation. Similarly in Germany workers in the huge iron and steel companies of the Ruhr, who sometimes lived in company housing and were often confronted by well organised and repressive employers who enjoyed a monopoly of the local labour market, were not those who unionised on any significant scale before the First World War. In fact when they did unionise, it was often in company unions, which in some areas of the Ruhr outstripped their socialist-affiliated Free Trade Union competitors.[138] It was not only the absence of a favourable position in the market-place, however, which deterred many from participation in strikes and trade union activity. There were other, more subtle, mechanisms at play. The provision of pension and insurance schemes by industrial magnates like Krupp and Stumm further helped to tie some workers to their employers; so did the system of 'locking-in', a system whereby an employee was guaranteed a steady improvement in his position and remuneration as long as he remained in the same factory and behaved himself.[139] Conversely a rapid turnover of labour from one firm to another militated against trade union organisation: workers simply were not in the same place long enough to form solid ties with the rest of the work-force.[140] A high turnover might also suggest that certain workers viewed their prospects of advancement as depending less upon collective action and more upon their personal initiative.

There is considerable evidence too that uprooting, distance migration from rural areas to new industrial areas, although perhaps alienating for the individual, was not propitious for collective action against capital. Thus German unions and socialist organisations were weak in the rapidly expanding industrial heartland of the Ruhr and much stronger in smaller towns;[141] the same appears to have been true in France.[142] The absence of well established networks of communication resulting from uprooting into an alien urban environment prevented worker solidarity: there seems to have been a time-lag between arrival in and adjustment to the new industrial order. It might seem that this contention falls on account of the Russian experience, in which newly arrived peasants have often been regarded as the basis of increasing industrial and political militancy in the large factories of Moscow and St Petersburg.[143] However, recent work has suggested that these new industrial workers possessed the ability to take collective action against their employers precisely because a large part of their existence was still rooted in the countryside, which provided the nexus of communications around which their solidaristic actions were based.[144] Again, therefore, it was not uprooting as such which constituted the stimulus to industrial protest.

A further crucial variable for any understanding of the relative quiescence of the unskilled labour force can be found in the absence of expectations and traditions of resistance to authority and economic exploitation. Groups from harsh rural backgrounds sometimes had relatively low expectations and often displayed a traditional resignation in the face of adversity; whilst even the appalling conditions in the early German factories were arguably no worse than the lot of the East Elbian farm labourer or of the domestic worker and his family. Similarly in France, urban wages were more or less double those in the countryside for most of the nineteenth century. Perhaps most obviously of all, low wages and a long and exhausting working day simply meant that most of the unskilled had neither the time, the energy nor the money to participate in economic and political organisation. In a sense it was improved living and working conditions, combined with adjustment to the new economic order and heightened expectations, which finally enabled these downtrodden groups to participate fully in the activities of the European labour movement.

There were many other, perhaps less tangible, factors which militated against independent labour activity and involvement in the work of trade unions and political parties. Age was one of these. As we will see later, radicalism among the working class at the end of the First World War was primarily located among younger workers. There were certain specific reasons for this in that particular historical conjuncture; but the phenomenon reflected more general realities of working-class existence as well. With age came increasing insecurity and declining wages for most manual trades.[145] An all-pervading insecurity, reinforced by the need to care for wife and children and roots which tied the worker to a particular locality, not surprisingly made older workers more cautious than their younger and unmarried colleagues. Religious attitudes also had a profound and far from defunct impact upon the economic and political activities of labour before the First World War. Confessional ties remained a crucial factor in Germany: the first strongholds of an emergent labour movement in the 1860s were on the Protestant northern seaboard, Berlin and Saxony, whilst Catholic workers both formed their own trade unions and remained loyal to the confessional Centre Party in the main until 1918. The only exceptions to this rule tended to be found in industrial areas in which the two major confessions were mixed, such as Dortmund, in Munich, which possessed cultural and political traditions very different to most of Germany, and in Alsace-Lorraine, where the SPD was the only party which did not give unconditional acceptance to the settlement of 1871. In totally Catholic areas which were none the less industrial, such as the Saarland, with its massive mining and metallurgical concerns, the SPD had little success in breaking the stranglehold of the Centre Party upon even the industrial proletariat.[146] It has also long been recognised that areas of high religious observance in France were areas in which the left fared badly at the polls and vice versa;[147] whilst in Italy anti-clericalism and working-class radicalism tended to overlap, as it did in Spain.[148] To some extent the wealth of the Church and its connections with right-wing politics might help to explain this, as might the simple fact that rapid urbanisation and the change in residential patterns left some working-class districts bereft of churches. However, the ability of the confessions to immunise the faithful against the evil doctrine of atheistic, materialistic socialism did not depend upon the residual strength of religious belief alone. It was partly a product of tying the worker into a whole nexus of confessional associations and culture, a product not just of the pulpit but of choral societies, insurance schemes, earthly as well as heavenly, educational associations, trade unions, political parties.

Confessional allegiance not only kept a significant section of the European working class away from socialist politics and certain kinds of trade union organisation; it also served to divide labour in its struggle against the employer. There were occasions on which Catholic and lay trade unions co-operated in the strikes of Ruhr miners, as in 1905; but there were others, as in 1912, in which the mutual hostility of the separate organisations doomed working-class resistance to failure. A further conflict which had a similar effect was that between different ethnic groups. In England many workers displayed a marked hostility to their Irish colleagues, a hostility which sometimes erupted in violence.[149] Similarly in Germany's Second Reich, Polish and German workers in the Ruhr rarely belonged to the same organisations and often revealed a profound mutual hostility, which sometimes led to fist-fights and was yet another issue preventing the formation of strong and united labour institutions.[150]

Residential factors could also play a part in helping to form or prevent the development of collective action. Carmaux glassworkers entered the ranks of labour protest in the 1880s not only when new technology transformed their situation in the factory but also when they came into closer residential contact with miners who had prior traditions of radicalism.[151] In the exploding Ruhr town of Bochum the residential solidarity of miners reinforced class consciousness, which seemed to be absent amongst metalworkers who lived in more socially mixed areas.[152] Conversely, Catholic workers in German towns who lived amongst their non-Catholic neighbours were to prove more amenable to the electoral appeal of Social Democracy than those of their faith who lived in confessionally homogeneous communities, as we have just seen.

In some cases the absence of certain workers from the ranks of protest might simply be explained by state legislation: in Germany, for example, state employees were expressly forbidden to join the Free Trade Unions or the SPD. On the other hand, the absence of expectations may have been the crucial factor, especially as far as women were concerned. Women did participate in various kinds of labour protest, as in the famous matchworkers' strike in Britain, where unions were beginning to have some success in mobilising them before the First World War.[153] In Germany too, Chemnitz witnessed an impressive strike of female textile workers and some women joined the ranks of the SPD.[154] However, such women tended to be the wives of labour aristocrats and not working themselves;[155] whilst the number of women engaged in European labour protest before the First World War remained disproportionately low. This is perhaps best explained by the fact that in many ways female workers were the archetype of the unskilled worker. They were exceptionally badly paid, worked exceedingly long hours in the factory and were then required to perform traditional housewifely duties in the home. Oppressed at home and at work, regarded as social inferiors by all but the most enlightened males, educated into obedience and limited expectations, it is hardly surprising that women so rarely participated in labour protest on the grand scale. Significantly, those women who did succeed in forming relatively strong unions themselves worked in more skilled trades and enjoyed certain bargaining assets.[156]

None of the above is intended to suggest that the unskilled were happy with their miserable lot. On the contrary, their usual failure to act may simply have been a consequence of a quite accurate assessment of the prospects of defeat. Furthermore, they did participate in certain kinds of sporadic and sometimes violent protest before 1890. To cite only a few examples, gangs of railway navvies and especially unskilled Irish labour often fought pitched battles against both one another and their employers in Britain in the 1830s and 1840s;[157] whilst there were riots of unskilled railway workers in the Rhineland and Westphalia between 1845 and 1848.[158] In France some unskilled workers fought on the barricades in June 1848, although they were not the typical insurgents and in any case the national workshops had helped to concentrate and politicise them in a way that was rather exceptional.[159] French textile workers and miners, whose inclusion in the unskilled category is admittedly problematic, also engaged in violent strike activity in 1869, although their participation in more organised forms of protest in general came later.[160]

What does seem to be true is that although dislocation, lack of bargaining power etc. may militate against organised and sustained protest, they none the less can produce a more volatile and direct response at particular points in time. Thus the activity of the major French trade union organisation, the Confédération Générale du Travail (CGT) changed markedly in style and was radicalised by an influx of new members after 1900; but equally rapidly a process of demobilisation set in.[161] In Germany the militancy of Ruhr miners and the growth of anarcho-syndicalist tendencies immediately prior to the First World War have likewise been attributed to the influx of the rural unskilled, as has the radicalism of chemical workers in the Leuna factory at Halle between 1919 and 1923.[162] In Russia the Bolsheviks were far more likely to recruit from workers of peasant origin than the Mensheviks; whilst the increase in direct action in Moscow and St Petersburg between 1911 and 1914 has also been attributed to the influx of peasant labour into the giant textile and metallurgical plants.[163]

In this last context the type of rural background from which the new factory work-force was recruited would seem to be of considerable significance. Where it came from rural labourers who were used to harsh discipline and had few traditions of protest, as in the case of those industrial workers in the Ruhr and Silesia recruited from East Elbian farms, violent reaction against factory life was far less common than in Russia, where traditions of peasant collectivism and radicalism − after the turn of the century − were strong. Whereas skilled workers in Russia in the 1860s and 1870s formed friendly societies, educational associations and trade unions, the unskilled expressed their discontents against the factory system in desertion, drunkenness and violence. In Spain the concentrated factory proletariat of the northern Basque provinces in heavy industry, recruited from a hierarchical background of strong conservative and clerical influence with no tradition of rural militancy, inclined to a strongly centralised and disciplined socialist movement; whereas the relatively backward textile industry of Catalonia produced a violent and uncontrollable work-force, at least in part because the origins of this work-force were to be found in Catalonia, where a rural proletariat experienced huge economic problems and had a strong tradition of violent, almost millenarian, protest. Furthermore, the nature of the Spanish Socialist Party changed dramatically in the early 1930s, with the influx of a violent rural proletariat from the latifundia of Extremadura and parts of Andalusia, and thus became far more radical and far less amenable to centralised control.[164] Thus different kinds of backgrounds and different levels of skill related to different styles of working-class protest.

Whether skilled or unskilled, however, organised protest involved but a small minority of European labour before 1890. As the disillusioned Julius Vahlteich, a founder of independent working-class organisation in Leipzig, remarked in the 1860s:

> If we look at close range at the great majority of workers, we find that they are dead to every earnest, enlightened, new and scientific idea ... they are not in the least interested in politics, in their own welfare, or in the conditions and rights of the working class. They live from day to day — for them it is only a question of working, eating, drinking and sleeping.[165]

It was to take time to change this situation.

This chapter has tried to do perhaps too many things. Its main objective, however, has been to identify the emergence of modern labour protest, characterised by strikes, trade union organisation and the formation of working-class political parties. It has become clear that this form of protest was no inevitable and unmediated consequence of the Industrial Revolution and most certainly not a direct response to intolerable poverty or feelings of alienation and disquiet at the new order. Only certain groups of workers responded to the process by engaging in protest; and these were overwhelmingly those with a highly developed set of values and expectations concerning their role in the world. These skilled men engaged in various activities, some of which might be construed as opposition to the new industrial order or at least the momentary forms of its organisation in private hands; but the shape of those activities depended upon the attitudes of employers and ruling classes as much as it did upon the worker's own situation in the factory. For most of the nineteenth century, therefore, the terrain of labour protest was determined more by the enemies of the working class than by its own volition. It was also a terrain occupied by relatively few workers before 1890. Thereafter things changed quite dramatically.

Notes

1. E.J. Hobsbawm and G.F.E. Rudé, *Captain Swing* (London, 1969).

2. Alan Booth, 'Food Riots in the North-West of England 1790-1801', *Past and Present*, no. 77 (1977), pp. 84-107; Louise Tilly, 'La révolte frumentaire, forme de conflit politique en France', *Annales*, vol. 27, no. 3 (1972), pp. 731-57; Charles Tilly, 'The Changing Place of Collective Violence' in M. Richter (ed.) *Essays in Theory and History* (Cambridge, Mass., 1970), p. 139; Richard Tilly, 'Popular Disorders in Nineteenth Century Germany', *Journal of Social History*, no. 1 (1970), pp. 25-30; Roger Wells, 'The Revolt of the South-West, 1800-1801', *Social History*, no. 6 (1977), pp. 713-44; George Rudé, *The Crowd in History* (New York, 1964), pp. 9-38 all discuss earlier food riots. For Italy see Richard Hostetter, *The Italian Socialist Movement*, vol. 1, *Origins (1860-1882)* (Princeton, 1958), pp. 128-35; for food riots in the First World War see Gerald D. Feldman, 'Socioeconomic Structures in the Industrial Sector and Revolutionary Potentialities 1917-22' in Charles L. Bertrand (ed.), *Revolutionary Situations in Europe, 1917-1922: Germany, Italy, Austria-Hungary* (Montreal, 1977), p. 161.

3. For a description of the typology of food riots see note 2.

4. Rudé, *Crowd*, p. 38; Louise Tilly, 'Révolte frumentaire', *passim*; and especially E.P. Thompson, 'The Moral Economy of the English Crowd in the Eighteenth Century', *Past and Present*, no. 50 (1971), pp. 76-136.

5. Thompson, 'Moral Economy', p. 108; Booth, 'Food Riots', p. 93f.

6. Thompson, 'Moral Economy', p. 108; Booth, 'Food Riots', p. 98.

7. Thompson, 'Moral Economy', p. 108 and 116; Booth, 'Food Riots', p. 98.

8. Wells, 'Revolt of the South-West', p. 717.

9. Thompson, 'Moral Economy', pp. 83-7; Louise Tilly, 'Révolte frumentaire', p. 757.

10. S.G. Checkland, *The Rise of Industrial Society in England 1815-1885* (Oxford, 1964), p. 368.

11. Robert J. Holton, 'The Crowd in History: Some Problems of Theory and Method', *Social History*, vol. 3, no. 2 (1978), p. 231.

12. E.P. Thompson, ' "Rough Music": Le Charivari anglais', *Annales*, no. 2 (1972), p. 308.

13. Holton, 'The Crowd', p. 223f.

14. Gareth Stedman Jones, *Outcast London* (Oxford, 1971), pp. 343ff.

15. Booth, 'Food Riots', p. 91; Wells, 'Revolt of the South-West', p. 740; Rudé, *Crowd*, p. 37.

16. William M. Reddy, 'The Textile Trade and the Language of the Crowd at Rouen 1752-1871', *Past and Present*, no. 74 (1977), p. 76.

17. Ibid., p. 80.

18. See Ch. 1, note 24.

19. Rudé, *Crowd*, Ch. 7.

20. See note 9 above.

21. Charles Tilly, 'The Changing Place', *passim*, and 'How Protest Modernised in France, 1845-1855' in William O. Aydelotte, Allen G. Borgue and Robert W. Vogel (eds.), *The Dimensions of Quantitative Research in History* (Oxford, 1972), *passim*.

22. See Chapter 1, note 7.

23. Friedrich Engels, *Condition of the Working Class in England* (trans. and ed. Henderson and Chaloner) (London, 1958).

24. Louis Chevalier, *Classes Laborieuses et Classes Dangereuses à Paris* (Paris, 1958).

25. Frank B. Tipton, *Regional Variations in the Economic Development of Germany during the Nineteenth Century* (Middleton, Conn., 1976), pp. 127-30.

26.　Jürgen Kocka, *Unternehmerverwaltung und Angestelltenschaft* (Stuttgart, 1969), p. 65.

27.　For examples of the regulations of German employers see Heilwig Schomerus, *Die Arbeiter der Maschinenfabrik Esslingen* (Stuttgart, 1977), pp. 315-29; also David Crew, *Town in the Ruhr. A Social History of Bochum* (New York, 1979), pp. 145-57.

28.　See T.S. Ashton, 'The Standard of Life of the Workers in England, 1790-1830' in a Supplement to the *Journal of Economic History* (1949); A.J. Taylor, 'Progress and Poverty in Britain 1780-1850', *History* (1960); R.M. Hartwell, 'The Rising Standard of Living in England, 1800-1850', *Economic History Review* (1961); E.J. Hobsbawm, 'The British Standard of Living, 1790-1850', *Economic History Review* (1963); E.P. Thompson, *The Making of the English Working Class* (London, 1978), Ch. 8; Brian Inglis, *Poverty in the Industrial Revolution* (London, 1972).

29.　Checkland, *Rise*, p. 231.

30.　Inglis, *Poverty*, passim.

31.　Crew, *Bochum*, pp. 46-58; Schomerus, *Die Arbeiter*, pp. 124-57; Jürgen Tampke, *The Ruhr and Revolution in the Rhenish-Westphalian Industrial Region 1912-1919* (London, 1979), Ch. 1.

32.　Inglis, *Poverty*, p. 30.

33.　For French real wages see George Dupeux, *La Société Française 1789-1960* (Paris, 1964), p. 145f.; Bernard Moss, *The Origins of the French Labour Movement* (Berkeley, 1976), p. 39f. For Germany see Theodor S. Hamerow, *Restoration, Revolution, Reaction* (Princeton, 1958), Ch. 5.

34.　Charles Tilly and Lynn H. Lees, 'The People of June, 1848' in Roger Price (ed.), *Revolution and Reaction, 1848 and the Second French Republic* (London, 1975), pp. 170-207; Richard Tilly, 'Popular Disorders', p. 31f.

35.　William Sewell, 'Social Change and the Rise of Working-Class Politics in Nineteenth Century Marseilles', *Past and Present*, no. 65 (1974), p. 84; Richard Tilly, 'Popular Disorders', p. 32; Christopher H. Johnson, 'Economic Change and Artisan Discontent: the Tailor's History, 1800-1848' in Price, *Revolution*, pp. 87f.

36.　E.P. Thompson, *The Making*, p. 217, 274-89 and 309-14; Hamerow, *Restoration*, Ch. 2; Peter N. Stearns, *The Revolutions of 1848* (London, 1974), pp. 20-8. pp. 20-8.

37.　This, indeed, is the central theme of E.P. Thompson's *The Making*. See also John Breuilly, 'Artisan economy – artisan values – artisan politics', unpublished MS. delivered to the fourth session of the SSRC Research Group on Modern German Social History at the University of East Anglia, July 1980.

38.　See below, pp. 70-80.

39.　Roger Penn, 'Skilled Manual Workers in the Labour Process', unpublished MS., University of Lancaster.

40.　See below, pp. 70-80.

41.　Hamerow, *Restoration*, p. 82f.; Hans Rosenberg, *Grosse Depression und Bismarckzeit* (Berlin, 1967), p. 40; Lawrence Schofer, *The Formation of a Modern Labour Force. Upper Silesia, 1865-1914* (Berkeley, 1975), pp. 131-6.

42.　Malcolm I. Thomis and Peter Holt, *Threats ⟨ Revolution in Britain 1789-1848* (London, 1977), pp. 31-6; Malcolm Thomis, *he Town Labourer and the Industrial Revolution* (London, 1974), pp. 77ff.; ⟨ ompson, *The Making*, Ch. 14; Rudé, *Crowd*, pp. 80-3; Richard Tilly, 'Popular ⟩ ⟨orders', p. 31; Charles Tilly, Louise Tilly and Richard Tilly, *The Rebellious Century* (London, 1975), p. 301f.; Jones, 'Economic Change' in Price, *Revolution*, p. 87; Edouard Dolléans, *Histoire du Mouvement Ouvrier*, vol. 1, *1830-1871* (Paris, 1936), p. 58; Patrick Kessel, *Le prolétariat Français avant Marx* (Paris, 1968), pp. 197, 236, 250; Hamerow, *Restoration*, pp. 33-6 and 84ff.; Dieter Dowe, *Aktion und Organisation* (Hanover, 1970), pp. 27-35.

43.　Hobsbawm and Rudé, *Swing*; David Jones, 'Thomas Campbell Fraser and the Rural Labourer: Incendiarism in East Anglia in the 1840s', *Social History*

(January 1976), pp. 5-43.

44. K.F. Donnelly, 'Ideology and Early English Working-class History: Edward Thompson and his Critics', *Social History* (May 1976), p. 227.

45. E.P. Thompson, *The Making*, pp. 529-60; Thomis and Hall, *Threats of Revolution*, pp. 33ff.; Jones, 'Thomas Campbell Fraser', pp. 14ff.; Rudé, *Crowd*, p. 83.

46. Jones, 'Thomas Campbell Fraser', p. 31.

47. Rudé, *Crowd*, p. 80.

48. Peter N. Stearns, *Lives of Labour. Work in a Maturing Industrial Society* (London, 1975), p. 126.

49. See Penn, 'Skilled Labour'; Dick Geary, 'The German Labour Movement 1848-1918', *European Studies Review*, vol. 6, no. 3 (1976), p. 298.

50. Joan Wallach Scott, *The Glassworkers of Carmaux* (Cambridge, Mass., 1974), pp. 53ff., 55-64 and 80-96.

51. Dick Geary, 'Radicalism and the German Worker: Metalworkers and Revolution 1914-1923' in Richard J. Evans (ed.), *Society and Politics in Wilhelmine Germany* (London, 1978), pp. 279-81; Klaus Tenfelde, 'Anarcho-Syndikalistische Strömungen in der Ruhr Bergarbeiterschaft 1906-1914', unpublished MS. for the second session of the SSRC Modern German Social History Research Group at the University of East Anglia, January 1979; James Hinton, *The First Shop Stewards' Movement* (London, 1973).

52. Hamerow, *Restoration*, Ch. 8; Paul Noyes, *Organization and Revolution* (Princeton, 1966); Georges Duveau, *1848: The Making of a Revolution* (New York, 1967).

53. Rudé, *Crowd*, pp. 66f.; Kessel, *Le Prolétariat*, Ch. 1.

54. Thomis, *Town Labourer*, p. 129; Thompson, *The Making*, p. 564 and 887ff.; David Jones, *Chartism and the Chartists* (London, 1975), pp. 138-43; Shorter and Tilly, *Strikes*, pp. 107-10; Richard Tilly, 'Popular Disorders', pp. 16-19, Dowe, *Aktion*, pp. 33-41. For 1848 see note 52 above.

55. The argument that the 'Great Depression' was little more than a myth may be true in aggregate economic terms. However, studies of the fortunes of specific sections of the working class suggest a very different picture. See what happened, for example, to employment and wage levels at an engineering factory in Esslingen: Schomerus, *Die Arbeiter*, Ch. III.

56. Geary, 'German Labour Movement', p. 302; Shorter and Tilly, *Strikes*, pp. 97-102; Dolléans, *Mouvement Ouvrier*, vol. 1, p. 181.

57. Thompson, *The Making*, p. 564; Shorter and Tilly, *Strikes*, p. 110; Bernard H. Moss, *The Origins of the French Labour Movement 1830-1914* (Berkeley, 1976), pp. 53ff.; Geary, 'German Labour Movement', p. 300f.

58. Thompson, *The Making*, p. 460; Thomis, *Town Labourer*, pp. 127-32; E.J. Hobsbawm, *Labouring Men* (London, 1979), Chs. 9 and 10; David Kynaston, *King Labour. The British Working Class 1850-1914*, pp. 51-4, Shorter and Tilly, *Strikes*, pp. 110ff.; Moss, *Origins*, pp. 11ff.; Kessel, *Le Prolétariat*, p. 201; Geary, 'German Labour Movement', pp. 300-4.

59. See below, pp. 74-80.

60. Mitchell and Stearns, *Workers*, pp. 165-81.

61. D. Vasseur, *Les Débuts du Mouvement Ouvrier dans la Région de Belfort-Montebehard* (Paris, 1967).

62. The Tillys, *Rebellious Century*, p. 20, 196 and 218ff.

63. See Ch. 1, notes 12 and 13.

64. Hedwig Wachenheim, *Die deutsche Arbeiterbewegung 1844 bis 1914* (Cologne and Opladen, 1967), p. 108.

65. See below, pp. 58-64.

66. Wachenheim, *Arbeiterbewegung*, p. 124.

67. Solomon M. Schwarz, *The Russian Revolution of 1905* (Chicago, 1967).

68.   See his remarks in *Karl Marx and Friedrich Engels on Britain* (Moscow, 1962), pp. 28-33 and 567f.

69.   David Footman, *Ferdinand Lassalle. Romantic Revolutionary* (New York, 1969), p. 201; Richard W. Reichard, *Crippled from Birth. German Social Democracy 1844-1870* (Iowa, 1969), pp. 165 and 190.

70.   For Proudhonist influence see Moss, *Origins*, pp. 48-54; Dolléans, *Mouvement Ouvrier*, vol. 1, pp. 280-310. For anarcho-syndicalism see Peter N. Stearns, *Revolutionary Syndicalism and French Labour* (New Brunswick, 1971).

71.   See below, pp. 74-80.

72.   Thomis, *Town Labourer*, p. 129; Thompson, *The Making*, p. 46; Dolléans, *Mouvement Ouvrier*, vol. 1, pp. 55, 73, 96; Günther Bergmann, *Das Sozialistengesetz im rechtsrheinischen Industriegebiet* (Hanover, 1970); Vernon L. Lidtke, *The Outlawed Party* (Princeton, 1966); Geary, 'German Labour Movement', p. 298f.; Hostetter, *Italian Socialist Movement*, p. 49; Allan K. Wildman, *The Making of a Workers' Revolution. Russian Social Democracy, 1891-1903* (Chicago, 1967), pp. 30-5; Franco Venturi, *Roots of Revolution. A History of the Populist and Socialist Movements in Nineteenth Century Russia* (London, 1960), p. 507; Ezra Mendelsohn, *Class Struggle in the Pale. The Formative Years of the Jewish Workers' Movement in Tsarist Russia* (Cambridge, 1970), pp. 35f.; Martin Blinkhorn, 'Industrialisation and Social Protest in Spain', unpublished MS.

73.   Jones, *Chartism and the Chartists*, p. 45f.; Asa Briggs, *Chartist Studies* (London, 1977), p. 4f.; Geary, 'German Labour Movement', p. 302f.; Dieter Dowe, 'Organisatorische Anfänge der Arbeiterbewegung' in Jürgen Reulecke (ed.), *Arbeiterbewegung an Rhein und Ruhr* (Wuppertal, 1974), pp. 113-67; Dowe, *Aktion und Organisation*, pp. 157 and 159; Wolfgang Schmierer, *Von der Arbeiterbildung zur Arbeiterpolitik* (Hanover, 1970) *passim* and esp. p. 56 and Ch. 4; Jörg Schadt, *Die Sozialdemokratische Partei in Baden* (Hanover, 1971), pp. 29ff.; Franz Osterroth, *Biographisches Lexikon des Sozialismus* (Hanover, 1960), p. 16; Frolinde Balser, *Sozial-Demokratie 1848/9 - 1863* (Stuttgart, 1965), pp. 29-33; Hugo Eckert, *Liberal- oder Sozialdemokratie. Frühgeschichte der Nürnberger Arbeiterbewegung* (Stuttgart, 1968), pp. 12 and 80-120.

74.   J.T. Ward (ed.), *Popular Movements c.1830-1850* (London, 1970), p. 102; Thompson, *The Making*, pp. 868-72; Moss, *Origins, passim*; Dolléans, *Mouvement Ouvrier*, vol. 1, pp. 74f. and 279ff.; George Lichtheim, *The Origins of Socialism* (London, 1969), pp. 75-82; George Lichtheim, *A Short History of Socialism* (London, 1970), p. 91f.; Footman, *Lassalle, passim*; Shlomo Na'aman, *Lassalle* (Hanover, 1970), *passim*; Schmierer, *Von der Arbeiterbildung*, p. 64; Schadt, *Sozialdemokratische Partei*, p. 31; Ursula Schulz, *Die deutsche Arbeiterbewegung 1848-1919 in Augenzeugen berichtet* (Düsseldorf, 1968), p. 123f.; Wachenheim, *Arbeiterbewegung*, p. 82f.

75.   Ward, *Popular Movements*, Ch. 4; Thomis, *Town Labourer*, pp. 127-43; Thompson, *The Making*, pp. 550-70; David Kynaston, *King Labour. The British Working Class 1850-1914* (London, 1976), pp. 17ff. and 52ff.

76.   Jacques Droz, *Le Socialisme Démocratique 1864-1960* (Paris, 1966), pp. 18ff.; Moss, *Origins*, pp. 10ff. and 40-54; R. Gossez, 'L'Organisation Ouvrière à Paris sous la Seconde République', *Revue des Révolutions Contemporaines*, vol. 42 (1950); Dolléans, *Mouvement Ouvrier*, vol. 1, pp. 55-82 and 279-335; Kessel, *Prolétariat*, pp. 200ff. and 313; Hostetter, *Italian Socialist Movement*, p. 123; Donald H. Bell, 'Worker Culture and Worker Politics: the Experience of an Italian Town, 1880-1915', *Social History*, vol. 3, no. 1 (1978), pp. 1-21; Donald Bell's review of Merlo in *Journal of Social History*, no. 1 (1976), p. 132f.; Giuliano Procacci, *La Lotta di Classe in Italia agli Inizi del Secolo xx* (Rome, 1972), pp. 23ff.; Venturi, *Roots of Revolution*, pp. 507-11.

77.   Noyes, *Organisation and Revolution, passim*; Ulrich Engelhardt, *'Nur vereinigt sind wir stark'. Die Anfänge der deutschen Gewerkschaftsbewegung*

1862/63 bis 1869/70 (Stuttgart, 1976), *passim*; Geary, 'German Labour Movement', pp. 298-301; Dowe, 'Organisatorische Anfänge', p. 59.f; Dowe, *Aktion*, pp. 248, 273 and 289-92; Schmierer, *Von der Arbeiterbildung*, p. 40 and Ch. 4; Balser, *Sozial-Demokratie*, pp. 33 and 66f.

78. Jones, *Chartism*, p. 138; Dolléans, *Mouvement Ouvrier*, vol. 1, p. 81; Dowe, *Aktion*, pp. 244-8 and 290f.; Schadt, *Sozialdemokratische Partei*, p. 32f.

79. Patricia Hollis (ed.), *Class and Class Conflict in the Nineteenth Century. 1815-1850* (London, 1973), p. 163; Kynaston, *King Labour*, p. 11 and *passim*; Geary, 'German Labour Movement', p. 163.

80. Thompson, *The Making*, p. 216 and *passim*; Robert J. Bezucha, 'The "Pre-Industrial" Worker Movement: the *Canuts* of Lyon' in Clive Emsley (ed.), *Conflict and Stability in Europe* (London, 1979), p. 62; Dolléans, *Mouvement Ouvrier*, vol. 1, pp. 172-9; John Plamenatz, *The Revolutionary Movement in France 1815-1871* (London, 1952), *passim*.

81. Lidtke, *Outlawed Party, passim*; Bergmann, *Sozialistengesetz, passim*; Geary, 'German Labour Movement', p. 304f.

82. V.I. Lenin, *Collected Works*, (Moscow, 1961), vol. 5, p. 383f.

83. John Foster, *Class Conflict in the Industrial Revolution* (London, 1974), *passim*; Central Committee of the East German Communist Party, *Geschichte der deutschen Arbeiterbewegung* (Berlin, 1966), *passim*.

84. For the reception of Marx and Lassalle in Germany see Footman, *Lassalle*; Na'aman, *Lassalle*; George Lichtheim, *Marxism. An Historical and Critical Study* (London, 1964), esp. Part 5; R.J. Geary, 'Karl Kautsky and the Development of German Marxism', unpublished Ph.D thesis, Cambridge, 1971. For the reception of French theorists, Lichtheim, *Origins*, Part 1. For Russia, Lichtheim, *Short History*, Chs. 7 and 8. For the social composition of anarchist support see below, pp. 79f. For Russian workers in 1905 see Schwarz, *Russian Revolution of 1905*, p. 111. For July 1917, Marc Férro, *La Révolution de 1917* (Paris, 1967), pp. 456-66. For Martov, J.L.H. Keep, *The Rise of Social Democracy in Russia* (Oxford, 1966), p. 46. Also Israel Getzler, *Martov. A Political Biography of a Russian Social Democrat* (Cambridge, 1967), *passim*. For the anti-intellectual sentiments of some Russian workers see Venturi, *Roots of Revolution*, pp. 517, 539 and 552; Wildman, *Making of a Workers' Revolution*, p. 94f.

85. Stearns, *Revolutionary Syndicalism, passim*.

86. Steinberg, *Sozialismus, passim*.

87. See the articles in *Journal of Social History* (1978). Also Guenther Roth, *The Social Democrats in Imperial Germany. A Study in Working Class Isolation and National Integration* (Totowa, NJ, 1963), *passim*.

88. R.P. Morgan, *German Social Democrats and the First International 1864-72* (Cambridge, 1965), *passim*; Susanne Miller, *Das Problem der Freiheit im Sozialismus* (Frankfurt am Main, 1964), *passim*; Geary, 'German Labour Movement', p. 302f.

89. Geary, 'Radicalism', pp. 270-3.

90. Erhard Lucas, *Arbeiterradikalismus, passim*; Eve Rosenhaft, 'The German Communists and Paramilitary Violence 1929-1933', unpublished Ph.D thesis, Cambridge, 1979.

91. This is the central thesis of Thompson, *The Making*.

92. Engels, *On Britain*, pp. 28-33; E.J. Hobsbawm, *Labouring Men* (London, 1979), Ch. 15; Kynaston, *King Labour*, p. 12; Harry J. Marks, 'Sources of Reformism in the Social Democratic Party of Germany, 1890-1914', *Journal of Modern History*, vol. XI, no. 3 (1939).

93. Hobsbawm, *Labouring Men*, Ch. 15; Thomis, *Town Labourer*, pp. 192ff.; Kynaston, *King Labour*, p. 12f.

94. Moss, *Origins*, pp. 14ff.

95. See below, pp. 107-26.

96.   A.E. Musson, 'Class Struggle and Labour Aristocracy 1830-1860' *Social History*, no. 3 (1976), pp. 335-56; Gareth Stedman Jones, 'England's First Proletariat', *New Left Review*, no. 90 (1975), pp. 35-69.
97.   Stedman Jones, 'First Proletariat', pp. 52ff.; Thompson, *The Making*, p. 325f.; Jones, *Chartism*, pp. 153-8; Ward, *Popular Movements*, pp. 7f., 108 and 121.
98.   Stearns, *Revolutionary Syndicalism, passim*; Shorter and Tilly, *Strikes, passim*; Theodore Zeldin, *France 1848-1945*, vol. 1 (Oxford, 1973), pp. 224 and 238ff.
99.   Frank Wilkinson, 'Collective Bargaining in the Steel Industry in the 1920s' in Asa Briggs and John Saville (eds.), *Essays in Labour History 1918-1939* (London, 1977), p. 102; J.T. Ward and W. Hamish Fraser, *Workers and Employers* (London, 1980), Ch. 6; Kynaston, *King Labour*, p. 152f.; Stearns, *Lives*, p. 180f.
100.   Stearns, *Lives*, pp. 180f. and 165; Geoff Eley, 'Capitalism and the Wilhelmine State', *The Historical Journal*, vol. 21 (1978), p. 742; Jürgen Kuczynski, *Die Geschichte der Lage der Arbeiter unter dem Kapitalismus*, Part 1, vol. 3, *Darstellung der Lage der Arbeiter in Deutschland von 1871 bis 1900* (Berlin, 1962), pp. 43ff.
101.   Kynaston, *King Labour*, p. 152.
102.   Ibid., pp. 157-62.
103.   Schwarz, *Russian Revolution of 1905, passim*; Robert Looker (ed.), *Rosa Luxemburg. Selected Political Writings* (London, 1972), pp. 117-34.
104.   Thompson, *The Making*, p. 216.
105.   See note 80 above.
106.   For 1848 see Duveau, *1848*, pp. 133-56; for the Commune see Moss, *Origins*, pp. 61ff. For later government activities, ibid., pp. 88 and 148. For the 1860s, Dolléans, *Mouvement Ouvrier*, vol. 1, pp. 279-300.
107.   Stearns, *Revolutionary Syndicalism, passim*; Albert S. Lindeman, *The 'Red Years'* (Berkeley, 1974), p. 6f.; Claude Willard, *Socialisme et Communisme Français* (Paris, 1967), pp. 51-73; Claude Willard, *Les Guesdistes* (Paris, 1965), *passim*; David Stafford, *From Anarchism to Reformism. Paul Brousse* (London, 1971), *passim*; Shorter and Tilly, *Strikes*, pp. 31ff. and 42f.
108.   Lidtke, *The Outlawed Party, passim*; Bergmann, *Sozialistengesetz, passim*; Alex Hall, 'By Other Means: the Legal Struggle Against the SPD in Wilhelmine Germany 1890-1900', *The Historical Journal*, vol. 17 (1974), *passim*; Geary, 'German Labour Movement', *passim*.
109.   Marks, 'Origins of Reformism', *passim*; Geary, 'German Labour Movement', pp. 305ff.; Carl E. Schorske, *German Social Democracy 1905-1917* (Cambridge, Mass., 1955), pp. 7-27 and Chs. 4, 5 and 6; Schadt, *Sozialdemokratische Partei, passim*; Georg Kotowski, *Friedrich Ebert* (Wiesbaden, 1963), *passim*; J.P. Nettl, 'The German Social Democratic Party as a Political Model', *Past and Present*, no. 30 (1965), pp. 65-95.
110.   See note 109 above.
111.   Adrian Lyttleton, 'Revolution and Counter-revolution in Italy, 1918-1922' in Charles L. Bertrand (ed.), *Revolutionary Situations in Europe, 1917-1922: Germany, Italy, Austria-Hungary* (Montreal, 1977), pp. 63ff.; the Tillys, *Rebellious Century*, pp. 97ff. and 143; Gerald Brenan, *The Spanish Labyrinth* (Cambridge, 1962), p. 156f.; Gabriel Jackson, *The Spanish Republic and the Civil War 1931-1939* (Princeton, 1965), pp. 276-309.
112.   Schwarz, *Russian Revolution of 1905, passim*; Oskar Anweiler, *Die Rätebewegung in Russland 1905-1921, passim*; E.H. Carr, *The Bolshevik Revolution 1917-1923* (London, 1966), Part I, *passim*.
113.   Thomis, *Town Labourer*, p. 26; Thomis and Holt, *Threats of Revolution*, p. 100; Jones, *Chartism*, p. 120f.; Briggs, *Chartist Studies*, pp. 38ff.
114.   Geary, 'German Labour Movement', p. 302f.; Schmierer, *Von der Arbeit-*

erbildung, passim and esp. p. 33; Balser, *Sozial-Demokratie, passim*; Reichard, *Crippled from Birth*, p. 128.

115.   Hans-Ulrich Wehler, *Das deutsche Kaiserreich 1871-1918* (Göttingen, 1973); H. Böhme, *Deutschlands Weg zur Grossmacht* (Cologne, 1966); Dirk Stegmann, *Die Erben Bismarcks* (Cologne, 1970); V.R. Berghahn, *Der Tirpitz-Plan* (Düsseldorf, 1971); Hans-Jurgen Puhle, *Agrarische Interessenpolitik und Preussischer Conservatismus im Wilhelmischen Reich* (Hanover, 1966).

116.   David Blackbourn, *Class, Religion and Local Politics in Wilhelmine Germany* (New Haven, 1980); Geoff Eley, *Reshaping the German Right* (New Haven, 1980).

117.   Eley, *Reshaping, passim*.

118.   Moss, *Origins*, p. 68.

119.   See above, p. 58.

120.   Leon Trotsky, *The History of the Russian Revolution*, vol. 1 (trans. Max Eastman) (London, 1967), Ch. 1.

121.   Bell, 'Worker Culture', p. 2.

122.   Penn, 'Skilled Manual Workers', p. 4 and *passim*.

123.   Kocka, *Unternehmerverwaltung*, p. 65.

124.   Thompson, *The Making*, pp. 457-64; Jones, *Chartism*, p. 24; Briggs, *Chartist Studies*, pp. 4-8; Thomis, *Town Labourer*, p. 132f.; Kynaston, *King Labour*, pp. 17ff.; Ward and Fraser, *Workers*, p. 104f.; Henry Pelling, *A History of British Trade Unionism* (London, 1966), p. 42f.; Wilkinson, 'Collective Bargaining', p. 103.

125.   Georges Dupeux, *La Société Française 1789-1960* (Paris, 1964), p. 152f.; the Tillys, *Rebellious Century*, p. 41f.; Shorter and Tilly, *Strikes*, pp. 110 and 154-60; Moss, *Origins*, pp. 9ff., 71, 125ff. and 151f.; Dolléans, *Mouvement Ouvrier*, vol. 1, pp. 55, 74-81 and 279-300; Kessel, *Prolétariat*, pp. 200f. and 347; Vasseur, *Les Débuts, passim*; Sewell, 'Social Change', p. 81.

126.   Na'aman, *Lassalle*, pp. 682ff.; Noyes, *Organization and Revolution, passim*; Hamerow, *Restoration*, Ch. 8; Geary, 'German Labour Movement', pp. 298-304; Dowe, *Aktion*, pp. 145 and 244-8; Schmierer, *Von der Arbeiterbildung*, pp. 55, 58ff. and 207-28; Schadt, *Sozialdemokratische Partei*, pp. 22, 32, 63, 76f., 94f. and 109; Bergmann, *Sozialistengesetz*, pp. 19, 73 and 91n.; Wachenheim, *Arbeiterbewegung*, p. 182; Balser, *Sozial-Demokratie*, pp. 20 and 92f.; Reichard, *Crippled from Birth*, p. 125f.; Eckert, *Liberal- oder Sozialdemokratie*, pp. 83, 157 and 249-70; Morgan, *German Social Democrats*, p. 4; Gerhard A. Ritter, *Die Arbeiterbewegung im Wilhelmischen Reich* (Berlin, 1959), p. 9; Helga Grebing, *The History of the German Labour Movement* (London, 1969), p. 48; Georg Gärtner, *Die Nürnberger Arbeiterbewegung 1868-1908* (Nuremberg, 1908), pp. 23 and 69-75.

127.   Hans Hautmann and Rudolf Kropf, *Die österreichische Arbeiterbewegung vom Vormärz bis 1945* (Linz, 1974), Chs. 3 and 4.

128.   Brenan, *Spanish Labyrinth*, p. 215.

129.   Bell, 'Worker Culture', pp. 2-7; Procacci, *La Lotta di Classe*, pp. 23ff.; the Tillys, *Rebellious Century*, p. 120.

130.   Venturi, *Roots of Revolution*, pp. 507-11 and 552; Wildman, *Making of a Workers' Revolution*, pp. 30-7 and *passim*; Mendelsohn, *Class Struggle*, p. 37.

131.   Kynaston, *King Labour*, p. 18.

132.   Moss, *Origins*, p. 11f.; Peter Stearns, 'Patterns of Industrial Strike Activity in France during the July Monarchy', *American Historical Review*, no. 70 (1965), pp. 371-94; Charles Tilly, 'How Protest Modernised', p. 203f.; Richard Tilly, 'Popular Disorders', p. 25ff.

133.   Thompson, *The Making*, p. 297; Thomis, *Town Labourer*, p. 90.

134.   Thompson, *The Making*, pp.297-337 and 529; Thomis and Holt, *Threats of Revolution*, pp. 31-6 and 100-22; Jones, *Chartism*, pp. 153-8; Briggs, *Chartist*

Studies, passim; Moss, *Origins*, pp. 125-35; Willard, *Socialisme*, pp. 67-73; Tilly and Lees, 'The People of June, 1848', pp. 170-207; Hamerow, *Restoration*, Ch. 8; Stearns, *Revolutions of 1848*, pp. 20-8 and Ch. 7; Schadt, *Sozialdemokratische Partei*, p. 22; Osterroth, *Biographisches Lexikon*, p. 17.

135.   Willard, *Guesdistes, passim*; Moss, *Origins*, p. 120.
136.   Geary, 'German Labour Movement', p. 310; Marks, 'Sources of Reformism', pp. 353ff.; J. Barrington Moore Jr., *Injustice. The Social Bases of Obedience and Revolt* (White Plains, NY, 1978), p. 183; Dieter Fricke, *Zur Organisation und Tätigkeit der deutschen Arbeiterbewegung (1890-1914)* (Leipzig, 1962), pp. 73ff. and 210f.
137.   Ward and Fraser, *Workers*, p. 108; Kynaston, *King Labour*, pp. 52ff.
138.   Vasseur, *Les Débuts, passim*; Barrington Moore, *Injustice*, p. 261n.; Klaus J. Mattheier, 'Werkvereine und wirtschaftsfriedlich-nationale (gelbe) Arbeiterbewegung' in Reulecke, *Arbeiterbewegung*, pp. 174-200.
139.   Karl Erich Born, *Staat und Sozialpolitik seit Bismarcks Sturz* (Wiesbaden, 1957), p. 67f.; Barrington Moore, *Injustice*, p. 189.
140.   Figures for exceptionally high labour turnover can be found in Crew, *Bochum*, Ch. 3.
141.   Barrington Moore, *Injustice*, p. 183.
142.   Charles Tilly, 'How Protest Modernised', p. 206; Richard Tilly, 'Popular Disorders', p. 25.
143.   Leopold Haimson, 'The Problem of Social Stability in Urban Russia, 1905-1917' in Clive Emsley (ed.), *Conflict and Stability in Europe* (London, 1979), pp. 240-6; Anweiler, *Rätebewegung*, p. 120; Benjamin Ward, 'Wild Socialism in Russia: the Origins', *California Slavic Studies*, vol. 3 (1964), p. 133; Theodor H. von Laue, 'Russian Labour between Field and Factory, 1892-1903' in ibid., pp. 33-65; Theodor H. von Laue, 'Russian Peasants in the Factory 1892-1904', *Journal of Economic History*, vol. 2 (1961), pp. 61-80.
144.   Robert Eugene Johnson, *Peasant and Proletarian: the Working Class of Moscow in the Late Nineteenth Century* (Leicester, 1980). There are problems with this argument, however. See the review of Johnson in *THES*, 18 April 1980, p. 20, by R.W. Davies, which points out that some recent research has located the sources of militancy amongst long-established skilled workers in the large factories of the metal industry. Such an analysis is perhaps even more consonant with the line of argument I have adopted here.
145.   Crew, *Bochum*, pp. 56ff.; Schomerus, *Arbeiter*, pp. 124-57.
146.   Geary, 'German Labour Movement', p. 310f.; Dieter Groh, *Negative Integration und Revolutionärer Attentismus* (Frankfurt am Main, 1973), p. 282f.; Ritter, *Arbeiterbewegung*, pp. 73-8.
147.   P.M. Jones, 'Political Commitment and Rural Society in the Southern Massif-Central', *European Studies Review*, vol. 10, no. 3 (1980), pp. 337-56; A. Siegried, *Tableau politique de la France d l'Ouest* (Paris, 1964); A. Siegfried, *Géographie Electrale de l'Ardèche sous la IIIe République* (Paris, 1949).
148.   Lyttleton, 'Revolution and Counter-revolution', p. 64f.; Brenan, *Spanish Labyrinth*, pp. 89f. and 152; Jackson, *Spanish Republic*, p. 289f.
149.   Thomis, *Town Labourer*, pp. 45, 49, 61, 109 and 194; Thompson, *The Making*, pp. 474-80.
150.   Ritter, *Arbeiterbewegung*, p. 74; Klaus Tenfelde, *Sozialgeschichte der Bergarbeiterschaft an der Ruhr im 19. Jahrhundert* (Bonn-Bad Godesberg, 1977), pp. 384ff.; Christoph Klessmann, *Polnische Bergarbeiter im Ruhrgebiet 1870-1914* (Göttingen, 1978).
151.   Scott, *Glassworkers*, pp. 117ff.
152.   Crew, *Bochum*, pp. 186-94.
153.   Hobsbawm, *Labouring Men*, pp. 180 and 191; Pelling, *British Trade Unionism*, pp. 94-8.

154.   Richard J. Evans, *Sozialdemokratie und Frauenemanzipation im deutschen Kaiserreich* (Bonn, 1979); Jean H. Quataert, *Reluctant Feminists in German Social Democracy, 1885-1917* (Princeton, NJ, 1979).
155.   Evans, *Sozialdemokratie*, pp. 203ff.
156.   Quataert, *Reluctant Feminists*, p. 21.
157.   Thompson, *The Making*, pp. 474-80.
158.   Dowe, 'Organisatorische Anfänge', p. 52; Hans-Gerhard Husung, 'Zum Protest der Eisenbahnarbeiter im Vormärz', unpublished MS.
159.   Charles Tilly and Lees, 'People of June', *passim*.
160.   The Tillys, *Rebellious Century*, p. 20; Shorter and Tilly, *Strikes*, p. 110; Dolléans, *Mouvement Ouvrier*, vol. 1, p. 329f.
161.   Moss, *Origins*, p. 152f.
162.   Tenfelde, 'Anarcho-syndikalistische Strömungen', *passim*; David W. Morgan, *The Socialist Left and the German Revolution* (Ithaca, NY, 1975), p. 72.
163.   David Lane, *The Roots of Russian Communism* (Assen, 1967), p. 21; Haimson, 'Problem of Social Stability', pp. 240-6; von Laue, 'Russian Labour', pp. 33-65; von Laue, 'Russian Peasants', pp. 61-80.
164.   Venturi, *Roots of Revolution*, pp. 507-11; Blinkhorn, 'Industrialisation and Social Protest in Spain'; Edward E. Malefakis, *Agrarian Reform and Peasant Revolution in Spain* (New Haven, Conn., 1970), Ch. 12; Jackson, *Spanish Republic*, p. 79f.
165.   Quoted in Reichard, *Crippled from Birth*, p. 182.

3 MATURATION AND ORGANISATION, 1890-1914

Introduction

The period that stretched from 1890 until the outbreak of the First World War was one in which strike activity reached unprecedented heights and the trade union movement came to embrace ever larger numbers of industrial workers. The French and German socialist parties also achieved national, even international, political importance, with the SPD becoming to all intents and purposes the first mass political party in history. At the same time a significant section of the British working class came to see the need for an independent political party of labour. To many contemporaries this was a period in which class conflict, the conflict between capital and labour, became increasingly obvious and increasingly bitter. In Britain the law courts and the House of Lords dealt a series of body blows to the trade union movement after the turn of the century. In France the government had contingency plans to arrest labour leaders in the event of war. As late as 1912 some sections of the German political establishment were advocating the forcible repression of the Social Democratic movement. Even more spectacularly, there was violence in the industrial cities of Spain in 1909 and barricades went up in parts of Italy five years later. Russia even lived through a revolution, albeit an abortive one, in 1905. And yet in August 1914 the working class of most European nations revealed its patriotism: the declaration of war was greeted by popular rejoicing in the streets of London, Paris, Berlin, Vienna and St Petersburg. With the sole exceptions of the Serbian and Russian parties, the official line adopted by the various socialist movements was support for their respective governments' war efforts. To some contemporaries and to many later historians the labour movement had sold its revolutionary soul for a mess of reformist pottage. Something strange had occurred in the ranks of the European working class: its revolutionary aspirations had somehow disappeared into thin air.[1]

90

Organised Growth

Between 1890 and 1914 the formal organisations of labour attracted a broad numerical support within the European working class and a degree of national and stable organisation they had not previously enjoyed. Admittedly large-scale expansion was only just beginning in some countries, such as Spain and Italy, on the eve of the First World War; but in Britain, France and Germany things were much more advanced.

Political Organisation

In virtually all European countries socialist parties were either established or continued to develop in the two decades before the outbreak of war; and in a few places the parties of the working class achieved real political significance. By 1914 the Austrian Social Democratic Party (SPÖ) had become the second-largest political group within the Austro-Hungarian Empire. In France, where a united Socialist Party had finally been formed from several pre-existing organisations, the SFIO succeeded in recruiting increasing support from the industrial proletariat: it had 35,000 members in 1905, and 91,000 nine years later, by which time it could also muster about one and a half million votes in elections to the Chamber of Deputies where it was now a force of some importance. Even more spectacular was the growth of the German Social Democratic Party (SPD), the existence of which was legalised in 1890, and which went from strength to strength in the Reichstag elections: it became the largest party in Wilhelmine Germany, securing over 4 million votes in 1912 and 110 seats in the Reichstag. In fact in some industrial towns such as Leipzig the SPD was winning over 50 per cent of the vote by this date. More factory workers voted socialist in Germany than in any other country in the world, in fact. This growth in electoral support was matched by an equally spectacular expansion of party membership: by 1906 the SPD had around 400,000 fee-paying members, 720,000 of the same in 1910 and over 1 million on the eve of the First World War.

It is important to realise that the German, and to a lesser extent the French, Socialist Party became far more than just an organisation that contacted its supporters at election time, as many of the older Continental liberal parties had done. The SPD developed a stable institutional framework employing full-time party officials and ran a massive press empire, publishing over 70 newspapers. It established choral societies, gymnastic and cycling clubs and instituted its own co-operative movement and insurance schemes. With the possible exception of the Roman Catholic Church, it was the only institution in Germany's Second Reich which cared for you from the cradle to the grave. In fact socialism in both France and Germany before the First World War became much more than a political creed; it became part and parcel of a whole sub-culture, often organised around the bar or the tavern, of a certain section of the working class.[2]

In Italy too the Italian Socialist Party really got off the ground in the 1890s in the north of the country, absorbing the various associations of the labour aristocracy already in existence, such as the friendly societies, and established a solid base first in the textile industry and subsequently amongst metal and car workers of the Turin-Genoa-Milan triangle, from which it recruited significant electoral support. Unlike its German counterpart, however, the PSI also succeeded in creating strong rural unions amongst some landless labourers and sharecroppers in the north, which through an apparatus of labour exchanges were able to exert a considerable influence upon the local rural economy, especially upon the hiring of labour. Also at the local level, the Italian Socialist Party managed to conquer some town councils before 1914.[3]

The growth of the Spanish Socialist Party (PSOE), founded by Lafargue in 1871, was rather slower and more painful. Its initial support came from printers in Madrid, who also constituted the rank and file of the trade union organisation, the UGT, which it helped to establish seventeen years later. Subsequently the party built a broader base of support amongst workers in the iron and steel industries of Bilbao and amongst radical miners in the mountainous Asturias in the north, although the major expansion of the party came only after 1910 and it remained numerically less impressive than its anarchist rival, the CNT.[4]

In Russia, perhaps most famously, the Social Democratic Party took over the revolutionary mantle from the populists, at least in the urban centres of Moscow and St Petersburg, in the 1890s, when industrial growth, the failure of terroristic assassination and the repeated refusal of the peasantry to overthrow Tsardom indicated that a new revolutionary understanding and tactic was required. Subsequently the party split into the opposing Menshevik and Bolshevik factions in 1903 but still played a significant role in the revolution of 1905. The Bolsheviks also enjoyed a rapid increase in their numerical strength in the large industrial towns of Russia between 1911 and 1914, as numerous peasants flocked into the giant textile and metallurgical plants.[5]

In Britain, of course, socialism seems to have interested only a minute percentage of the industrial work-force before the First World

War. Most workers continued to vote for the Liberal Party and to a lesser but still significant extent the Conservative Party; and although various socialist parties were formed in the 1880s, such as Hyndman's Social Democratic Federation (SDF), they remained small and without real political significance. However, although socialism concerned few Englishmen, the call for *independent* labour politics became more and more insistent. By 1892 there were three independent Labour MPs in the House of Commons. Six years later came the most important breakthrough of all, namely the decision by the Trades Union Congress (TUC) to support the election of independent working-class representatives to Parliament. The Labour Representation Committee was formed in the following year; and although it did not receive the immediate backing of all unionists — the miners only gave their support in 1906, for example — there were no fewer than 45 Labour MPs in the House of Commons by 1908.[6]

The nature of the various political parties described above obviously varied enormously from country to country and even from region to region within the same country. In some countries, as in Britain, Italy and Germany, there were close contacts between working-class politics and the major trade union organisations; whilst in France and Spain socialist parties found themselves in competition and at odds with trade union movements which espoused the doctrine of revolutionary anarcho-syndicalism.[7] In some countries a single socialist party incorporated both revolutionary and reformist elements: this can be said of Austria, France, Germany, Italy and Spain.[8] On the other hand the Russian Social Democratic Party split as early as 1903 at the instigation of Lenin; and to a certain extent the split between Bolsheviks and Mensheviks did mirror a division between revolutionaries and reformists, although far from perfectly.[9] A similar split had occurred, albeit over slightly different issues, within the Dutch socialist movement before the First World War.[10] In some countries the politics of labour were primarily concerned with no more than the defence of the immediate economic interests of the working class within the prevailing social and political order and had little time for socialist rhetoric; this was most obviously the case in Britain. In others that rhetoric was of considerable importance, especially in Germany and Russia. Here, though, one encounters a further difficulty and difference. Even in some of the socialist parties that espoused a revolutionary ideology, daily activities became increasingly dominated by electoral considerations, as in the case of the SPD and the SFIO.[11] Such was obviously not true, on the other hand, of the Bolsheviks.

The stimuli both to political activity in general and radical political activity in particular have already been discussed at a general level;[12] and they remained much the same in this period. The indiscriminate use of violent repression in Spain on occasion led to working-class insurrection, as in the 'tragic week' of 1909.[13] The frequent resort to military action on the part of Italian governments and the absence of voting rights for workers before 1912 produced a 'peculiar revolutionary sensitivity' amongst the population of the Romagna, Ancona and some parts of north-west Tuscany.[14] On the other hand, the more relaxed policies of the Giolitti government were to a certain extent successful in integrating the reformist wing of Italian socialism, based upon workers in industries with strong craft traditions like printing and sections of the building industry, into the prevailing political order.[15] Germany and Austria remained intermediate between liberal England, with its reformist labour movement, and autocratic Russia with its revolutionary opposition.

Again the resort to political action was often a function of industrial impotence. In Britain the trade unions decided to support independent Labour parliamentary candidates in the wake of an employers' offensive involving the use of blackleg labour and lock-outs, and above all in response to a number of decisions in the law courts and the House of Lords which restricted trade union activity and awarded considerable damages against individual unions as a result of industrial action. It has also been suggested that the turn to politics on the part of some British workers came from those who were rendered marginal by a second wave of technological modernisation, whereas the secure and well organised continued to look to the older parties to represent them.[16] Similarly in France: it was precisely the previously unorganised and depressed textile workers in the Nord who turned to the Socialist Party of Jules Guesde.[17] In Germany the massive electoral gains of the SPD must be weighed against the fact that only a minority of trade union members were actually prepared to join the party; and this may again suggest that the economically strong did not require political support and that the high socialist poll came from, amongst others, unorganised workers in heavy industry seeking an outlet for their grievances in politics, given that the strength of their employers prevented effective unionisation and strike action.[18] In this last case, however, such an explanation clearly lacks general validity, in so far as the most active Social Democrats in Germany were also skilled workers.

In fact, if we now turn to the social composition of these parties, the dominance of the skilled worker in long-established trades becomes clear. In France most socialist groups recruited predominantly from skilled workers in the construction industry and from metal-, wood- and leather-work.[19] In Italy the PSI drew its major support from small-scale artisan production in the textile and metal trades until just before the First World War.[20] An enormous amount of evidence from Germany gives the same impression. The SPD's membership was over- whelmingly working-class (between 77.4 and 94 per cent in individual branches); but the great majority of these workers were skilled men working in small or medium-sized concerns, often in small towns. In 1904 in the party's Leipzig branch the membership was composed of the following: 138 lower-middle-class, 200 unskilled workers and over 1,300 skilled bookbinders, printers, plumbers, painters, masons and the like. In Baden metalworkers, woodworkers and printers predominated, as did masons, printers and woodworkers in the Hamburg branch of the SPD in the early twentieth century.[21] In Spain too printers constituted the backbone of the PSOE in its early days.[22] The Social Democratic Party in Russia began life as a movement of skilled workers, but after its division in 1903 some interesting differences in social composition arose between the Bolshevik and Menshevik factions. Whereas the Mensheviks were more likely to recruit from skilled workers of urban origin, the Bolsheviks had more success with less skilled workers in larger factories and from rural backgrounds. It was also the latter who benefited from the rapid expansion of the labour force of rural origin in the large factories of Moscow and St Petersburg between 1911 and 1914.[23]

The French and Italian socialist parties were distinguished from some of their counterparts in the rest of Europe in this period by their success in recruiting both members and voters from rural areas. In the case of Italy this is perhaps not too difficult to explain. The inhabitants of the countryside who proved amenable to socialist propaganda in areas like Emilia were landless labourers and to a certain extent share- croppers subject to agrarian capitalism. They benefited directly from the labour exchanges through which the PSI was able to exert a considerable influence on the hiring and firing of rural labour. This rural mobilisa- tion was further facilitated by the proximity of the main industrial area of Italy to those areas in which rural capitalism was creating a landless proletariat and strengthened by the cultural contacts between the northern industrial area and the rural north through local migration.

The situation in France, however, was somewhat different. As might be expected, some agrarian radicalism was generated amongst a rural proletariat of impoverished woodcutters in the Cher and the Nièvre, amongst wage labourers who sometimes went on strike in the 1890s for higher wages. However, much rural support for the nascent socialist movement in the Midi came not from landless labourers but from land-owning peasants. This puzzling phenomenon has elicited a wide variety of explanations. One of the most common states that a radical 'tradition' can be identified amongst the peasantry of the south of France going back to the days of the great French Revolution.[24] There were peasant risings not only then but later, in 1849 and in 1851. Even if this expla-nation holds water, we are still left with the question of how this 'tradition' came about in the first place and then what enabled it to survive. However, there are also reasons to doubt the force of such a tradition in explaining socialist support; for as Tony Judt has shown in an exhaustive study, the peasants who voted socialist in the early nine-teenth century in the Department of the Var were not those who had supported radical republican causes earlier.[25] We will have to find other explanations.

One contender is religion. Some of the Languedoc peasantry were or had been Protestant heretics and had suffered vicious persecution at the hands of the established authorities. However, such considerations were hardly relevant to the anti-clerical practices of Third Republican govern-ments after the turn of the century; and in any case large areas of the south in which peasant radicalism was rife were not Protestant. Here it is possible that anti-clericalism played a role: areas of low religious observance were also areas which normally recorded a strong left-wing vote, as in the Var and the Hérault. Of greater importance almost certainly was the very different social world and home environment of the peasant of the Midi compared to that of his more conservative counterpart in, for example, Brittany. The peasants of the Var and the Hérault did not live in isolated hamlets remote from urban influence, but in relatively large villages in densely populated (by rural standards) areas which enjoyed a reasonable network of communications. Hence they encountered urban ideas more regularly than the isolated peasant of Finisterre and also lived in a community which possessed a fair sprinkling of rural artisans, such as blacksmiths and coopers. Further-more, the Mediterranean peasantry enjoyed a collective social life around the local bar and café, and possessed democratic traditions of collective assembly to decide upon local matters. Here the priest and the local aristocrat had never wielded the same power and influence as in other parts of France.

Perhaps the most important single factor in determining the political behaviour of the socialist peasantry, however, was their material situation; for most of them were *vignerons*. These wine-growers were subject to the fluctuations of a national and even international market from the days of the railway, i.e. from about the 1860s onwards. Production of wine was not for the grower himself but for a broader market. As a result the *vigneron* suffered from the agricultural depression of the 1870s and 1880s (which was also accompanied by the devastation of the phylloxera) and from the over-production of inferior wines thereafter. Under these circumstances the wine-grower felt increasingly exploited by merchant intermediaries, who purchased either his grapes or his wine, and gained an insight into class conflict that was denied the isolated and self-sufficient peasant farmer of the north-west. Peasants in the Midi thus felt the need for protection, for state intervention to protect them against the vicissitudes of the market and the exploitation of greedy merchants. In a sense this is what socialism meant to them: opposition to the untrammelled dominance of market forces. Thus they demonstrated for state aid and protection against cheap foreign wines in 1903, 1904 and 1907 on a significant scale and began to vote socialist at about the same time.[26]

In spite of the enormous growth in working-class political organisation documented above, it must be remembered that it was still only a minority of male factory workers who voted socialist, even in Germany, before the First World War and that considerably fewer ever took the trouble to become party members. We have seen that the unskilled remained outside the ranks of organised protest almost everywhere until the war. In Germany they first became active in the revolutionary upheavals of the post-war period. In France it was not until the era of the Front Populaire that such workers entered the political scene on any significant scale; whilst in Italy the rapid expansion of heavy industry in the war and immediate post-war period saw the involvement of the new factory working class in radical politics.[27]

Thus skill remained a major determinant of participation in working-class political organisation, although the socialist parties may have found a stronger resonance amongst the unskilled at the polls: voting in a secret ballot was less risky and involved few of the sacrifices that went with party membership. Ethnic variables also continued to obstruct the formation of strong labour organisations. In Austria-Hungary the SPÖ recruited almost exclusively from ethnic Germans, whilst Germany's Poles rejected the advances of the SPD and formed their own organisations. Confessional allegiance further continued to frustrate the aims of socialists. In Wilhelmine Germany, for example, it is true that Social

Democracy began to make some headway in areas that were industrial *and* Catholic after 1903. In fact in that year the SPD won almost 43 per cent of the vote in Dortmund and also made an impact in Cologne, Krefeld and Essen, all towns with a sizeable Catholic population. In 1907 the party won six seats that were overwhelmingly Catholic and industrial in the Reichstag elections; and 12 of 28 such seats in 1912. However, it still did much better in confessionally mixed towns like Dortmund than it did in solidly Catholic industrial areas like the Saarland. In fact as late as 1912 60 per cent of all Catholic males were voting for the Centre Party and in the same year some SPD electoral gains were partially offset by losses to that latter organisation.[28] Working-class political organisation, therefore, still found itself fragmented in several countries on the eve of the First World War; and it had still not succeeded in mobilising significant numbers of the unskilled or female work-force.

Trade Union Organisation

If the growth of working-class political parties was impressive between 1890 and 1914, that of the trade unions was staggering. By 1914 British trade union membership had soared to the impressive figure of 4,145,000. In Germany in the same year the socialist-affiliated Free Trade Unions had about 2.6 million members; and although the figures for France were considerably lower, they none the less indicated a major advance: in 1890 fewer than 250,000 workers belonged to the *syndicats* but by 1912 there were around 1 million French trade union members. The figures for that part of the Austro-Hungarian Empire that subsequently became Austria after the peace settlement of 1919 were far more impressive: in a country of little more than 6 million inhabitants, union membership embraced no fewer than 415,195 workers by the end of 1913.[29] Admittedly growth on this scale had yet to come to Spain and Italy.

This was not only a period of growth for the trade union movement throughout Europe. It was also one in which effective national federations of labour were established for the first time in France and Germany, although the process in Britain had begun four decades earlier with the creation of the New Model Unions. In France this occurred between 1892 and 1902: the CGT, a national federation of craft-based *syndicats*, was founded in 1895 and fused seven years later with the national federation of *bourses du travail*, initially government-funded labour exchanges which had become umbrella organisations for locally based trade union activity, and which were more financially viable than the *syndicats.* In Germany the demise of the exceptional anti-socialist law in 1890 enabled the creation, under SPD auspices, of strong and centralised national trade unions with a united direction from what became known as the General Commission of Free Trade Unions. The majority of these unions were craft-based, as we shall see, but a few, as in the case of building and metalwork, were genuinely industrial unions, embracing or at least attempting to embrace all workers in a particular industry, whatever their level of skill. In a drive to extend membership Karl Legien, the chairman of the General Commission, adumbrated the unions' position of political neutrality. This did not denote a formal break with German Social Democracy; on the contrary, the links of the Free Trade Unions with the SPD remained of the utmost importance until the destruction of the organised labour movement by the Nazis in 1933. What it signified, however, was the intention of these new unions to recruit members from all political persuasions. It was one amongst many indications that the likes of Legien did not see their role as the propagation of socialist revolution but rather the defence of the immediate interests of the working class within the prevailing economic and social order.

It is of some interest and was subsequently to be of some importance that the centralisation and depoliticisation of the union movement in Germany met with considerable resistance in the early days. The so-called localist unions, which had emerged from the necessarily decentralised struggles of the period of persecution in the 1870s and 1880s and which were especially strong in metalworking and the building industry in Berlin and some parts of the Rhineland, had been radicalised by the harassment of governmental authorities under the exceptional law; and in consequence they found themselves bitterly opposed to the centralising activities of Legien's paid officials and their doctrine of political neutrality. With considerable foresight the localists realised that the creation of a full-time bureaucracy of trade union officials would lead to political conservatism and give rise to a gulf separating the bureaucrats from the ordinary worker. They even went so far as to reject the conclusion of wage agreements with employers as class collaboration and actually expelled the printers' union for engaging in such activity in 1896. By that date it was clear that the localist unions had lost their battle with the powerful General Commission; but they continued to survive until the First World War and enjoyed something of a revival in 1913, as we will see.[30]

As might be imagined from earlier comments on political developments, the French and Italian labour movements also managed to recruit some significant support in the countryside. After 1900 several agricultural *syndicats* were formed amongst the wine-growers and impoverished woodcutters of southern France; whilst the Italian labour leaders succeeded in creating a network of strong rural unions amongst day labourers and sharecroppers in the north of their country.[31]

The growth of the trade union movement was thus striking in many respects; and what made it possible was that new groups of workers, including some of the unskilled, began to see the benefits of organisation. In Britain following the great dock strike of 1889 a veritable host of unskilled workers joined the trade union ranks: dockers, of course, gasworkers, local authority employees, railway workers, tramway workers, people employed in confectionery.[32] In France too after the 'time-lag' discussed earlier workers in mining and manufacture began to organise on a significant scale between 1884, when unions were legalised, and 1914. Especially after the turn of the century workers in larger-scale concerns gave their allegiance to the CGT: miners and textile workers were joined by dock and railway workers and above all by metalworkers. Even the formerly conservative engine-drivers became involved in the general strike of 1910.[33] In Germany the Free Trade Union of Metalworkers (DMV) had recruited no fewer than 556,939 members by 1913. In the same year the figures for the other major Free Trade Unions were as follows: 229,785 transport workers (principally in the docks), 326,631 construction workers, 141,484 textile operatives, 104,113 miners, 195,441 woodworkers (excluding a further 62,069 carpenters), and 210,569 unspecified 'factory workers'.[34]

The degree of success enjoyed by trade unions in mobilising the work-force, however, is easily exaggerated. The rapid recruitment of unskilled workers in Britain in 1889/90 failed to outlive the subsequent onset of economic depression. In France as late as 1905 the average *syndicat* had no more than 170 members, a fair proportion of whom did not bother to pay their union dues. In fact the annual income of the French National Federation of Printers in 1910 was itself ten times greater than that of all the unions in the CGT combined! By the outbreak of the First World War under 10 per cent of the total French labour force had been drawn into economic or political organisations. In Italy the national trade union federation, the CGL, had less than a quarter of a million members on the eve of war; whilst the infinitely larger trade union movement in Germany had still failed to attract support from the overwhelming majority of lesser skilled workers in heavy industry by the same date.[35] It was only in the course of the First World War, in fact, and in the years immediately thereafter that huge numbers of the previously unorganised in these last three countries entered the ranks of labour protest for the first time and with very radical consequences.[36] In Spain too the anarcho-syndicalist CNT, which could boast no more than 15,000 members in 1914, also experienced rapid expansion in the next six years.[37]

Not only did the trade unions remain limited in their numerical strength before 1914; they also retained much of their traditional nature. The great majority of trade unions in England, France, Austria, Germany, Italy and Spain remained craft-based and continued to pursue highly restrictive practices. Even in Britain in the 1880s and 1890s the 'new unionism' only succeeded in mobilising about 13 per cent of total trade union membership; and some of the new unions owed their success to the fact that they confined their recruitment to certain occupational groups rather than others. In fact they became almost as sectional in their interests as the older craft unions had been.[38]

It should further be noted that many of the European trade union organisations which existed in the three decades before the outbreak of the First World War had no connection with any kind of left-wing politics. This is most obviously the case in Britain, where, as we have seen, trade union commitment to the fledgeling Labour Party was primarily defensive. In Russia before the revolution of 1905 the only unions which were allowed a legal existence were the so-called police unions of Zubatov, an attempt by the Tsarist state to direct economic grievances into loyalist channels, and those unions which followed the orthodox priest Father Gapon, which again were loyal to the Tsar, at least initially. In Austria there existed a powerful and anti-socialist Catholic trade union organisation, as was also the case in Wilhelmine Germany: in 1914 the *Christliche Gewerkschaften* in the latter country had succeeded in recruiting no fewer than 343,000 members. At the same time the German liberal trade union movement could still boast over 100,000 members, whilst the hold of the 'yellow' company unions upon the work-force of large firms in heavy industry was even more impressive, often outnumbering the support enjoyed by the SPD-affiliated Free Unions. Germany's Second Reich saw many other anti-socialist labour organisations, such as a monarchist bakers' union and above all the largest trade union of white-collar workers there, the Deutschnationaler Handlungsgehilfenverband (German National Union of Commercial Employees), which subscribed to an ideology that was not only anti-socialist but also nationalist, imperialist and expressly racist.[39]

This last point raises the important question of the increasingly large sector of non-manual industrial workers spawned in the later nineteenth century. In France the teachers' union acquired some significance, as did the National Union of Clerks and the Railway Clerks' Union in Britain; but before the First World War such white-collar workers were grossly underrepresented in the ranks of labour protest, their unions were small and their strikes relatively isolated. Indeed, in Central Europe the mobilisation of white-collar workers often took place under the auspices of political reaction. Enjoying closer contact with at least middle management, greater security of employ, a system of seniority which guaranteed some improvement in income in later years and pension rights rarely vouchsafed to the average manual worker, the clerk quite often saw his route to advancement as lying along lines of individual rather than collective action and often had highly developed status anxieties which demarcated him from the industrial proletariat. Such cleavages within working-class consciousness were rarely overcome and often reinforced by the deliberately differential treatment of white- and blue-collar employees by their employers.[40]

Not all unions were politically conservative or quiescent, however: as we have already seen, close contacts existed between trade union organisation and socialist politics in Italy and Germany before 1914. In other places, in Spain and France in particular, the major confederations of trade unions refused to limit their activities to the exclusive pursuit of immediate material gain but committed themselves to the revolutionary doctrine of anarcho-syndicalism. Crudely stated, this view of the world condemned political activity in general and participation in parliamentary elections in particular as inescapably bourgeois and corrupt. Indeed, it despised all co-operation with middle-class elements and fervently believed that proletarian emancipation could only be the result of the workers' own activity, an activity rooted in the factory and the union rather than the political party. For anarcho-syndicalists the union, the *syndicat*, was not only the organ of struggle under capitalism but the seed from which the future society, rid of private ownership of the means of production and freed from the oppressive control of a central state apparatus, would grow. This millenarian transformation would be brought about through a revolutionary general strike.[41] To this revolutionary doctrine the French CGT committed itself at several congresses before the First World War, whilst its millenarian rejection of reformism seemed to inform the daily activities of the Catalonian working class in the same period. Why?

In the case of both Spain and France ideological variables clearly have some importance. In the first, Fanelli carried the anarchist message to discontented workers before socialist agitators had arrived on the scene, whilst France possessed a strong anarchist tradition which stretched back to the writings of Proudhon. In fact it has even been argued that most varieties of French socialism with any degree of working-class support before the advent of Guesde's Marxism in the 1880s fundamentally demanded some form of small-scale co-operative association.[42] However, the purely ideological explanation lacks conviction. It does so first because anarchism penetrated certain European labour movements but subsequently retreated in the face of socialist recruitment: such was the case in Italy, where anarchism took a certain hold in some cities in the late 1860s and 1870s, especially amongst the dockers and porters of Ancona, Genoa, La Spezia and Leghorn, and amongst artisans in the small manufacturing towns of the Romagna and parts of Tuscany, and gave way to organised socialism.[43] More importantly, it becomes clear from the French and Spanish examples that the appeal of anarcho-syndicalism was to certain groups of workers rather than others. Whereas the factory proletariat of north-eastern France provided the backbone of the Guesdiste movement, French anarchism found its strongest bastions amongst the Parisian artisanate working in small units of production and to a lesser extent amongst the depressed and ancient textile trades of Roubaix, Roanne, Reims and Lyons.[44] In Spain it was workers in the long-established and equally depressed, small-scale textile industry of towns like Barcelona and Saragossa, not those in the larger-scale heavy industry of Bilbao, who formed the rank and file of the anarcho-syndicalist CNT. Clearly the decentralised vision of the future made more sense to workers whose own economic livelihood was rooted in small units of production rather than huge modern factories. However, there were further reasons why anarcho-syndicalism found a responsive audience in Catalonia. The national, historical and linguistic differences which separated Catalans from Castillians made the former highly suspicious of any form of central Spanish state apparatus, now or in the future. Perhaps even more important, however, was the background from which the Catalan working class was recruited: many came from a rural background in Andalusia which itself possessed a long history of violent social conflict and anarchist allegiance.[45] Finally, the strength of anarcho-syndicalist support in both Spain and France doubtless had a great deal to do with the nature of politics in both countries. Not only had the political representatives of the French bourgeoisie betrayed working-class aspirations on more than one occasion, as we have already seen;[46] politics in the Third Republic were manifestly corrupt, staggering from financial scandal to financial scandal. The Chambre des Députés did seem remote from the concerns of ordinary working men and more concerned with lining the pockets of its bourgeois notables.[47] Similarly in Spain, a democratic franchise did not succeed in destroying the power of the *caciques*, who with government aid controlled the distribution of local patronage and tax privileges in rural areas and hence election results. Of course, this system of manipulation caused increasing resentment; and it certainly made a mockery of supposedly 'free' elections.[48]

Thus the nature of the trade union movement varied in its scale and ideological identity enormously from place to place. However, it may again be appropriate to conclude with a word of warning, namely that it is dangerous to take ideological labels too seriously. As we have seen, the behaviour of French workers in anarcho-syndicalist organisations did not differ wildly from that of their non-anarchist colleagues.[49] In Spain rural and urban anarchism were arguably very different phenomena;[50] whilst the rapid influx of rural labourers from Extremadura into the ostensibly socialist movement in Spain in the early 1930s transformed it into something remarkably like its anarchist cousin.[51] Nor could the violent insurrectionary activities of Asturian miners in the early twentieth century square neatly with the overall perspectives of the Spanish Socialist Party.[52] Likewise in the small manufacturing towns of Italy anarchists tended to re-emerge as the leading lights of violent insurrection in the period immediately before the First World War, despite the apparent hold of organised socialism.[53]

Whatever the ideological leanings of trade union organisations before 1914, however, their social composition remained primarily the reserve of the skilled. It also remained the case that such organisations could not control all forms of industrial protest, as in the case of strikes.

Strikes

What contemporaries would have noticed more than any other aspect of labour activity in the three decades before the First World War was the massive increase in the incidence of strikes and in their scale. More and more workers attempted either to defend or improve their living standards through industrial action. In most cases the first consideration was uppermost in the minds of strikers; but for some skilled and well organised groups such as printers and engineering workers complaints were made about nervous exhaustion as a result of new techniques of production and demands of an offensive nature, such as a share in the higher profits that accrued from increased productivity, could be heard. Issues of trade union recognition, harsh treatment at the hands of inconsiderate foremen and other questions relating to work practices and authority on the shop floor also raised their head from time to time.[54] Whatever the reason, there can be no doubt that industrial disputes reached unprecedented proportions after the turn of the century. Britain saw massive strikes on the railways and in the docks in 1911; in fact the first national railway strike paralysed the country in that year. Even more days were lost in the following twelve months as a result of industrial disputes.[55] In France the average annual strike rate never dropped below 500 disputes between 1900 and 1915, the first effective industry-wide strikes were staged in 1902 and four years later there came the first attempts to organise national stoppages. (It still remained true, however, that the average French strike was localised and small in scale before 1914.[56]) In Germany the number of industrial disputes escalated in the following way: 1,468 strikes involving 321,000 workers in 1900, 3,228 strikes (681,000 strikers) in 1910, and 2,834 strikes involving 1,031,000 two years later. It must be admitted that these years were the high points of German industrial conflict; but it remains true, none the less, that more and more workers, often from industries new to strike action, became involved in this particular form of labour protest. As in France, so in the Second Reich some of these strikes were nation- and industry-wide. In 1905, for example, no fewer than three-quarters of Ruhr miners downed tools in the same dispute, thus indicating that the strike had the support of many men who were not actually members of either the Catholic or the Free Trade Union miners' organisations. Indeed, throughout this period many strikes were called without guidance from formal labour organisations and, as we shall see, in some cases against the express wishes of an increasingly cautious trade union bureaucracy.[57]

The overwhelming majority of these strikes arose from wage disputes, especially between 1910 and 1914 when inflation threatened to erode working-class living standards. However, the issue of the length of the working day also assumed a new importance with the introduction of more rigorous controls over labour in the factory and the employment of new techniques of production which increased the pace of work.[58] In France the major trade union confederation, the CGT, took up the demand for an eight-hour day. In Germany some metalworkers complained of nervous exhaustion. In Hamburg there was an unprecedented protest for more regular and reduced hours in the 1890s amongst dockers, as there was also in London in 1889. In some cases what was at issue was the increased control and regulation to which factory work was now made subject, as in the docks.[59] In fact the distribution of authority within the workplace was often the principal concern of French strikes between 1880 and 1910, according to Shorter and Tilly.[60] There were even cases where strikes were called to achieve specifically political purposes. In Belgium in 1902 workers went out on strike in an attempt to force an extension of the franchise; whilst only four years later the Free Trade Unions and Social Democrats adopted the same weapon to combat a proposed restriction of the suffrage in Hamburg.[61]

The timing of strike activity between 1890 and 1914 continued to follow familiar patterns. The relatively high level of unemployment in Britain between 1900 and 1910 militated against strikes, which remained concentrated in times of a relatively tight labour market, as in 1889-93 and 1910-13.[62] In the Ruhr mining town of Bochum the great strikes of German miners followed in the wake of periods of a long and sustained rise in working-class living standards, as in 1889 and 1912.[63] Similarly in France, strike levels peaked in the periods 1890-3 and 1899-1907, though political variables also played an important role here: in 1893, 1899 and 1906 political changes raised workers' expectations of governmental support. That support was all the more necessary, of course, because industrial impotence led French workers to turn to government authorities to bring pressure to bear upon recalcitrant employers.[64]

Less traditional, however, were the groups of workers who now participated in strike action. In Britain the great London dock strike of 1889 and subsequent industrial action on the part of other transport workers and those employed in the gas industry have been identified as the major turning-point.[65] The period 1890-1914 also marked a decisive shift in industrial militancy on the other side of the Channel. The relative importance of printers, textile workers and woodworkers in French labour protest declined. At the same time metalworkers, construction workers and above all transport workers went on strike as never before, as did postmen. Metalworkers achieved a further prominence in a new wave of industrial militancy in Italy and Germany on the eve of the First World War, as we will see.[66]

The incorporation of new groups of labour into the ranks of industrial protest is hardly surprising, given what we have seen already. In a sense the 'time-lag effect' came into operation: these people began to adjust to their new-found situation and could see how collective action had furthered the interests of other sections of the work-force. They were also in a position to act as a result of greater material security and a shorter working day than had been vouchsafed to all but a few in the earlier days of the Industrial Revolution. However, some of the new activists found the stimulus to participate in industrial protest from a combination of new pressures. Technological modernisation, the increasing pace and regulation of work in some sectors of industry, decasualisation in the docks placed many in a novel dilemma, as we will see.[67]

Embourgeoisement

It has been widely held that the working class of the more advanced industrial states of Europe became less radical in the course of time and increasingly contented with its relatively comfortable lot within affluent capitalist society. The days of barricades and insurrections were gone — except in underdeveloped Russia — and even when workers did complain, their demands were restricted in scope and certainly constituted no real challenge to the existing order. Some have even gone so far as to claim that the working class, or at least its ostensible representatives, lost any revolutionary consciousness they may once have possessed and in certain respects became 'bourgeois' in their aspirations.

Before criticising both the assumptions and substance of this argument, it will first be necessary to ascertain why a process of deradicalisation has been identified by some historians and the kinds of explanations they have offered for this supposed phenomenon.

The Case for Deradicalisation

The argument that European labour lost its revolutionary initiative between 1890 and 1914 assumes two related forms. The most common constitutes a set of statements about the leaders of organised unions and political parties, about formal institutions, for example 'the SPD moved to the right'. The second is far more ambitious and states that it was not only the formal institutions of labour but the working class of the advanced nations of Western Europe in general that became sucked into the prevailing economic, political and social order.

The classic evidence for the former thesis rests upon the demonstration that with few exceptions the major socialist parties voted for the war efforts of their respective governments in 1914, and this despite the fact that organised socialism in France and Germany was theoretically wedded to revolutionary Marxism. Only the Russian and Serbian parties voted as parties to oppose the war from the start and espoused the doctrine of 'revolutionary defeatism'. In some other countries small anti-war minorities formed within the socialist camp, as in Britain, France and Germany;[68] but these were very definitely the exception rather than the rule before the later stages of the war. What this appeared to show was that the official internationalism of these parties, an internationalism proclaimed in national party programmes and at the congresses of the Second International to which they belonged, was a hollow sham. The events of August 1914 seemed to demonstrate that the socialist ideology of internationalist class conflict was weaker than the forces of nationalism and patriotism; and that the representatives of organised labour had retreated from their uncompromising revolutionary stance of 'not a penny, not a man to the system', as the German Social Democrats used to say.

A wealth of other evidence can then be produced to reinforce the impression that the political parties of labour reneged on their revolutionary commitments. The German Social Democratic Party has often been seen as the clearest embodiment of this move to the right. It was a party which had adopted revolutionary Marxism at its Erfurt Congress of 1891 and possessed a significant number of Marxist theorists in its leading ranks, people such as Karl Kautsky, Rosa Luxemburg, Rudolf Hilferding, Parvus. Yet this supposedly Marxist party not only found itself voting for the German war credits on 4 August 1914; it had also voted for part of the Reich's military budget in the previous year, albeit because that expenditure was to be covered by some kind of progressive taxation. Within the ranks of this same organisation an increasing number of 'revisionists', of intellectuals around Eduard Bernstein, began to assert that the SPD should abandon its maximalist revolutionary aims and concentrate on piecemeal reform within the existing order, preferably in alliance with the more progressive elements of the German bourgeoisie. More significantly, reformists, practical politicians like the leaders of Social Democracy in the relatively liberal states of southern Germany (Baden especially, but also Bavaria and Württemberg) and trade union leaders, concerned with immediate bread and butter questions and disclaiming any interest in distant revolution, came to play an increasing role in the SPD. The same applied to the ever greater numbers of paid bureaucrats in the party, men like Friedrich Ebert who rose to prominence not on the barricades or through flights of rhetoric, unlike an earlier generation of leaders, but through the performance of routine administrative tasks. Such men, it might be argued, had taken over German Social Democracy by 1914, despised the revolutionary theorists and simply saw the maintenance of the party's organisational empire as an end in itself. The SPD's refusal to launch a general strike to achieve a reform of the iniquitous three-class franchise in Prussia, its passivity in the face of harassment from government authorities, its failure to denounce imperialist adventures in Morocco in 1911 all seemed to indicate that the SPD had indeed lost its revolutionary soul. In fact this was even apparent in the party's cultural activities, which to a large extent were concerned with the dissemination of traditional artistic values rather than the propagation of revolutionary ideals.[69]

Although this process of deradicalisation was perhaps most notoriously apparent in the action, or rather inaction, of the SPD, it was certainly not exclusive to Germany. In France the insurrection of 1871, which subsequently became known as the Commune, was the last of the old-style barricade revolts; and it was produced by a peculiar set of circumstances determined by French defeat in the Franco-Prussian war.[70] Furthermore, the Socialist Party, which had ostensibly adopted Guesde's rather castrated brand of Marxism, seemed to become increasingly preoccupied with electoral victories. In the party the more restrained eclecticism of Jean Jaurès, which integrated relatively well with the establishment of the Third Republic, effectively triumphed over even the muted revolutionary rhetoric of Guesde. At the same time, French anarcho-syndicalist trade unions concentrated upon the formulation of immediate economistic demands in practice, despite their noises about a revolutionary general strike, and behaved no differently to reformist union organisations.[71] In Italy a significant section of the PSI and its affiliated trade union federation (CGL) were prepared to co-operate with Giolitti's politics of *transformismo* in the hope of making material gains; in Spain the perspective of the Socialist Party and its trade union organisation (UGT) was also predominantly reformist until the First World War.[72] Most obviously of all, the major institutions of British labour eschewed revolutionary theory. The bitter conflicts of the first half of the nineteenth century seemed dead and gone. Trade unions remained dominated by the concern to achieve only limited, even sectional, economic gains for their membership; whilst the emergent labour Party only committed itself to socialisation after the war.[73]

Such is the evidence as far as the organised leadership of European labour is concerned. But there is more evidence which implicates the working-class rank and file in this process of deradicalisation. Despite the occasional insurrection in Spain and Italy, and the 1905 revolution in Russia, all events in what were arguably underdeveloped countries, the European working class did seem to abandon the barricade for the strike and insurrection for peaceful organisation. The industrial workers of Britain, France and Germany, and most of their counterparts in Italy and to a lesser extent Spain, did not mount a frontal assault on capitalist society or the bourgeois state before 1914. Moreover, it has been argued that the success of cautious trade unions and political parties indicates that the reformists were giving the rank and file what they wanted. Certainly the French Socialist Party did best at the polls when at its most reformist and the same could be said of the SPD. Support for the war was also an accurate reflection of ordinary working-class sentiment in the belligerent countries in August 1914: there was popular rejoicing on the streets of London, Paris, Berlin, Vienna and St Petersburg when war was declared.

What ordinary workers thought is extremely difficult to ascertain, of course, especially as the overwhelming majority of them participated in *no* form of protest, industrial or political, organised or unorganised, before 1914. It has been suggested for the British case that the old artisan values of independence, pride in one's craft etc. were being replaced by a popular culture that maintained a stricter division between work and leisure; and this privatisation produced a less radical view of the world. Workers' concerns revolved less around images of their rights as 'free-born Englishmen' and more around soccer and similar activities.[74] In Germany we know that even SPD and trade union members rarely borrowed books from party and union libraries; but when a minority of them did so, what they borrowed was not *Das Kapital* but works of escapist fiction.[75] We have already seen in the case of France that membership of the supposedly revolutionary anarcho-syndicalist movement was not sufficient to guarantee what might have been regarded as the requisite revolutionary thought and action.[76]

In the case of German Social Democracy a great deal of work has been done in an attempt to establish the ideological identity of the party's working-class rank and file. Guenther Roth and Peter Stearns have amassed large numbers of working-class quotations which seem to indicate the reformist stance of many party members; and many contemporaries reported the same. Levenstein's surveys of German metalworkers in 1907 and 1910 revealed limited ambitions;[77] whilst Paul Göhre, a clergyman who spent some time working in a factory, reported that, for 'the majority, especially of the more intelligent, thoughtful, practical, experienced and mature men, neither the official republicanism nor economic communism were really popular. These were things for which most of them had no real understanding or enthusiasm.'[78] One worker who had joined the officially Marxist SPD and presumably took the trouble to pay his membership dues could even say the following:

> You know, I never read a social democratic book and rarely a newspaper. I used not to occupy myself with politics at all. But since I got married and have five people to feed at home, I have to do it. But I think my own thoughts. I don't go in for red ties, big round hats and other similar things. All that doesn't amount to much. We really don't want to become like the rich and refined people. There will always have to be rich and poor. We would not dream of altering that. But we want a better and more just organisation at the factory and in the state. I generally express what I think about that, even though it may not be pleasant. But I do nothing illegal.[79]

Various analyses of the content of working-class strike demands, especially of those of German miners, have further stressed their limited and economistic nature.[80] There can be no doubt, therefore, that at least significant sections of the German working class did appear to lack any real enthusiasm for truly revolutionary action by 1914.

Any number of explanations have been proffered for this supposed process of deradicalisation and embourgeoisement and it is to these that we must now turn.

Explanations of Deradicalisation

One major variable which may have influenced European workers and their representatives and persuaded them to abandon a position of complete hostility to the prevailing economic and political order was the relative political relaxation that occurred in several states in the later nineteenth and early twentieth centuries. This has already been discussed in the case of Britain, where various pieces of legislation progressively facilitated strike action and trade union organisation.[81] It is also true that much repressive legislation was abolished in France, Germany and Italy in the same period. In France strikes and unions were effectively legalised in 1884. In Italy the extension of the suffrage to the working class combined with Giolitti's wooing of some sections of the leadership of the CGL and PSI did serve to attract certain elements to reformism. In Germany in particular the ending of the anti-socialist law in 1890 served to undermine certain kinds of radicalism and to produce expectations of peaceful improvement within the existing system. Almost immediately after the ending of the law the formerly radical leader of Bavarian Social Democracy, Georg von Vollmar, advocated a change in the party's attitude towards the state and urged the SPD to concentrate on the achievement of immediate reforms within the prevailing order. Much the same was said by Eduard Bernstein and his fellow revisionists. Conversely, the absence of real liberal and demo- cratic reform in the Tsarist autocracy before the First World War left the labour movement no option but outright revolution.

There were several ways in which the existence of a liberal or demo- cratic political system could further the politics of reformism. The very existence of parliamentary institutions combined with parliamentary sovereignty in Britain and France meant that it was possible to argue with some conviction that workers' interests could be served by the existing state. It was even possible to imagine that the parties of labour could come to power through the ballot box alone and without recourse to various forms of extraparliamentary action. In Germany the situation was rather different; for parliamentary sovereignty only became a reality in 1918 and this may explain why the German labour movement could never espouse totally reformist politics before that date. However, even in the Second Reich the right to exist as a legal political organisa- tion and to participate in elections to the Reichstag had a not dissimilar effect to the existence of parliamentary institutions in France and Britain. Allowed to bid for votes in open elections the SPD, SFIO and the PSI were often forced to dilute their pristine and radical ideologies to attract electoral support from a variety of non-proletarian social strata, such as the independent peasantry of south Germany and France's large lower middle class. To a certain extent simply participating in elections and parliamentary debates led to an absorption of the refor- mist rules of the game, as the anarchists were already arguing. Certainly persistent electoral successes seems to have bred a rather blind optimism amongst the leadership of the SPD and some sections of the French Socialist Party.[82] In France, Germany, Italy and Britain trade union and socialist organisations were further sucked into the system through their participation in municipal politics, co-operation with government institutions involved in welfare activities and the like.

One factor which encouraged caution amongst trade union and party leaders was the creation of large-scale paid bureaucracies. For example, both the Italian Socialist Party and German Social Democracy succeeded in forming huge organisational empires before 1914; and as Robert Michels, a former SPD member who became disillusioned with the party's inaction, argued, the creation of such empires had profoundly conserva- tive results.[83] This was so for a number of different reasons. The kind of people who came to the fore in bureaucratic labour organisations, people like Friedrich Ebert and Philipp Scheidemann, were not revolutionary firebrands but rather dull, hard-working but petty-minded types, obsessed by routine duties. Furthermore, the privileged lives of such bureaucrats, who received higher remuneration and greater security than the ordinary worker, separated them from any real understanding of grass-roots misery and radicalism. Above all, the preservation of the party organisation, which guaranteed their jobs and in which they had invested so much time and energy over the years, became an end in itself; and the ultimate goal of revolution was thus displaced by an instinct of bureaucratic survival. Such an argument certainly has a great deal of force as far as the leaderships of German Social Democracy and the Free Trade Unions are concerned. Time and time again they pursued cautious policies so as not to provoke government suppression of the beloved organisation; and this was certainly one of several reasons why the SPD voted for the German war credits on 4 August 1914.

A further contribution to the increasingly reformist stance of the political parties of labour may be found in the growing influence and importance of pragmatic union leaders. That the British Labour Party was largely 'a weapon of the trade-union leaders devised for the reversal of the Taff Vale decision'[84] implied a reformist perspective from the start. In Italy the leaders of the CGL often gave their support to the reformist elements within the socialist movement.[85] In Germany trade union membership overtook that of the SPD in 1902; and the increasing bargaining power this conferred upon the union leaders in their dealings with the party was used to prevent the strict observance of May Day, to reject decisively the calling of political strikes for suffrage reform and to discipline and control an emergent and radical socialist youth movement.[86]

There was yet another mechanism, so it is argued, whereby the organisation of labour paradoxically guaranteed the stability of the existing social and political order. It seems clear that the ability to protest peacefully and the discipline involved in union organisation served to reduce both the number of strikes and the use of violence in them.[87] Even more significantly, the very creation of formal labour organisations, the foundation of socialist choral societies, gymnastics associations, cycling clubs, pubs, etc. actually served to integrate the working class 'negatively' into Wilhelmine society.[88] In both France and Germany, in fact, socialism was not merely a political movement which appeared on the scene at election time; it became part and parcel of a whole working-class subculture. This subculture constituted an alternative society in what was otherwise a hostile world, providing the worker with a realm of action and self-respect which would otherwise have been denied him. In a sense the rank and file of the French and especially of the German socialist movement were cocooned against a harsh reality, at least outside the factory.

There is some evidence to support this theory of 'negative integration'. The older workers with a long involvement in socialist politics, those, therefore, to whom this process should have applied, were not those who occupied the factories and mounted the barricades in France, Germany and Italy at the end of the First World War. Those who participated in such radical activities and who went on to form the rank and file of the Communist parties of the inter-war period were precisely younger workers, often in new industries or new industrial areas, who had not been strongly represented in the ranks of organised labour before 1914.[89] The extent to which German Social Democracy actually functioned as a mechanism of social control is perhaps best attested by an analysis of crime statistics in both the Wilhelmine period and the Weimar Republic: the leaders of the SPD took pride in the fact that areas dominated by their organisation had remarkably low rates of criminal activity![90]

These various arguments — 'negative integration', bureaucratic goal displacement, the role of pragmatic trade unionists, participation in democratic politics and political liberalisation — go some way towards explaining the reformism of labour leaders. However, this is only one part of the argument about embourgeoisement, which in its most ambitious form states that the working class as a whole and not only its political representatives became 'integrated' into the fabric of capitalist society. When the emphasis shifts from labour organisations to the ordinary worker, then the explanation has to change tack as well. In particular it becomes necessary to understand the changing material conditions of working-class life in Europe in the period before 1914. In this context the overall improvement in working-class living standards after the early stages of the Industrial Revolution has been regarded as crucial. Its effect upon the reformist aspirations of the British labour aristocracy has already been discussed;[91] but many Continental workers also saw considerable increases in their real wages in the late nineteenth century. In Germany there was a sustained improvement in the real earnings of labour from the mid-1870s until the outbreak of the First World War;[92] whilst in France the average worker enjoyed a 50 per cent increase in real wages between 1870 and 1914.[93] Various kinds of welfare legislation, as in Germany in the 1880s and Britain in the first decade of the twentieth century, combined with relative job security in the European economic boom after 1896 further reduced dissatisfaction on the part of workers, or so it is claimed.[94] Not only did the worker enjoy security; he also had to spend less time in the factory: the length of the average working day decreased significantly between 1890 and 1914. In Silesia, for example, 45 per cent of miners had worked a twelve-hour day in 1891. By 1910 only 9.4 per cent did so and for over 70 per cent of them ten hours was now the norm.[95]

The affluence argument is augmented by that of the labour aristocracy: in both Britain and Germany wage differentials between the skilled and the unskilled remained high until the outbreak of the First World War. Indeed, in the case of Britain it has even been claimed that such differentials were continuing to widen until 1914;[96] whilst in Germany as late as 1913 the differential between the wages of skilled and unskilled labour, although less than in 1900, was still significant: almost 27 per cent in the building industry, 33 per cent in mining and 41 per cent in woolspinning.[97] In consequence, so the argument goes, the old obstacles which prevented the formation of a solidaristic working-class consciousness remained. A significant section of labour was still being bribed away from the snares of political radicalism. In Britain many of these well paid labour aristocrats refused to have anything to do with the Labour Representation Committee until the unions themselves came under attack from the law courts and the House of Lords after the turn of the century.[98] In Germany, on the other hand, it cannot be denied that the same kinds of skilled workers formed the rank and file of ostensibly Marxist Social Democracy; but they have also been held responsible for that party's lack of real revolutionary initiative.[99]

Thus affluence, political relaxation and organisational developments are believed to have lain behind the apparent deradicalisation of labour in the two decades before the First World War, a process witnessed by the absence of revolution in the advanced states, the increasingly reformist perspectives of the major socialist parties and the final act of patriotism in August 1914. Just how convincing is this argument?

The Case against Deradicalisation

In the first place some of the supposed indicators of deradicalisation and embourgeoisement are more than a little misleading. Exactly what the patriotism of the European working class in August 1914 tells us, apart from the fact that it was in the main patriotic, is difficult to see. It may well be that in a fully articulated and systematic political theory nationalism and domestic radicalism are mutually exclusive. But it is far from clear that such is the case in daily reality. There were South

Wales miners with traditions of domestic militancy who none the less volunteered to fight for the British Empire in 1914, just as some former radicals in Germany supported the war effort of the Reich.[100] These workers may have been 'nationalist'. Yet their nationalism, their view of what they were fighting for, may well have been very different to that of the ruling elite. To support the fatherland in its hour of need did not imply satisfaction with prevailing social and political arrangements. This was clearly the case for many of the German Social Democrats who supported their government's war effort. They did so because they believed that such support would oblige the Wilhelmine state to make concessions to the political and economic aspirations of the German working man.[101] Furthermore, much working-class support for Germany's war effort in August 1914 stemmed from the genuine belief that their country was about to be invaded not only by a foreign power but by Russia, by the bulwark of European reaction, the arch-enemy of progressive labour, Tsarist despotism. Thus the SPD's initial declaration of support for the Reich government on 4 August 1914 was conditional upon the defensive nature of Germany's war.[102] In short, nationalism meant different things to different people and it is misleading to read too much into working-class support for national war efforts in August 1914. Hence the behaviour of the European working class at this time cannot be taken as irrefutable proof that a process of deradicalisation had in fact taken place.

This is so for a further reason. It cannot be assumed that this same working class had been uniformly radical at an earlier date and had then undergone a unilinear process of deradicalisation which culminated in the events of August 1914. If one looks in some detail at the attitudes and behaviour of workers and their representatives in earlier periods, then the picture is far from clear. Although it is true that *some* sections of the English working class had become involved in radical politics in the 1830s and 1840s, it is also true that others remained aloof from such activity and pursued a reformist path through trade unions and friendly societies, even in those bitter years.[103] In France as early as the 1880s the so-called 'possibilist' party of Paul Brousse, which subscribed to reformist tenets, enjoyed greater electoral fortunes than the more revolutionary organisation of Jules Guesde.[104] When the various socialist groups of France did finally unite to form the SFIO in 1905, the new party was thus composed from its very inception of a plethora of political persuasions, some possibilist, some Marxist, some eclectic and far from doctrinaire in their socialism, as in the case of the group of Independents whose most famous representative was Jean Jaurès. In Germany the SPD's adoption of an ostensibly Marxist programme at its Erfurt congress in 1891 should not be regarded as an unequivocal commitment on the part of all members of the party to revolutionary socialism. In fact even in the period of the anti-socialist law from 1878 to 1890, when repression was most marked, certain elements within German Social Democracy were already pursuing reformist politics in the Reichstag and in some of the states of south Germany.[105] There was considerable internal feuding within the party even then. Thus no simple, unilinear process of the displacement of radical goals had taken place: the attitudes of workers and their ostensible leaders in parties and trade unions were never monolithic.

This last point perhaps needs to be emphasised above all else. As we have seen, the French labour movement found itself divided between anarcho-syndicalists and socialists, between Marxists and reformists throughout its existence; and in a sense the division of that movement into Social Democratic and Communist wings after the First World War was a continuation of pre-war ideological conflicts.[106] If this was true of the situation in France, it was even truer of that across the Rhine. German Social Democracy certainly possessed a conservative trade union and party bureaucracy, and a revisionist wing of intellectuals; but it also embraced radical party organisations in Prussia and Saxony, together with a significant number of Marxist theorists of great distinction. Again the post-war split built upon pre-war divisions.[107] In Spain a relatively reformist trade union organisation (UGT) and Socialist Party in some areas found itself in competition with insurrectionary anarcho-syndicalism in Catalonia and revolutionary socialism amongst the miners of the Asturias.[108] In Italy too the reformists could not claim to dominate the institutions of labour before 1914. Not only did an insurrectionary tradition survive in Ancona, the Romagna and parts of north-west Tuscany, but the maximalist wing of the PSI clearly took control of the party in the wake of the Libyan war of 1911/12.[109] Again, therefore, it will not do to describe the European labour movement as a whole as 'integrated' into the prevailing economic and social order before 1914.

That this should have been so can be explained at least in part by the fact that many of the explanations of deradicalisation are themselves rather one-dimensional. For example, the role of the state in most European countries before 1914 could hardly be described as sympathetic to labour. Admittedly the scale of repression varied, with Tsarist Russia standing on the extreme of the spectrum, but labour still confronted hostile legislation in several places. Although Germany's Second

Reich abandoned its anti-socialist law in 1890, there remained innumerable legal obstacles to complete freedom of speech and association:
many SPD newspaper editors spent a good deal of time in prison after
convictions for 'insulting the Kaiser', for example.[110] Members of the
Free Trade Unions and the SPD also remained ineligible for employment
by the state until the war. Above all, Germany's constitutional system
remained semi-autocratic until the revolution of 1918, when parliamentary sovereignty was finally achieved. Thus Bernstein's vision of a gradual
road to socialism made little sense to many of his contemporary Social
Democrats and thus his views were regularly rejected at SPD party
conferences. Furthermore the Wilhelmine state still sent sabre-swinging
troops to deal with strikers: in this way several miners were killed in
violent clashes in the Ruhr in 1912.[111] In the same year the German
government tightened up the law concerning picketing. In France a
republican government elected by universal manhood suffrage and with
radical credentials from the past did not hesitate to use troops to break
the strikes of electrical workers, railway employees and postmen in the
period between 1906 and 1910, and had still passed little social legislation before the outbreak of war in 1914.[112] Even in 'liberal' Britain
after the turn of the century the relative absence of violent or overt
repression did not necessarily imply a friendly attitude towards labour
on the part of the authorities. In the first place, electoral qualifications
and registration procedures effectively disenfranchised a significant
section of the British working class.[113] Second, the Taff Vale and
Osborne judgments struck at the very heart of trade union organisation
and action and were, of course, the prologue to the formation of an
independent Labour Party with trade union backing. The formation of
that party may well have been primarily defensive in aim; and the party
did not adopt a socialist platform until after the First World War. However, its formation hardly tallies with the idea that British labour was
becoming progressively *more* integrated into the prevailing political
system. Amongst certain sections of the work-force, especially in the
docks and in some parts of Wales, the period immediately before 1914
also witnessed the growth of syndicalist attitudes, as we will see.[114] Thus,
whilst it is true that repression became more muted in some European
states and whilst this obviously had some impact on the formulation of
strategies by some labour leaders, it would have been equally difficult
for the observer to identify the European state positively with the
interests of the working class before 1914.

The extent to which the creation of formal labour organisations
served to strengthen the hand of reformism is equally unclear. Robert

Michels, a disillusioned former member of the SPD, was certainly correct when he argued that the massive organisational empire erected by the party between 1900 and 1914 produced a narrow-minded bureaucracy which became obsessed with the preservation of that empire as an end in itself.[115] However, the extent to which the process of bureaucratisation *initiated* conservatism within the ranks of the SPD is another matter. We have already seen that there were powerful reformist elements within the party even during the 'heroic' struggle against the anti-socialist law. More relevant is the fact that at the very point of its inception, the SPD bureaucracy was created for reformist purposes – to win elections – and thus cannot be regarded as the initial *cause* of reformist sentiments. Furthermore, it can also be argued that it was not organisation as such which gave rise to reformism as an inevitable reflex but rather the specific kind of organisational structure adopted by German Social Democracy, an organisational structure in which the radical membership of the party branches of large industrial towns was grossly underrepresented.[116] This leads to a further point: there were places in which the SPD retained a radical orientation and expressed disquiet about the rather cautious policies of the national party leadership. Such was the case in the SPD branches of Greater Berlin, Brunswick, Bremen, Stuttgart, i.e. many of the largest and most important organisations within the party. Furthermore, the fact that some leading Social Democrats were never that radical or had moved to the right over the years tells us less than might be imagined about the ideological identity of the rank-and-file party member. Some towns were represented successively by right-, then left-wing parliamentary deputies. In others the reverse was the case. Thus there seems to have been a Social Democratic consciousness at the base of the party which transcended the ideological divisions at the level of leadership.[117] There is evidence that lower party functionaries at a local level were often a good deal more radical than regional or national SPD organisers, as was the case in Dortmund, for example;[118] whilst Saxon and Prussian party conferences were invariably more leftist in tone than those of south German Social Democracy or at a national level. Clearly, therefore, the massive organisational growth of the SPD did not guarantee a uniformly reformist party; and thus to talk of the integration of the SPD *as a whole* into the fabric of capitalist Wilhelmine society is most unsatisfactory. This is true for another reason: if the ranks of German Social Democracy had undergone some mysterious process of embourgeoisement, why did the Wilhelmine working class choose to form their own cultural, social and political organisations, rather than unite with those of other social groups?[119]

Admittedly what the ordinary working-class member of European socialist parties thought in this period cannot be established with any degree of accuracy. But we have already seen that in parts of Italy and Spain, as well as Russia, an insurrectionary spirit had not been extinguished by 1914. In the case of Germany, as we have also seen, it is possible to assemble rows of quotations from contemporary commentators and from some working-class Social Democrats themselves which suggest something far removed from revolutionary sentiment.[120] Some may have joined the SPD because they were lonely or because they wished to enjoy its wide range of leisure and cultural activities; or for more materialistic motives, to derive benefit from pension and insurance schemes. Indeed, Guenther Roth has amassed a wealth of such quotations to validate his theory of 'negative integration' and show that the SPD did not constitute a revolutionary threat in Imperial Germany. Such evidence, however, is of limited value. It not only chooses to ignore rival radical quotations and the substance of many resolutions at party congresses but emanates in the main from either the atypical working-class autobiography or the observations of commentators with a political axe to grind.[121] Most important of all, perhaps, is the need to realise that the failure of the German working class to mount the barricades before 1914 does not necessarily indicate that it lacked any revolutionary commitment or was totally in the grip of reformism. Rather the inaction indicated a simple grasp of objective reality: the SPD not only confronted the most powerful military machine in the world and a reactionary aristocratic elite, but also an elite that had the backing of a mighty and feudalised industrial bourgeoisie and significant sections of the German lower middle class of peasants, artisans and some white-collar workers. In a sense, therefore, the SPD did not imagine its impotence before 1914; it was impotent. In this context it is revealing to look at what happened in the wake of the First World War, when the previous structures of economic and political control were removed: then there was a revolutionary movement, although its precise nature is problematic.[122] Furthermore, the rhetoric adopted by workers' and soldiers' councils in the post-war upheavals does demonstrate at least some contact with the age-old and on occasion radical aspects of Social Democratic ideology: democratisation, demilitarisation, socialisation, a 'Social' or 'Socialist Republic'.[123]

That the European labour movement split into hostile camps after the First World War, not only in Germany, but in France and Italy as well, again points to deep-seated divisions of both an ideological and social nature within its ranks, divisions that were present before the war but which could more easily come into the open as genuinely revolutionary situations developed in some countries and the old order collapsed. Once again those pre-war divisions testify to the danger of regarding European labour as uniformly reformist — or for that matter monolithically revolutionary — before the outbreak of war. It was not the case, therefore, that organisation bred reformism of necessity. No more did an improvement in the standard of living of the European working class.

There can be no doubt that the standard of living of labour in most European countries improved between 1800 and 1914. However, within this overall improvement significant variations took place. In Britain an earlier period of rising average real wages was succeeded between 1900 and 1914 by one in which they fell.[124] In France the years immediately prior to the outbreak of war in 1914 saw prices rise faster than wages.[125] In Germany a sustained rise in working-class living standards between about 1873 and 1890 was followed by a period of real-wage stagnation, again partly as a consequence of price inflation.[126] The problem for the worker, however, was not just one of inflation. Another factor played an increasing role, especially in Wilhelmine Germany: employers increasingly came to form their own powerful organisations to combat labour and resorted with ever greater success to the lock-out to force workers into submission. Thus strikes became less and less effective in some industrial sectors and more and more costly. Indeed, this was precisely one of the reasons why the leadership of German trade unions became so cautious in the pre-war period.[127] To a lesser extent the same development can also be detected in Britain at the same time. Employers imported blackleg labour to break strikes and instituted an extremely effective lock-out against the ASE in 1897/8, despite the fact that this had traditionally been the most successful of all labour unions.[128] Even where real wages were rising on average, however, there remained huge differences of income between different sectors of the labour force. We have already seen that wide pay differentials survived in Britain and Germany in this period, differentials between the skilled and unskilled, male and female, and between similar workers in different regions.[129] Furthermore, the earnings curve of industrial workers — the fact that their earnings were at a maximum for a period of time of varying length after initial training but then fell with increasing age — not only meant increasing insecurity and poverty with old age but different patterns of poverty for different groups of workers, whose earnings curves adopted a different shape.[130] Insecurity was generated by other factors too, by illness, accident and the like, as well as by the scale of heavy employer fines in some places.[131]

The greatest threat to security, however, perhaps came from cyclical and structural unemployment, from the vagaries of the business cycle or technological modernisation. In years of depression in the European economy, in 1901/2 and 1908/9 in Germany, for example, there was a good deal of overall unemployment; whilst certain trades also had to tolerate high annual unemployment − 5 per cent in the case of German printers.[132]

Thus there was no vast and no universal improvement in the standard of living of the European working class, at least as far as wages were concerned. The same might be said of the length of the working day. There were certainly some improvements here, as we have seen already, but again there were wide variations. Between 1890 and 1914 German textile workers still worked an average week of 63 to 66 hours, whilst Silesian miners had to bear a longer working day than their more fortunate counterparts in the Ruhr.[133] However, even if such a huge improvement in the standard of living of European labour could be identified, it is more than a little questionable to assume that such affluence would necessarily produce reformism or quietism. If this affluence theory of reformism held water, than those most liable to protest would have been the most impoverished; and the relatively prosperous worker would have remained outside the ranks of militancy. This is far from the truth, however. On the contrary, we have already seen that some of the poorest unskilled factory labourers failed to organise or protest on any significant scale before 1914 and that the trade unions and political parties of labour recruited predominantly from skilled and relatively affluent workers. In fact the immediate pre-war and war years saw the relatively well paid engineering worker emerge as arguably the major vehicle of revolutionary ardour.[134] In fact it could be argued that the sustained rise in real wages up to 1900 led to rising expectations amongst some sections of the European working class and that this became a major cause of the vast wave of industrial militancy in the four years immediately before the First World War: the inflation of those years robbed the worker of that improvement in his living standards that he had come to regard as his just deserts.

In any case, in these pre-war years many workers not only faced the traditional problems of industrial society but also new threats to their livelihood. The emergence of a class of white-collar workers standing between management and the shop floor produced both more impersonal labour relations and an obstacle to the mobility prospects of the skilled manual worker. More importantly, the two decades before the First World War saw a great range of technological innovations which once again threatened to strike at the status, skills and security of some sections of the old labour aristocracy and also some of the unskilled as well. The introduction of mechanical saws, prefabricated wooden units and the use of iron and concrete as building materials produced something of a revolution in the construction industry. Glass bottling plants revolutionised work processes in the glass-making industry. Gasoline motors threatened the unskilled in lifting and hauling occupations. Milling and grinding machines, more specialised lathes and mechanical drills and borers disposed of some of the traditional skills in engineering and formed the background to the great surge in industrial unrest and political militancy on the part of metalworkers which was to be of crucial importance throughout Europe, as we will see. In the 1890s the hand manufacture of shoes also found itself displaced by new technology.[135]

As in an earlier period of industrialisation, the problem was not simply and not necessarily one of new technology, however, but often the reorganisation of work structures, involving increased competition from sweated immigrant labour in the textile industry, as in London's East End, the decasualisation of dock labour, the increased supervision and pace of work, use of piece-rates and the removal of traditional holidays. Not surprisingly, therefore, workers protested for a shorter working week on an unprecedented scale. Some German engineering workers actually complained of nervous exhaustion and in some cases workers appear to have deliberately lowered productivity in protest against the new pressures of work. Some French workers struck against Taylorism, as did some printers and engineers in Britain.[136] Not only did such problems give rise to industrial conflicts between capital and labour. There is also evidence to suggest that an old union leadership, reared in craft traditions, proved incapable of comprehending the problems of a younger work-force and that this in turn generated a good deal of independent militancy at the shop-floor level.[137]

This leads to a further and crucial point: much of the industrial and even political protest which took place at the end of the First World War and in the subsequent two decades cannot simply be regarded as the product of the deprivations and misery of war but is rather to be seen as a consequence of the long-term change in the structure of European industry which had already begun before 1914. In fact, far from detecting any decline in the radicalism of European labour in the decade before the First World War, I would suggest that the reverse was the case. The few years before 1914 witnessed an utterly unprecedented surge in the scale and militancy of industrial and in some cases even political protest on the part of labour. In Britain inflation provoked an upsurge of industrial militancy: 1908 saw miners' riots and a fatality at Tonypandy, 1911 witnessed both the first national rail strike and clashes between striking dockers and troops in Liverpool, in which two men were killed. In fact between 1910 and 1914 syndicalism made some headway in the British docks and certain groups of workers, as in the case of railwaymen and Welsh miners, became increasingly restive against their official and cautious trade union leadership.[138] In June 1914 in Italy there occurred a succession of local risings and industrial workers mounted the barricades in the so-called 'red week'; whilst in Russia the influx of former peasants into the giant metallurgical and textile factories of Moscow and St Petersburg between 1911 and 1914 brought an increase in the strength of the radical Bolshevik party and an increase in industrial militancy.[139] Even in the supposedly disciplined labour movement of Germany's Second Reich one contemporary was led to speak of the growth of a 'syndicalist undercurrent' amongst broad sections of the work-force in 1913 and the official newspapers of the SPD were full of accounts of and discussions about rank-and-file alienation from the inactive party leadership. From 1905 in the German building industry, in the mines and in particular in the rapidly expanding metalworking industries there occurred a significant number of wildcat strikes in defiance of national union instructions and in some places a marked hostility between rank-and-file unionists and their official leaders developed, a hostility which reached extreme proportions in the great Hamburg dock strike of 1913, in which the local stewards demanded an increasing say in union policy-making. Now it would be ridiculous, of course, to claim that any of this represented a real threat of revolution in Wilhelmine Germany on the eve of war; however, such action within the trade union movement did mark the start of opposition to the official bureaucracy in certain industries which led to demands for some form of shop-floor control. Hence it is neither surprising nor without significance that the councils' movement which emerged in the German Revolution of November 1918 found fruitful soil in precisely those industrial sectors which had witnessed such conflicts between trade union leaders and the rank and file. Furthermore, the growth of radicalism among metalworkers may constitute a more important factor making for the later split of the labour movement in Germany than the ideological divisions within the leadership of the SPD that have more normally dominated the attention of historians: for the newly formed and more radical Independent Social Democratic Party (USPD), which was created in 1917 in opposition to the war, developed most strongly in those industrial centres where there had been significant rank-and-file opposition to the official leadership of the German Metalworkers' Union (DMV) before the First World War.[140] Similarly, it is possible to detect the growth of syndicalist attitudes and industrial unrest in the mining community of the Ruhr before 1914, an unrest which again formed the prologue to later radicalism.[141] Again it is significant that one of the few groups of French workers to oppose the First World War from its start was another organisation of metalworkers, Merrheim's Fédération des Métaux;[142] whilst the triumph of *maximalismo* within the Italian Socialist Party derived some of its support from the new semi-skilled auto workers of the Milan-Turin-Genoa triangle.[143]

This wave of pre-war militancy and radicalism seems to have been generated by some of the same phenomena that have been held responsible for the even greater upheavals at the end of the First World War, namely the deskilling of some previously skilled engineering workers on the one hand, and the influx of new and young elements, often in semi-skilled occupations, into rapidly expanding industries on the other.[144] The absence of traditions of disciplined organisation on the part of the latter and their youthfulness contributed to this wave of unrest, as did spiralling inflation and the reorganisation of work structures discussed above. It has also been claimed that preindustrial backgrounds amongst new Russian factory workers and Ruhr miners also contributed to the uncontrollable nature of the new wave of protest.[145] If we take a considered look at developments within the political parties and trade unions of European labour before the First World War, therefore, it is clear that no uniform process of deradicalisation or embourgeoisement took place.

Having said this, we must now remember that the overwhelming majority of the European working class belonged to no economic or political organisations before 1914. In Britain only about a quarter of the industrial work-force had been mobilised by such organisations, and the figure for Germany was much the same. In France over 90 per cent of industrial workers were unorganised; and the figure for Italy, Spain and Russia was even higher. Yet we must not assume that workers who belonged to no formal organisation or who never went on strike were necessarily happy with their lot, peacefully 'integrated' into the social and political fabric of European capitalism. Many of the workers who joined the insurrections of 1918-23 in Germany, many of those who participated in the *biennio rosso* of 1919/20 in Italy, many of those who occupied factories in France in 1936 were precisely those who had played no part in labour protest previously.[146] This might indicate that their earlier inaction was less the consequence of an acceptance of the prevailing social and political order but was rather the result of economic and political controls exercised by employers and the state, not only through overtly repressive institutions but also through company-provided housing, employer monopoly of the labour market, etc. When these controls were undermined in the course of the war or as a result of political changes, as in France in 1936, then it became much easier to express dissatisfaction and engage in various forms of protest. In fact studies of individual concerns have revealed seething discontent surviving beneath an apparent sea of calm;[147] whilst it is striking that some of the most ultra-leftist adventures in the Ruhr in the post-war period were initiated by those who had previously belonged to the yellow unions of the bosses.[148] Thus even belonging to a company union may not necessarily indicate conservative values but could simply indicate a recognition of prevailing economic realities. What happened during and after the First World War was that many of the previous impediments to protest disintegrated; and the European working class attempted to seize this chance to improve its lot.

Notes

1.   The belief that at least certain sections of European labour had accepted their lot within the prevailing order can be found in Rosa Luxemburg's critique of the caution of the SPD leadership, repeated and developed into the classic argument concerning the effects of bureaucratisation in Robert Michels, *Political Parties* (New York, 1959). Michels was a former member of the SPD who became disillusioned. Deradicalisation characterises the traditional account of the history of the SPD to be found in later writing as well. See Carl E. Schorske, *German Social Democracy 1905-1917* (Cambridge, Mass., 1955); Harvey Mitchell and Peter N. Stearns, *Workers and Protest. The European Labour Movement, the Working Classes and the Origins of Social Democracy 1890-1914* (Itasca, Ill., 1971); Harry J. Marks, 'Sources of Reformism in the Social Democratic Party of Germany, 1890-1914', *Journal of Modern History*, vol. XI, no. 3 (1939).

2.   Hans Hautman and Rudolf Kropf, *Die österreichische Arbeiterbewegung vom Vomärz bis 1945* (Linz, 1974), Chs. 4, 5 and 6; Georges Lefranc, *Le Mouvement Socialiste sous la IIIe République* (Paris, 1963), pp. 14-196; Edouard Dolléans, *Mouvement Ouvrier*, vol. 2, *1871-1936* (Paris, 1946); Jacques Droz, *Le Socialisme Démocratique 1864-1960* (Paris, 1966), pp. 63-75; Dick Geary, 'The German Labour Movement 1848-1918', *European Studies Review*, vol. 6, no. 3 (1976), pp. 304-15; Schorske, *German Social Democracy*; Guenther Roth, *The Social Democrats in Imperial Germany. A Study in Working Class Isolation and National Integration* (Totowa, NJ, 1963); Helga Grebing, *The History of the German Labour Movement* (London, 1969); Hedwig Wachenheim, *Die deutsche Arbeiterbewegung 1844 bis 1914* (Cologne and Opladen, 1967).

3.   Martin Blinkhorn, 'Industrialisation and Social Protest in Italy', unpublished MS.; Richard Hostetter, *The Italian Socialist Movement*, vol. i, *Origins*

(1860-1882) (Princeton, 1958); Giuliano Procacci, *La lotta di classe in Italia agli inizi del secolo xx* (Rome, 1972).

4.   Gerald Brenan, *The Spanish Labyrinth* (London, 1962), Chs. 8 and 10; D. Ruiz, *El Movimiento Obrero en Asturias* (Gijon, 1980); Tunon de Lara, *El Movimiento Obrero en la Historia de Espana* (Madrid, 1972); Martin Blinkhorn, 'Industrialisation and Social Protest in Spain', unpublished MS.

5.   Franco Venturi, *Roots of Revolution* (London, 1960); Allen K. Wildman, *The Making of a Workers' Revolution. Russian Social Democracy, 1891-1903* (Chicago, 1967); Solomon M. Schwarz, *The Russian Revolution of 1905* (Chicago, 1967); David Lane, *The Roots of Russian Communism* (Assen, 1967); Richard Pipes, *Social Democracy and the St Petersburg Labour Movement, 1885-1897* (Cambridge, Mass., 1963); J.L.H. Keep, *The Rise of Social Democracy in Russia* (Oxford, 1966); Israel Getzler, *Martov. A Political Biography of a Russian Social Democrat* (Cambridge, 1967); Donald W. Treadgold, *Lenin and his Rivals* (London, 1955); Samuel Baron, *Plekhanov. The Father of Russian Marxism* (London, 1963); E.H. Carr, *The Bolshevik Revolution* (London, 1966), pp. 15-81; Isaac Deutscher, *Trotsky*, 3 vols. (London, 1954-63); L.H. Haimson, *The Russian Marxists and the Origins of Bolshevism* (Cambridge, Mass., 1955); David Shub, *Lenin* (London, 1966); Adam B. Ulam, *Lenin and the Bolsheviks* (London, 1969); Leopold Haimson, 'The Problem of Social Stability in Urban Russia, 1905-1917' in Clive Emsley (ed.), *Conflict and Stability in Europe* (London, 1979); Theodore H. von Laue, 'Russian Peasants in the Factory 1892-1904', *Journal of Economic History*, vol. 2 (1961), pp. 61-80.

6.   Henry Pelling, *The Origins of the Labour Party* (Oxford, 1965); David Kynaston, *King Labour. The British Working Class 1850-1914* (London, 1976), p. 65.

7.   For a fuller treatment of this see below, pp. 98-104.

8.   See notes 2, 3 and 4 above.

9.   See note 5 above.

10.   See the introduction to D.A. Smart (ed.), *Pannekoek and Gorter's Marxism* (London, 1978), p. 10f.

11.   See notes 1 and 2 above. Also see below, pp. 108f.

12.   See above, pp. 47-70.

13.   Brenan, *Spanish Labyrinth*, p. 220.

14.   Adrian Lyttleton, 'Revolution and Counter-revolution in Italy, 1918-1922' in Charles L. Bertrand (ed.), *Revolutionary Situations in Europe, 1917-1922: Germany, Italy, Austria-Hungary* (Montreal, 1977), p. 65.

15.   Ibid., p. 64f.

16.   Kynaston, *King Labour*, p. 66.

17.   Claude Willard, *Les Guesdistes* (Paris, 1965); Bernard Moss, *The Origins of the French Labour Movement* (Berkeley, 1976), p. 120f.

18.   See above, pp. 56f.

19.   Moss, *Origins*, pp. 120-35.

20.   Charles Tilly, Louise Tilly and Richard Tilly, *The Rebellious Century* (London, 1975), p. 120; Donald H. Bell, 'Worker Culture and Worker Politics: the Experience of an Italian Town, 1880-1915', *Social History*, vol. 3, no. 1 (1978), pp. 2-7; Procacci, *Lotta di Classe*, pp. 23ff.

21.   Geary, 'German Labour Movement', pp. 310ff.; Jörg Schadt, *Die Sozialdemokratische Partei in Baden* (Hanover, 1971), p. 150; Dieter Fricke, *Zur Organisation und Tätigkeit der deutschen Arbeiterbewegung (1890-1914)* (Leipzig, 1962), pp. 73ff. and 210f.; Marks, 'Sources of Reformism', pp. 353ff.; Georg Gärtner, *Die Nürnberger Arbeiterbewegung 1868-1908* (Nuremburg, 1908), *passim*.

22.   Brenan, *Spanish Labyrinth*, p. 216f.

23.   See above, pp. 75f.

24.　Leo A. Loubère, *Radicalism in Mediterranean France: its Rise and Decline, 1848-1914* (New York, 1974).

25.　Tony Judt, *Socialism in Provence, 1871-1914* (Cambridge, 1979).

26.　Ibid.

27.　Dick Geary, 'Radicalism and the German Worker: Metalworkers and Revolution 1914-1923' in Richard J. Evans (ed.), *Society and Politics in Wilhelmine Germany* (London, 1978), pp. 276-83; David W. Morgan, *The Socialist Left and the German Revolution* (Ithaca, NY, 1975), p. 72; Dolléans, *Mouvement Ouvrier*, vol. 3, *De 1921 à nos Jours* (Paris, 1953), p. 153; Edward Shorter and Charles Tilly, *Strikes in France 1830-1968* (Cambridge, 1974), pp. 132-6; Antoine Prost, *La CGT à l'Époque du Front Populaire* (Paris, 1964), pp. 95-104; Ronald Tiersky, *French Communism 1920-1972* (New York, 1978), p. 58; Daniel R. Brower, *The New Jacobins* (Ithaca, NY, 1968), p. 87, 135 and 156; P. Spriano, *L'occupazione della fabbriche* (Turin, 1964); P. Spriano, *Storia del partito communista italiano* (Turin, 1967); John M. Cammett, *Antonio Gramsci and the Origins of Italian Communism* (Stanford, 1967). For a fuller discussion see below, pp. 151f.

28.　Gerhard A. Ritter, *Die Arbeiterbewegung im Wilhelmischen Reich* (Berlin, 1959), pp. 73-8; Dieter Groh, *Negative Integration und Revolutionärer Attentismus* (Frankfurt am Main, 1973), p. 282f.

29.　Pelling, *British Trade Unionism*, Ch. 7; J.T. Ward and W. Hamish Fraser, *Workers and Employers* (London, 1980), p. 364f.; Geary, 'German Labour Movement', p. 311f.; H. Varain, *Freie Gewerkschaften, Sozialdemokratie und Staat* (Düsseldorf, 1956); Fricke, *Zur Organisation*, pp. 225ff.; Georges Lefranc, *Histoire du Mouvement Syndical Francais* (Paris, 1937); Paul Louis, *Le Syndicat en France* (Paris, 1963); Theodor Zeldin, *France 1848-1945* (Oxford, 1973), pp. 218-67; Moss, *Origins*, pp. 151ff.; Peter N. Stearns, *Revolutionary Syndicalism and French Labour* (New Brunswick, 1971); Dolleans, *Mouvement Ouvrier*, vol. 2, p. 208; Hautmann and Kropf, *Die österreichische Arbeiterbewegung*, Chs. 5 and 6.

30.　Geary, 'German Labour Movement', pp. 312ff.; Schorske, *German Social Democracy*, p. 10f., 128ff., 200, 203, 208, 218n., 229f., 260f. and 270; Klaus Tenfelde, 'Anarcho-syndikalistische Strömungen in der Ruhr Bergarbeiterschaft 1906-1914', unpublished MS. for the second session of the SSRC Modern German Social History Research Group at the University of East Anglia, January 1979.

31.　Dolléans, *Mouvement Ouvrier*, vol. 2, p. 143; the Tillys, *Rebellious Century*, p. 121; Shorter and Tilly, *Strikes*, p. 120; Judt, *Socialism in Provence*; Michel Augé-Laribé, *La Révolution Agricole* (Paris, 1955); pp. 220ff. and 260ff.; Gérard Walter, *Histoire des Paysans de France* (Paris, 1963), pp. 422ff. and 426-9; Blinkhorn, 'Italy'; L. Lotti, *La settimata rossa* (Florence, 1965), pp. 27ff.

32.　E.J. Hobsbawm, *Labouring Men* (London, 1979), Chs. 9, 10 and 11; Pelling, *British Trade Unionism*, Ch. 6.

33.　Lefranc, *Mouvement Syndical*; Louis, *Les Syndicats*; Stearns, *Revolutionary Syndicalism*; Zeldin, *France*, pp. 218-67.

34.　Fricke, *Zur Organisation*, pp. 225ff.

35.　Kynaston, *King Labour*, pp. 139-43; Hobsbawm, *Labouring Men*, Ch. 8; Zeldin, *France*, p. 239f.; Blinkhorn, 'Italy'; Geary, 'German Labour Movement', p. 311f.; J. Barrington Moore Jr., *Injustice. The Social Bases of Obedience and Revolt* (White Plains, NY, 1978), p. 183.

36.　See below, pp. 151f.

37.　Blinkhorn, 'Spain'; Brenan, *Spanish Labyrinth*, Ch. 8.

38.　Kynaston, *King Labour*, pp. 139-44; Hobsbawm, *Labouring Men*, Ch. 10.

39.　Geary, 'German Labour Movement', p. 311; Barrington Moore, *Injustice*, p. 260f.; Klaus J. Mattheier, 'Werkvereine und wirtschaftsfriedlich-nationale (gelbe) Arbeiterbewegung' in Reulecke, *Arbeiterbewegung*; Fricke, *Zur Organisation*, p. 254f.; Geoff Eley, 'The Wilhelmine Right' in Evans, *Society and Politics*, p. 121f.

40. Mitchell and Stearns, *Workers and Protest*, p. 148f.; George Sayers Bain, *The Growth of White-Collar Unionism* (Oxford, 1970), pp. 11-21; T. Pierenkemper, 'White-Collar Workers in Germany before 1900', unpublished MS. delivered to the third meeting of the SSRC/DFG North West Forum on German Economic and Social History at the University of Liverpool, 1980; Jürgen Kocka, *Unternehmerverwaltung und Angestelltenschaft* (Stuttgart, 1969); David Crew, *Town in the Ruhr. A Social History of Bochum, 1860-1914* (New York, 1979), p. 86f.

41. Brenan, *Spanish Labyrinth*, Ch. 8; Stearns, *Revolutionary Syndicalism*; F.F. Ridley, *Revolutionary Syndicalism in France* (Cambridge, 1970).

42. Brenan, *Spanish Labyrinth*, Ch. 7; Moss, *Origins*.

43. Hostetter, *Italian Socialist Movement*; Tillys, *Rebellious Century*, pp. 97-120; Blinkhorn, 'Italy'; Lyttleton, 'Revolution and Counter-revolution', p. 68.

44. Moss, *Origins*, p. 128; Stearns, *Revolutionary Syndicalism*, pp. 12 and 19f.; Claude Willard, *Socialisme et Communisme Français* (Paris, 1967), pp. 67-73.

45. Blinkhorn, 'Spain'; Brenan, *Spanish Labyrinth*, Chs. 7 and 8; Gabriel Jackson, *The Spanish Republic and the Civil War 1931-1939* (Princeton, 1965), pp. 17-24.

46. See above, pp. 67f.

47. For accounts of French politics in the Third Republic see David Thomson, *Democracy in France since 1870* (Oxford, 1969); Alfred Cobban, *History of Modern France*, vol. 3, *1871-1962* (London, 1965).

48. Brenan, *Spanish Labyrinth*, pp. 7ff. and 220.

49. See above, pp. 50f.

50. See note 45 above.

51. Jackson, *Spanish Republic*, p. 79f.

52. Adrian Shubert, 'Revolution in Self-Defence: the Radicalization of the Asturian Coal Miners, 1921-1934', unpublished MS.; Ruiz, *El Movimiento Obrero*.

53. Lyttleton, 'Revolution and Counter-revolution', p. 65.

54. For tabulation of strike demands see Peter N. Stearns, *Lives of Labour. Work in a Maturing Industrial Society* (London, 1975), Ch. 9.

55. Pelling, *British Trade Unionism*, pp. 135ff.

56. For a massive compilation of statistical data see Shorter and Tilly, *Strikes*, Appendix B; Stearns, *Revolutionary Syndicalism*, p. 5; Stearns, *Lives*, Ch. 9.

57. For this last point see below, pp. 123ff.; for strike figures see Albin Gladen, 'Die Streiks der Bergarbeiter' in Reulecke, *Arbeiterbewegung*, pp. 113-46; Fricke, *Zur Organisation*, pp. 257-63; Jürgen Kuczynski, *Die Geschichte der Lage der Arbeiter unter dem Kapitalismus*, Part I, vol. 3, *Darstellung der Lage der Arbeiter in Deutschland von 1871 bis 1900* (Berlin, 1962), p. 205; Kuczynski, *Geschichte der Lage*, Part I, vol. 4, *Darstellung der Lange der Arbeiter in Deutschland von 1900 bis 1917/18* (Berlin, 1967), p. 155.

58. For a discussion of such changes see below, pp. 122f.

59. Shorter and Tilly, *Strikes*, pp. 68-80; Stearns, *Lives*, p. 3.

60. Shorter and Tilly, *Strikes*, pp. 68-80.

61. Mitchell and Stearns, *Workers and Protest*, pp. 168f.; Richard J. Evans, ' "Red Wednesday" in Hamburg', *Social History*, vol. 4, no. 1 (1979).

62. Stearns, *Lives*, pp. 372-8; Kynaston, *King Labour*, pp. 132 and 163f.

63. Crew, *Bochum*, Ch. 6.

64. Shorter and Tilly, *Strikes, passim*.

65. Hobsbawm, *Labouring Men*, Chs. 9, 10 and 11; Pelling, *British Trade Unionism*, Ch. 6.

66. See below, pp. 122f.

67. See below, pp. 122ff.

68. There is a vast literature on the attitude of socialist parties towards the war and the divisions which arose during it. Walter Bartel, *Die Linken in der deutschen Sozialdemokratie im Kampf gegen Militarismus und Krieg* (Berlin, 1958);

A.J. Berlau, *The German Social Democratic Party 1914-1921* (New York, 1949); Carr, *Bolshevik Revolution*, vol. 1, Chs. 3 and 4; Merle Fainsod, *International Socialism and the World War* (Cambridge, Mass., 1934); Hermann Heidegger, *Die deutsche Sozialdemokratie und der nationale Staat, 1870-1920* (Göttingen, 1956); James W. Hulse, *The Forming of the Communist International* (Stanford, 1964); James Joll, *The Second International* (London, 1955); William Maehl, 'The Triumph of Nationalism in the German Socialist Party on the Eve of the First World War', *Journal of Modern History*, vol. 24, no. 1 (1952); Karl W. Meyer, *Karl Liebknecht* (Washington DC, 1957); Susanne Miller, 'Zum dritten August 1914' in *Archiv für Sozialgeschichte*, no. 4 (1964), pp. 515-23; John W. Mishark, *The Road to Revolution* (Detroit, 1967); Eugen Prager, *Geschichte der USPD* (Berlin, 1921); A.J. Ryder, *The German Revolution of 1918* (Cambridge, 1967); Schorske, *German Social Democracy*; Robert Wohl, *French Communism in the Making* (Stanford, 1966); Annie Kriegel, *Aux Origines du Communisme Français* (Paris, 1964); Georges Haupt, *Socialism and the Great War* (Oxford, 1972); Helmut Trotnow, *Karl Liebknecht* (Cologne, 1980); Kenneth R. Calkins, *Hugo Haase* (Durham, North Carolina, 1979); Susanne Miller, *Burgfrieden und Klassenkampf* (Düsseldorf, 1974); Gilbert Badia, *Le Spartakisme* (Paris, 1967); Warren Lerner, *Karl Radek* (Stanford, 1970); Ursula Ratz, *Georg Ledebour* (Berlin, 1969); Morgan, *Socialist Left*; Robert F. Wheeler, *USPD und Internationale* (Frankfurt am Main, 1975); Albert S. Lindemann, *The 'Red Years'* (Berkeley, 1974).

69.   Michels, *Political Parties*; J.P. Nettl, 'The German Social Democratic Party as a Political Model', *Past and Present*, no. 30 (1965), pp. 65-95; Schorske, *German Social Democracy*; Marks, 'Sources of Reformism'; Roth, *Social Democrats*; articles in *Journal of Contemporary History*, vol. 13, no. 2 (1978); Geary, 'German Labour Movement', pp. 305-15.

70.   Willard, *Socialisme et Communisme*, pp. 42-8; Roger Williams, *The Commune of Paris, 1871* (New York, 1969).

71.   Willard, *Socialisme et Communisme*, pp. 51-85; Lindemann, *'Red Years'*, p. 6f.; David Stafford, *From Anarchism to Reformism. Paul Brousse* (London, 1971); Stearns, *Revolutionary Syndicalism*.

72.   Blinkhorn, 'Italy'; Lyttleton, 'Revolution and Counter-revolution', p. 64; Blinkhorn, 'Spain'; Brenan, *Spanish Labyrinth*, Ch. 10.

73.   Pelling, *Origins of the Labour Party*; Pelling, *British Trade Unionism*.

74.   Gareth Stedman Jones, 'Working-class Culture and Working-class Politics in London, 1870-1900', *Journal of Social History*, vol. 7, no. 4 (1974), pp. 460-508; Kynaston, *King Labour*, pp. 101-9.

75.   Steinberg, *Sozialismus*, Ch. 6; Klaus Schönhoven, 'Arbeiterbibliotheken und Arbeiterlektüre im Wilhelmischen Deutschland', *Archiv für Sozialgeschichte*, vol. XVI (1976), pp. 135-204.

76.   See above, pp. 50f.

77.   Adolf Levenstein, *Die Arbeiterfrage* (Munich, 1912).

78.   Roth, *Social Democrats*, p. 195.

79.   Mitchell and Stearns, *Workers and Protest*, p. 211.

80.   See above, p. 15.

81.   Ward and Fraser, *Workers*, pp. 104, 160, 164 and 167.

82.   Schorske, *German Social Democracy*; Geary, 'German Labour Movement', pp. 305-11; Lindemann, *'Red Years'*, p. 6f.

83.   Michels, *Political Parties*; Nettl, 'German Social Democratic Party'.

84.   Pelling, *British Trade Unionism*, p. 126.

85.   Blinkhorn, 'Italy'; Lyttleton, 'Revolution and Counter-revolution', p. 64.

86.   Schorske, *German Social Democracy*, pp. 88-115.

87.   Or at least so argues Peter Stearns in Mitchell and Stearns, *Workers and Protest*, pp. 164-81. However, Shorter and Tilly find a more positive correlation

between organisation and the proclivity to strike: Shorter and Tilly, *Strikes*, p. 10 and *passim*.

88.　This is the central argument of Roth, *Social Democrats*.

89.　See below, pp. 151ff.

90.　Mary Alice Walters (ed.), *Rosa Luxemburg Speaks* (New York, 1970), p. 149f.

91.　See above, p. 53.

92.　Kuczynski, *Geschichte der Lage*, vol. 3, pp. 408ff. and vol. 4, pp. 330f.; Gerhard Bry, *Wages in Germany 1870-1945* (Princeton, 1960).

93.　Lindemann, *'Red Years'*, p. 3.

94.　For social welfare legislation in Germany see Born, *Staat und Sozialpolitik*; Marks, 'Sources of Reformism', pp. 341ff.

95.　Lawrence Schofer, *The Formation of a Modern Labour Force. Upper Silesia, 1865-1914* (Berkeley, 1975), p. 117.

96.　Malcolm Thomis, *The Town Labourer and the Industrial Revolution* (London, 1974), pp. 192ff.

97.　Kuczynski, *Geschichte der Lage*, vol. 4, p. 360f.

98.　Thomis, *Town Labourer*, p. 193f.

99.　Marks, 'Sources of Reformism', p. 341f.

100.　This was the case with Konrad Haenisch and Paul Lensch in the SPD. For Britain see Ward and Fraser, *Workers*, p. 193f.

101.　Gerald Feldman, *Army, Industry and Labour in Germany, 1914-1918* (Princeton, 1966), p. 30.

102.　Ryder, *German Revolution*, p. 42f.

103.　A.E. Musson, 'Class Struggle and Labour Aristocracy 1830-1860', *Journal of Social History*, no. 3 (1976), pp. 335-560.

104.　Stafford, *Anarchism to Reformism*, p. 206 and *passim*.

105.　This is the major point which arises from Vernon L. Lidtke, *The Outlawed Party* (Princeton, 1966).

106.　For an account of the different wings within pre-war French socialism see Willard, *Socialisme et Communisme*, pp. 51-75. However, it has to be admitted that the actual division of socialists at the Congress of Tours in 1920 into Communist and Social Democratic wings did not correspond neatly to ideological divisions. See Kriegel, *Aux Origines*.

107.　Geary, 'German Labour Movement', pp. 305-15; Schorske, *German Social Democracy*, *passim*. Again, however, some caution must be exercised here. Not all radical pre-war SPD branches affiliated to the USPD or the KPD and the divisions between the parties in the immediate post-war period were far from clear-cut. See Geary, 'Radicalism', pp. 270-3.

108.　Blinkhorn, 'Spain'; Brenan, *Spanish Labyrinth*, Chs. 8 and 10.

109.　Lyttleton, 'Revolution and Counter-revolution', p. 64.

110.　Alex Hall, 'By Other Means: the Legal Struggle Against the SPD in Wilhelmine Germany 1890-1900', *The Historical Journal*, vol. 17 (1974).

111.　Geary, 'German Labour Movement', p. 308.

112.　Moss, *Origins*, p. 148.

113.　Alastair Reed, 'Politics and Economics in the Formation of the British Working Class', *Social History*, vol. 3 (1978), pp. 327-36.

114.　See below, p. 124.

115.　Michels, *Political Parties*.

116.　Schorske, *German Social Democracy*, Ch. 5.

117.　Th. Nipperdey, *Die Organisation der deutschen Parteien* (Düsseldorf, 1961), p. 337f.

118.　Ralf Lützenkirchen, *Der sozialdemokratische Verein für den Reichstagswahlkreis Dortmund-Hörde* (Dortmund, 1970).

119.　Richard J. Evans, 'The Sociological Interpretation of German Labour

History', unpublished MS.
120.   See above, pp. 110f.
121.   For criticisms of Roth, see Geary, 'German Labour Movement', pp. 305-15; Evans, 'Sociological Interpretation'.
122.   Geary, 'Radicalism'. For different views of the German Revolution see Ryder, *German Revolution*; Morgan, *Socialist Left*; F.L. Carsten, *Revolution in Central Europe* (London, 1972); Allan Mitchell, *Revolution in Bavaria* (Princeton, 1966); Badia, *Le Spartakisme*; Eric Waldman, *The Spartacist Rising of 1919* (Milwaukee, Wis., 1958); J.S. Drabkin, *Die Novemberrevolution 1918 in Deutschland* (Berlin, 1968); Pierre Broué, *Révolution en Allemagne 1917-1923* (Paris, 1971); R. Rürup, 'Problems of the German Revolution', *Journal of Contemporary History* (1968); Richard Comfort, *Revolutionary Hamburg* (Stanford, 1966); Sebastian Haffner, *Die verratene Revolution* (Frankfurt am Main, 1971); Eberhard Kolb, *Die Arbeiterräte in der deutschen Innenpolitik* (Düsseldorf, 1962); Peter von Oertzen, *Betriebsräte in der Novemberrevolution* (Düsseldorf, 1963); Wheeler, *USPD*; Manfred Bock, *Syndikalismus und Linkskommunismus von 1918-1923* (Meisenheim an Glan, 1969); Gottfried Mergner, *Arbeiterbewegung und Intelligenz* (Starnberg, 1973); Gerhard Schmolze (ed.), *Revolution und Räterepublik in München* (Düsseldorf, 1969); Gerhard A. Ritter and Susanne Miller, *Die deutsche Revolution* (Frankfurt am Main, 1968); Erhard Lucas, *Arbeiterradikalismus: Zwei Formen von Radikalismus in der deutschen Arbeiterbewegung* (Frankfurt am Main, 1976); Jürgen Tampke, *The Ruhr and Revolution in the Rhenish-Westphalian Industrial Region 1912-1919* (London, 1979).
123.   Geary, 'Radicalism', pp. 268ff.
124.   Kynaston, *King Labour*, p. 163; Pelling, *British Trade Unionism*, p. 131; Ward and Fraser, *Workers*, p. 160.
125.   Stearns, *Revolutionary Syndicalism*, p. 18.
126.   Bry, *Wages in Germany*, p. 73; Kuczynski, *Geschichte der Lage*, vol. 4, p. 330f.
127.   For the statistics of German lock-outs see Kuczynski, *Geschichte der Lage*, vol. 4, p. 143.
128.   Kynaston, *King Labour*, p. 152f.
129.   See above, p. 115; also Kuczynski, *Geschichte der Lage*, vol. 4, pp. 360f. and 372.
130.   See above, p. 76.
131.   Schofer, *Modern Labour Force*, p. 134f.
132.   Stearns, *Lives*, Ch. 3.
133.   Schofer, *Modern Labour Force*, pp. 111-18; Stearns, *Lives*, pp. 195-200.
134.   See below, p. 151ff.
135.   Kynaston, *King Labour*, pp. 65ff.; Stearns, *Lives*, pp. 122-6; Hobsbawm, *Labouring Men*, pp. 355-62.
136.   Kynaston, *King Labour*, pp. 65ff.; Stearns, *Lives*, pp. 126-69, 193f. and 219f.
137.   Gerald D. Feldman, 'Socio-economic Structures in the Industrial Sector and Revolutionary Potentialities, 1917-1922' in Charles L. Bertrand (ed.), *Revolutionary Situations in Europe, 1917-1922: Germany, Italy, Austria-Hungary* (Montreal, 1977), p. 160f.
138.   Pelling, *British Trade Unionism*, pp. 134-8; Stearns, *Lives*, pp. 322ff.
139.   Lyttleton, 'Revolution and Counter-revolution', pp. 64ff.; Lotti, *Settimata Rossa*. For Russia see above, p. 79.
140.   Geary, 'Radicalism', p. 279f.; Fritz Opel, *Der deutsche Metallarbeiterverband* (Hanover, 1962); Comfort, *Revolutionary Hamburg*, *passim*.
141.   Tenfelde, 'Anarcho-syndikalistische Strömungen'.
142.   C. Gras, 'La Fédération des Métaux, 1913-14' in *Mouvement Social* (December 1971).

143.   M. Degl'Innocenti, 'La guerra libica, la crisi del riformismo e la vittoria degli intransigenti', *Studi storici*, no. 3 (1972), pp. 502-6.

144.   Geary, 'Radicalism', pp. 276-83; Hobsbawm, *Labouring Men*, p. 360; Spriano, *L'occupazione*; Cammett, *Gramsci*; Feldman, 'Socio-economic Structures', pp. 160-6; James Hinton, *The First Shop Stewards' Movement* (London, 1973); B. Pribicevic, *The Shop Stewards' Movement and Workers' Control* (Oxford, 1959); Wheeler, *USPD*, p. 255f. However, the extent to which deskilling was central to the militancy of German metalworkers has been questioned. Robert F. Wheeler, 'Zur sozialen Struktur der Arbeiterbewegung am Anfang der Weimarer Republik' in Hans Mommsen, Dietmar Petzina and Bernd Weisbrod (eds.), *Industrielles System und politische Entwicklung in der Weimarer Republik* (Düsseldorf, 1974), p. 185, claims that deskilling was irrelevant in Solingen but was relevant to the fears of the revolutionary shop stewards in Berlin.

145.   Tenfelde, 'Anarcho-syndikalistische Strömungen'; for Russia see note 143 to Ch. 2 and the qualifications in note 144 to Ch. 2.

146.   Geary, 'Radicalism', pp. 276-83; Blinkhorn, 'Italy'; Lindemann, *'Red Years'*, pp. 253-70; Hans-Ulrich Ludewig, *Arbeiterbewegung und Aufstand* (Husum, 1978), p. 84; Dolléans, *Mouvement Ouvrier*, vol. 3, pp. 152ff.; Shorter and Tilly, *Strikes*, pp. 132-6; Antoine Prost, *CGT*, pp. 66 and 104.

147.   A classic demonstration of this point occurs in Rudolf Vetterli, *Industriearbeit, Arbeiterbewusstsein und gewerkschaftliche Organisation: Dargestellt am Beispiel der Georg Fischer AG (1890-1930)* (Göttingen, 1978).

148.   George Eliasberg, *Der Ruhrkrieg von 1920* (Bonn, 1974), p. 48; Geary, 'The Ruhr: From Social Peace to Social Revolution' *European Studies Review*, no. 4 (1980).

4 WAR, REVOLUTION AND THE RISE OF COMMUNISM

The First World War has often been regarded as a watershed, indeed sometimes *the* watershed, in European history, as a traumatic break with the politics of the pre-war *ancien régime*. This applies as much to the history of the labour movement as to other areas of investigation and in particular to those historians of European labour who believe that the working class had become overwhelmingly reformist in the period before 1914. For the inter-war years were to see the greatest social and political upheavals in living memory. Many contemporaries, in fact, looked back to the supposed serenity of Edwardian England or Wilhelmine Germany and compared contemporary circumstances with it unfavourably. Obviously much of such thinking was illusory, an upper-class nostalgia for a society in which wealth differentials had been huge and in which large sections of European mankind — and even more womankind — had been disenfranchised. But it was true that the politics of the inter-war period became unprecedentedly violent in many European countries. On the political right, authoritarian regimes seized power in most of eastern Europe, whilst more rabid and popular reaction brought Mussolini to power in Italy in 1922 and saw the triumph of Nazism in Germany eleven years later. On the left, mass Communist parties emerged in France, Germany and Italy; whilst a new revolutionary international movement, the so-called Third International, was formed under the auspices of Lenin and the Russian Bolsheviks. Most famously of all, there were two revolutions in Russia in 1917. The first, the February revolution, merely displaced the Tsarist autocracy; but the second, the seizure of power by the Bolsheviks in October 1917, instituted the first socialist workers' state in the world and struck terror into the hearts of the European bourgeoisie. Further revolutions followed in Austria and Germany in 1918, in which power was seized by armed workers' and soldiers' councils; and although neither country witnessed successful proletarian dictatorship thereafter, there were a series of working-class insurrections in Germany throughout the next five years. Hungary experienced its abortive socialist revolution in 1919, whilst rural and urban Italy was gripped by massive unrest in 1919 and 1920, an unrest characterised by land seizures on the part of a rural proletariat and factory occupations in industrial Milan and Turin. French miners, metalworkers and building labourers engaged in massive strike waves in 1919/20; and some anarcho-syndicalists believed that the capitalist Republic was about to be overthrown by a revolutionary general strike, which would in turn inaugurate the socialist millennium. In 1934 the First Austrian Republic was racked by a vicious civil war, in which a courageous labour movement was defeated at the hands of united conservative-clerical and Fascist opposition. In Spain an even bloodier and more famous conflict began two years later and witnessed radical revolutionary experiments in anarchist-controlled Catalonia: to survive the local bourgeoisie had to resort to proletarian dress! In the same year the formation of the Popular Front government in France initiated the greatest strike wave in French history before 1968, a strike wave that involved over 2 million workers, many of whom occupied their factories. In comparison with all this inter-war Britain enjoyed a relative absence of bitter social conflict; but only a *relative* absence. At the end of the war on 'Red Clydeside' there developed a militant shop stewards' movement for workers' control in industry, whilst Glasgow witnessed local Communist electoral gains. Between 1919 and 1923 over 35 million days a year were lost in Britain as a result of strike action; whilst in the five years following 1920 miners engaged in a host of industrial disputes which sometimes led to demands for the nationalisation of the mines and culminated in the somewhat inappropriately named 'general strike' of 1926. Subsequently the admittedly minute Communist Party began to recruit members rapidly, whilst the National Minority Movement sought to build up opposition within the unions to the existing leadership.

Although the labour movement was far from universally revolutionary in this period, it once again enjoyed an unprecedented numerical expansion. By 1939 the British Labour Party, now committed to nationalisation in Clause IV of its constitution, had an individual membership of 450,000, whilst its affiliated trade union membership was, of course, infinitely greater. In Germany the Free Trade Unions achieved a membership of over 9 million workers for a time in the 1920s. In Spain the CNT, which had only succeeded in recruiting 15,000 workers in 1914, had achieved an impressive membership of over 1 million only four years later, whilst the Spanish Socialist Party increased in size very rapidly in the early 1930s. The expansion of the Italian union organisation, the CGL, was equally impressive: from a membership of around a quarter of a million in 1914, it managed to recruit over 2 million workers by October 1920. During the French political upheavals of 1936 the French Communist Party (PCF) acquired no fewer than 200,000 members in a single year, whilst the reunified trade union movement, which had split into socialist and Communist organisations in early 1921, increased its membership from three-quarters of a million workers to the staggering figure of 4 million within a few months.[1]

Clearly, therefore, something happened after 1914 both to radicalise some sections of the European working class and to involve ever larger sections of the work-force in the politics of protest. One explanation, to which historians have frequently had resort, is that the events of the First World War played a crucial role in these processes.

The Impact of War

The initial enthusiasm for the war exhibited by the working class of most European nations evaporated relatively rapidly, especially in Central and Eastern Europe, for a number of fairly obvious reasons, most clearly those associated with material distress. The blockade of Germany by the fleets of the Western allies led to a quite dramatic deterioration in food supplies, a shortage reinforced by the withdrawal of combatant labour from the countryside. Significantly this effective blockade of a country which had long been heavily dependent upon the import of foreign foodstuffs continued after the armistice and until the final signing of the Versailles peace treaty in mid-1919. Starvation or inadequate diet, combined with a major influenza epidemic which sent thousands to their graves in 1918/19, produced appalling conditions in many parts of the Reich: in January 1919 one in every three new-born children died within a few days, whilst the figure of such infant mortality in Düsseldorf, which suffered especially badly from the shortage of food and fuel, reached a gruesome 80 per cent in that dreadful winter.[2] The even harsher Russian winters, combined with food and fuel shortages, which were in turn exacerbated not only by the problems of war but also by labour unrest, formed the backcloth to those famous revolutions of 1917 which successively overthrew Tsarism and then the Provisional government of Kerensky.[3]

Such levels of starvation were not encountered in Western Europe, of course; but even there food shortage was one of several causes of another bane of working-class existence and one which provoked massive industrial unrest: inflation. The best-recorded incidence of this disease struck especially hard at Central Europe. In Germany the cost-of-living index (1900 = 100), which had stood at 130 in 1913 after a three-year burst of unprecedented inflation, had shot up to 407 by the

end of the war; but this was nothing compared to subsequent developments, especially the hyper-inflation of 1922/3. As a result rising prices
far outstripped wage increases: average real wages in Germany fell by
55 per cent in the course of the First World War and were still 10 per
cent below their pre-war level as late as 1921.[4] This formed a crucial
stimulus to strike action, which in the immediate post-war German
context was in turn often a prologue to political radicalism, as we will
see.[5] The French worker suffered far less from the ravages of inflation
than his German neighbour, but he suffered none the less: the index
of the cost of living, which had stood at 100 on the eve of the First
World War, had risen to 600 by April 1920 and was again a major factor
in the generation of the massive strike wave of that year.[6] Rampant
price inflation also formed the background to the seizure of factories
in Milan and Turin in 1920 by engineering workers.[7] In so far as the
shortages of war and the government indebtedness it engendered
generated inflation, so the war was an agent in the radicalisation of
labour.

In other ways too the conditions of life of the European working
class were adversely affected by the war. In order to prosecute the war
more successfully and to maintain armaments production at a peak,
governments suspended protective labour legislation and lengthened
the working day. One concomitant of this was not only dissatisfaction
on the shopfloor but also higher accident rates: in Germany the rate
increased by 50 per cent on average.[8] A further source of working-class
discontent in Germany at the same time was the attempt to restrict
labour mobility through the provisions of the Auxiliary Service Law
of 1916, which was particularly resented by skilled metalworkers, who
used their strong position in the labour market to extract relatively high
remuneration from employers who had to compete for their services.
This last point leads to another — rather paradoxical — one. Such
skilled workers resented the increased control in the factory, were confronted with levels of inflation which rapidly outran even their relatively
high wages and thus had cause to complain; but their skills gave them
such a strong bargaining position in the context of their nation's
striving to maximise munitions production that strikes became all the
more probable.

Food shortage, inflation, longer working hours, increased governmental regulation of mobility, all these things served to fuel working-
class discontents, which then translated themselves into industrial militancy, despite the existence of 'foreign' enemies. In Britain engineering
workers struck for two weeks on the Clyde in February 1915 in defiance

of official union instructions. Three months later 200,000 miners in south Wales followed suit.[9] In France 1917 saw a wave of unrest in the factories.[10] The Austrian and German governments found themselves confronted with strikes, especially amongst metalworkers in the munitions factories, from 1916 onwards; and by January 1918 there were strike waves of a huge dimension in both states. Furthermore, these strike waves no longer made demands that were simply economistic in nature but also desired the ending of the war and political reforms, in particular the democratisation of both the Austrian and the German Reich.[11]

This last point is of especial significance. In the context of war, economic grievances almost of necessity led to political as well as trade union action. In the first place, workers would begin to demand an answer to the question of why they should make sacrifices to save a state which was in no way representative of their interests on account of its undemocratic structure. Thus it was no accident that Austrian, German and Russian strikers not only concerned themselves with the size of the bread ration and their pay packets but also with political reforms. Second, the fact that many of the material problems of the period could be ascribed directly to the impact of the war again led workers to make demands of their governments: for wars are waged and peace treaties concluded by governments. A government's refusal to end the war could lead to its overthrow: this is essentially what happened in Russia in both February and again in October 1917. Similarly, the fact that President Wilson and his allies refused to conclude peace with the Kaiser gave a powerful impetus to the movement for democratic reform in Germany in November 1918.

The war created economic difficulties, therefore, and these sometimes spilled into the political arena. However, it was not simply problems of appalling factory conditions and inflation which generated discontent on the scale that exploded in Europe in the period between 1917 and 1920. A further factor related to structural changes in the industries of some European states in the course of the war. One such change was a massive influx of new labour into those industrial sectors which underwent spectacular expansion between 1914 and 1918. The Spanish economy enjoyed a massive boom in the war years, partly as a consequence of Spain's neutrality which rendered her a supplier of manufactured goods to the whole of Europe.[12] In Italy wartime demand generated a huge expansion of the heavy industrial sector in the north of the country and a consequent massive increase in the size of the work-force of large iron, steel and metalworking plants in Milan,

Turin and Genoa.[13] Such developments were partly responsible for the increase in levels of union mobilisation described at the beginning of this chapter. They were also the prologue to militancy in a number of ways. The backbone of industrial militancy and political radicalism in Italy now shifted from the small towns with radical artisan traditions to engineering workers, both skilled and semi-skilled, in the large plants: these were the workers who seized their factories in 1920, often without and sometimes against official union instructions, and who became the rank and file of the Italian Communist Party.[14] Similar developments can also be detected in wartime Germany. The sudden concentration of workers in giant plants characterised the Essen concern of Krupp, where the work-force rose from the already considerable 34,000 men in 1914 to 100,000 only four years later. Similarly Thyssen's engineering plant at Mülheim in the Ruhr expanded from 3,000 to 26,500 in the same period. Large engineering and electrotechnical works also developed in Berlin, whilst new concentrations of chemical workers emerged in Leverkusen and Merseburg, most famously of all in the giant BASF plant of Leuna. These new factories in metalworking, chemicals and the electrical industry often employed modern flow or serial techniques of production of the kind pioneered by Henry Ford in the United States. They were also manned by a younger generation of workers: in German metalwork in 1913 the number of 14- to 16-year-old employees had stood at 10,728, but rose to over 18,000 in the next four years, whilst the chemical industry, which first achieved real significance as an employer of labour in the war, increased its number of youths of the same age from 1,179 to 4,204. An equally dramatic increase occurred in terms of the employment of female labour between 1914 and 1918, though demobilisation decrees at the end of the war then forced many of the new women workers to return to their homes.[15] There appears to have been a high degree of correlation between the new work-force in large factories and both industrial militancy and political radicalism.[16] The young workers were neither like the old skilled labour aristocracy which had served a lengthy apprenticeship and had traditions of organisation in trade unions and, in the case of Continental Europe, in socialist parties; nor were they similar to the traditional unskilled and apathetic labour force. They were semi-skilled, given a minimal training on the shop floor and relatively underrepresented hitherto in the ranks of organised labour. This massive and rapid influx of new blood into the factories created a host of difficulties for an elderly trade union and party elite reared in craft traditions, as we will see.[17]

The militancy of engineering workers and their like cannot be explained solely in terms of the role of the semi-skilled worker, however; certain skilled sections of the labour force also played a crucial role. In Britain the movement for workers' control on Clydeside was initiated by a group of highly skilled engineering workers, whilst the Revolutionary Shop Stewards organisation, which emerged in the major industrial cities of Germany in the course of the war and went on to play a major role in the revolution of 1918, was based upon the turners' section of the DMV. Between 1914 and 1918 the position of these skilled workers was threatened in a variety of ways: by the 'dilution' of labour, the employment of the less skilled to do jobs normally undertaken by skilled groups of workers, by the erosion of wage differentials, the introduction of piece-rates, by the sacrifice of traditional manning agreements for the sake of national defence. It was such things which radicalised British engineering workers, the revolutionary stewards in the large munitions factories of Berlin and their counterparts in the giant Putilov works of St Petersburg, in the car factories of Milan and Turin and in Merrheim's revolutionary Fédération des Métaux.[18]

The war not only served to radicalise certain sections of the European labour movement; it also led to a host of new tensions which ultimately produced the fateful division of that movement into two hostile camps. This was first of all because the issues involved in support for national war efforts called forth various ideological perspectives and built upon earlier divisions. Some of the pre-war Marxist radicals such as Lenin and Rosa Luxemburg argued that the war was nothing other than a struggle between equally culpable imperialist powers struggling to control markets and investment potential. In such a situation the concept of a 'defensive war', manipulated by many supposed socialists to justify their support for the national war effort, was simply untenable. For Lenin the war was not to be supported but rather to be ended by proletarian revolution. As Karl Liebknecht, one-time Social Democrat and subsequently founder of the German Communist Party (KPD), put it: 'the real enemy is within'. Workers were not to fight one another but to turn their weapons against the domestic enemy, the capitalist class. For Lenin and those who thought like him, therefore, the decision of most European socialist parties to support their national war efforts was nothing less than an act of betrayal and indicated the need to break with the theoretical bankruptcy of the past. A new International, purged of 'reformist' and 'centrist' elements and with tighter central direction to guarantee a truly 'international perspective', was to be erected. Thus the Communist

Third International came into existence after meetings between disaffected and radical socialists in the course of the First World War. The question of whether or not to affiliate to this new organisation, the world revolution incarnate, was precisely the issue which led to the division of the French Socialist Party at the Congress of Tours in 1920 and to the subsequent break-up of the PSI. It was the issue which led to the foundation of Communist parties in both France and Italy. In Germany the situation developed in a rather different fashion. The different attitudes towards the war had already produced a split in 1917 when the Independent Social Democratic Party (USPD) was formed in opposition to the majority Social Democrats (MSPD), who supported the German war effort, and called for 'peace without annexations'. However, this new party was itself split in 1920, when a majority decided to affiliate to the Third International and join with what hitherto had been a relatively insignificant KPD. Now the German Communist Party, founded by the Spartacist League (Liebknecht and Luxemburg) and other leftist factions in Bremen, Hamburg and Berlin, became a mass party for the first time.[19]

Such divisions within the European socialist movement, however, were not exclusively ideological in origin. Other developments in the war created other kinds of tensions, tensions not just between radicals and non-radicals within the various party leaderships but also between the official trade union leaderships on the one hand and rank-and-file working-class members on the other. For at the same time as inflation and starvation radicalised the Central European worker, his ostensible leaders were being sucked into the prevailing order by a number of concessions forced upon the traditional authorities by the exigencies of war. Even reactionary army commanders of the German Reich realised that a modern war could not be fought without some degree of support from the representatives of labour. If such support had not been forthcoming, then the arms supply simply could not have been maintained. Thus the German authorities granted to the Free Trade Unions and to the SPD the right to recruit members for the first time from those employed by the state. Trials against leading trade unionists were abandoned and such men were exempted from conscription. Furthermore, the Auxiliary Service Law of 1916 forced employers to accept trade unionists as legitimate partners on factory committees and thus began a move towards union recognition which culminated in November 1918. Not surprisingly, therefore, the union officials attempted to ban strikes for the duration of the war and to prevent labour unrest. They even reported the names of strike leaders to the

German High Command! Similarly, leading members of the SPD found new opportunities for recruitment, were allowed to circulate their publications to the troops and for the first time found themselves consulted by senior Ministers. For such rewards the SPD found a generous response: it continued to support the war effort, refused to comment on the barbaric treatment of Belgians as forced labour and even sent some of its members to argue Germany's case before the neutral nations.[20] Thus the union and party leadership became increasingly remote from the material problems which gripped their membership with increasing severity in the last years of the war. It was local stewards who now took the initiative in the organisation of strikes, not the traditional organisational hierarchy. The road to the counter-revolutionary role of the Free Trade Unions and the SPD in the November revolution of 1918 and the subsequent five years was already being laid, just as the defection of many workers to the radical left was prepared precisely by this 'betrayal'.[21] A further cause of this growing chasm between the union leadership and rank and file has also been identified: as Gerald Feldman has written:

> The trade unions were poorly structured both in personnel and in organizational character to assimilate the influx of new members that began everywhere in 1917 and reached massive proportions at the end of the war. There was a serious shortage of functionaries, and a long history of craft traditions and craft organization not easily adapted to the mass factory and to the new impulses in the direction of the industrial rather than the craft union.[22]

Such tension between a working-class base bombarded by economic difficulties and a cautious and patriotic political and trade union leadership were perhaps most marked in Germany, but they were not absent elsewhere. There is evidence from 1917 that many English workers had lost confidence in their official leaders;[23] whilst the French strikes of 1917 testify to similar sentiments.[24] The concrete experience of ordinary workers who saw that the old institutions of labour were not defending their interests but collaborating with wartime governments in attempting to discipline the work-force obviously formed a prologue to the abandonment of Social Democracy on the part of some sections of the European working class.

Thus the First World War provided a stimulus to the tragic division of the organised labour movement, a division which doomed it to ultimate failure in the inter-war years. It also served to brutalise social mores on both sides of the political spectrum. Men came back from the front sometimes appalled by the killing and mutilation; but others came back inured to such brutality. Some came back demanding compensation for the sacrifices they had made; and at least some of the general dissatisfaction in France and Italy after 1918 can be attributed to the failure of victory to bring the expected rewards: peace, security and higher living standards. Furthermore, it may be platitudinous to say that these men came back armed; yet it is a fact of the utmost importance. Without such weaponry it is difficult to see how the workers and peasants of Central and Eastern Europe could have matched their willingness to fight with the ability to do so. For many the return to a humdrum peacetime existence and for some to unemployment was difficult, to say the least.

Finally, the First World War paved the way for revolution and revolt not only by its impact on the masses of industrial Europe but also by the way in which it undermined the power of the traditional ruling elite through defeat. In 1905 in Russia the army had put an end to proletarian insurrection. In 1917 the Russian Army could no longer be relied upon to do the same. Not only was it engaged against a foreign enemy at the same time as workers seized power in the industrial centres; it was not the same army. Significant sections of the old officer corps had been obliterated and the call-up of the war years had brought disaffected peasants into the ranks. Furthermore, cracks were beginning to appear within the ruling circles themselves, both over the conduct of the war and the role of the Tsar. In Germany the realisation of defeat came as a huge shock to the loyal middle class, which had been fed a diet of military success stories by the authorities until the very last hours. This shock, and the disillusionment with the old order which it bred, at least in part explain the stupefaction and inaction of significant non-revolutionary groups in German society which enabled power to be seized so bloodlessly by workers' and soldiers' councils in November 1918. Furthermore, some of the classes who had previously been remote from the propaganda of socialists or even their affiliated trade unions were now less prepared to mobilise behind the ranks of reaction than previously. Many German peasants resented government attempts to regulate food prices during the war. In fact in Bavaria this economic resentment reinforced particularist grievances against central direction from Berlin.[25] At the same time, the erosion of wage differentials and the increasingly proletarian situation of many white-collar workers in large firms between 1914 and 1918 reduced some of the antagonism that had previously existed between them and the blue-collar work-force and led some of them to join the Free Trade Unions. In some cases they even began to vote socialist for the first time.[26] By thus removing some of the obstacles to revolt, by destroying the traditional repressive apparatus of the state – even the German Army disintegrated after crossing the Rhine in mid-December and thus was not available for the implementation of the counter-revolutionary schemes of some high-ranking officers[27] – and by demobilising potential hostility from other social groups, the First World War made revolution at least conceivable, even if it did not guarantee revolutionary success. This opening of possibilities confronted the European socialist parties with the first real opportunity to think about revolution seriously; and hence it was precisely in the immediate post-war years that the divisions between radicals and reformists which had remained at best latent but at least not completely destructive within the various socialist parties, within the SFIO, the SPD and the PSI, now came to the surface. What had previously been merely theoretical alternatives now became real.

There can be little doubt, in view of the above, that the physical deprivations of war stirred working-class discontents and that it took the First World War to weaken the traditional ruling authorities. What is questionable, however, is the extent to which these developments were the result of war alone. Even in the context of the declining power of the old authorities it has been argued with some force that the Tsarist autocracy not only lost some credibility in the wake of defeat in the Russo-Japanese war but that various divisions within the ruling elite were coming to the surface *before* 1914: privileged society and the Tsarist regime were drawing further apart.[28] Likewise in Germany, although no-one could describe the Welhelmine regime as weak, in so far as it possessed a formidable army and the backing of significant sections of the agrarian and industrial elite, many contemporaries felt that political life had reached a dead end: there was a revival of liberal fortunes in the Reichstag elections of 1912, the Social Democrats registered huge victories at the polls, becoming the largest party in the Empire and winning a third of all votes cast, and it was becoming increasingly difficult for government to command the majority necessary in Parliament for the passing of certain Bills, especially those concerned with finance. It was far from clear that the political system could survive unchanged. Similar remarks could be made about that other military monarchy, Austria-Hungary, which not only faced a growing socialist threat but an even more potent challenge to the integrity of its Empire: the nationalism of the ethnic minorities. The destruction of these three empires in 1917/18, therefore, although in many ways a consequence of wartime developments, had roots which stretched back into the period before 1914. In Italy, of course, a democratic governmental system survived the turmoil of 1914 to 1918 and finally disintegrated in the face of Fascist rather than proletarian radicalism. Yet even in Italy Giolitti's consensus had already broken down in the aftermath of the Libyan war of 1911/12.[29] George Dangerfield's vision of an England saved from the threat of labour, radical feminists and the Irish *by* rather than in spite of the First World War may be somewhat far-fetched; but his work does highlight the fragility of social peace even in Edwardian England.[30]

The security of government systems in pre-war Europe was thus far from guaranteed. In addition, many of the economic problems of inter-war Europe were certainly exacerbated by wartime developments but were far from exclusively caused by them. In some cases they were the result of the class-determined economic policies of governments before the war. The great German inflation, for example, and to a lesser extent the lesser inflation in France, were a consequence of the refusal of conservative regimes to cover vastly increased state expenditure by a progressive income tax. Conversely, other economic problems really owed their origins to post-war developments rather than the events of 1914: a further stimulus to the great post-war inflation in both Weimar Germany and the First Austrian Republic was the heavy social expenditure of Social Democratic governments, as well as the reparations exacted by the victorious Entente powers.[31] Similar remarks apply to the unemployment which plagued numerous proletarian existences between the two world wars and which certainly fuelled the fires of working-class radicalism: in Britain the radical left had a limited degree of success in mobilising the unemployed, whilst on a much more spectacular scale in Germany the Spartacists of 1918 and then the KPD, 80 per cent of whose membership were unemployed by April 1932, benefited from this human misery.[32] Some of the immediate post-war unemployment was obviously the direct consequence of the ending of the war, demobilisation and the transition from a war to a peace-time economy; but subsequent high levels of the disease were most obviously the result of the great depression of the late 1920s and early 1930s. They were also the result of much longer-term developments: rationalisation and technological modernisation led to the closure of unproductive units and the replacement of human labour with new machines. As a result of such rationalisation and a slump in demand the Frankfurt metalworking industry halved the size of its work-force in 1923/24.[33] The outcome of such structural economic changes was that levels of unemployment between 1919 and 1939 were higher even in boom periods than they had been in the years of depression before the First World War.[34]

If some of the economic distress experienced by the European working class between the wars cannot be laid at the door of the holocaust of 1914-18, the same can be said for the radicalisation of significant sections of European labour from 1914 onwards. It has already been established that for some groups of workers the years *before* the war saw a resurgence of industrial militancy and political radicalism, in particular in the docks, the mines and, above all, in the engineering industry,[35] and furthermore that the root cause of this radical resurgence lay in precisely those phenomena that continued to operate during and were indeed accelerated by the First World War and subsequent developments, namely the deskilling of some sections of labour, the emergence of a young and semi-skilled work-force, etc. Milan, Turin, Berlin, Stuttgart, Vienna, Linz, even Budapest saw the emergence of mass industries employing a huge semi-skilled labour force in electro-technology, engineering and automobile production before 1914. This early such a labour force was subjected to experiments in 'Taylorism', increased control over and monitoring of mechanised production on the shop floor.[36] As we have already seen too, divisions between the rank and file and the leadership of the trade unions and labour parties were becoming apparent even before 1914 and were not novel to the war years, as is testified by the syndicalism of some British workers, by tensions within the Ruhr mines between the ostensible representatives of labour and those whom they claimed to represent, and by the great Hamburg dock strike of 1913.[37] From the outset of the war in France the radical metalworkers' union opposed the war effort; whilst its German counterpart, or rather its shop-floor representatives, refused to accept a moratorium on strikes, the so-called *Burgfrieden* (civil truce) dictated by the official union leaders and the SPD. Significantly the USPD subsequently derived its strongest support from those areas which had seen radical rank-and-file opposition to the official leadership of the DMV before 1914. We have also seen that the barricades were erected in some parts of Italy in 1914; and that in Russia the large factories of Moscow and St Petersburg had witnessed a marked increase in Bolshevik support between 1911 and 1914, although the precise origins of this support are debated.[38] Thus some of those groups of workers who were to play a significant role in the upheavals of 1918 to 1920 were stirring before the outbreak of the First World War.

It is equally true to say that the ideological divisions which in part produced the fateful division of the European labour movement into Communist and Social Democratic camps were prefigured in the ideological debates of the pre-war years. Thus to a certain, though far from unqualified, extent, the splitting of the German Social Democratic Party mirrored earlier conflicts between revisionists (Eduard Bernstein), centrists (Karl Kautsky) and radical Marxists (Rosa Luxemburg).[39] Similarly in Italy divisions within the PSI between the so-called maximalists and less radical elements around Turati had long existed;[40] whilst the SFIO also experienced tensions between possibilist and Marxist traditions.[41] Thus what happened between 1914 and 1918 was that a series of previously uncomfortable alliances between radicals and reformists was broken by changed circumstances, by the emergence of genuinely revolutionary opportunities, and fired by the dissolution of the old regimes and the example of the Russian proletariat. The origins of the French, German and Italian Communist parties was therefore to be found not only in Lenin's spirited attack on the bankrupt Second International but also in indigenous revolutionary sentiment within the pre-war socialist parties of France, Germany and Italy. Indeed, if this had not been the case, it is difficult to see how the Communists could claim to be the real inheritors of pre-war socialism and accuse their former Social Democratic allies of betraying the past.

In conclusion, therefore, the First World War certainly helped to radicalise some sections of the working class in several European countries, especially in those which experienced defeat and the subsequent humiliation of dictated peace treaties; but longer-term economic developments and more deeply rooted convictions on the part of some workers presaged the tragic division of European labour before and independently of the war.

The Division of Labour: Socialism versus Communism

Perhaps the most salient feature of working-class protest in Europe between the two world wars was the division that occurred in most, though by no means all, countries between Social Democratic and Communist labour organisations, and the subsequent emergence of mass Communist parties in France, Germany and Italy. To explain this crucial development we must examine events before, during and after the First World War.

In one very obvious sense the origins of the post-war Communist parties were inextricably linked to the successful Bolshevik seizure of power in Russia in October 1917. This event gave Lenin and his colleagues a disputed prestige within other European socialist parties, which, unlike that of Russia, had not split into more and less revolutionary wings before 1914.[42] This prestige and the results of wartime experience, which to the radicals appeared to demonstrate the bankruptcy of traditional Social Democracy in the light of its abandonment of internationalism and its collaboration with national governments at war, Lenin exploited to create a new revolutionary international organisation, the so-called Third International. The Communist organisations which emerged from the French SFIO Congress of Tours in 1920, from the USPD congress at Halle in the same year and from the Leghorn conference of the PSI in 1921 were composed of those groups within those existing parties who chose to affiliate to Lenin's Third International and accepted the famous — or in Social Democratic circles infamous — 21 conditions of entry. These committed them to the formation of a 'party of the new type', a party purged of reformist and 'centrist' elements, and one which accepted the need for stronger central direction — critics said Moscow control — in order to overcome nationalist prejudice and create a genuinely international and revolutionary movement. In a sense, therefore, the decision to affiliate to the Third International was meant to sort out the sheep from the goats, the revolutionaries from their more feeble-minded and weaker-spirited colleagues.[43] Subsequently Moscow did come to exert increasing control over these new Communist parties.[44] Events in Russia had a further influence upon developments in other European labour movements: the more the prospects of successful domestic revolution receded in France, Germany and Italy, the more socialists there were forced to look to Russia as the one example of successful proletarian revolution.

Having said this, however, it would be incorrect to imagine that the splitting of the socialist movements of France, Italy and Germany constituted a clear-cut and irreparable breach between a revolutionary left and a reformist right. This is indicated by the very rapid reversal of the fortunes of the French Communist Party (PCF) in the 1920s, for example. At the Congress of Tours in 1920 something in the order of two-thirds of the socialist delegates voted to affiliate to the Third International. Yet within three years the balance of strength between the rump of the SFIO and the former majority who had constituted the PCF had been reversed. In fact the PCF only really recouped its strength in the 1930s in the wake of depression and in the context of the Popular Front alliance between socialists and Communists. This rapid reversal of fortunes suggests that the initial majority vote to constitute a Communist Party was somewhat misleading; and close analysis of the events at Tours reinforces this impression. Delegates voted to affiliate to the Third International not necessarily because they subscribed to the specifics of Leninist ideology but for a host of confused reasons. Peasant delegates, who constituted the major support for affiliation, simply disliked the traditional agrarian programme of the SFIO; whilst others saw in Communism an attack upon parliamentary tactics and could be better described as anarcho-syndicalists than Bolsheviks. Hence it was hardly surprising that many of the pro-affiliation groups within the SFIO soon became disillusioned with the new PCF and either left of their own accord or were forced out of the ranks of the faithful for dissent. In short, the initial division between the SFIO and the PCF was far from a clear-cut break between reformists and revolutionaries. Lenin himself was forced to confess that there was no such thing as a 'Leninist party' in France in 1923. It took seven more years for a reliable Leninist leadership and new party structure to emerge in France under Maurice Thorez.[45]

If events were confused in France, they were positively chaotic in Germany. In the first place, the German Social Democratic Party had already split into a majority which supported the government's war effort (MSPD) and a sizeable minority (USPD) which opposed it in 1917. However the separating line which ran between the two organisations did not correspond to a simple division between reformists and revolutionaries. Some radical branches remained within the MSPD, whilst the USPD was only united in its opposition to the war and included within its ranks not only genuine revolutionaries such as Rosa Luxemburg and Karl Liebknecht and the high priest of centrist Marxism, Karl Kautsky, but also former revisionists such as Eduard Bernstein. It is true that the radical left within the USPD, the Spartacists, did break away in December 1918 to join with other groups who had long been urging the formation of a new party, namely the Hamburg Left, the Bremen Left and Julius Borchardt's International Socialists in Berlin, to form the German Communist Party. However, not only did the constitution of the KPD in late December 1918 precede Lenin's formulation of the 21 conditions; there is once again evidence of considerable ideological diversity amongst its founders. There was a clear ultra-leftist majority at the founding conference of the KPD which refused to participate in parliamentary elections and wished to leave the traditional trade unions. Until late 1919 this ultra-left remained dominant within the party and finally broke away from it in that year when the party first began to resemble a Leninist organisation more approximately.[46] Furthermore, the nature of the various socialist factions in Germany between 1918 and 1923 varied enormously from place to place. In some towns the SPD, USPD and KPD came together to demand socialisation. In others the USPD and the Communists worked together; whilst in certain areas the two parties were at loggerheads. In Saxony the local SPD engaged in radical actions which appalled the cautious national party leadership in 1923. Furthermore, there are cases of rank-and-file MSPD members behaving in a way that might have rather suggested Communist affiliation. Thus to ordinary workers the boundaries between the socialist factions were far from clear to say the least; and there is considerable evidence in the early days that they found it difficult to distinguish between the different positions of their ostensible leaders. There were even miners in the Ruhr who belonged to both Communist and anarcho-syndicalist organisations simultaneously![47] Thus the initial division of the various socialist parties in Europe in the immediate post-war period cannot be assumed to indicate an unambiguous break between radicals and reformists, at least in the earliest days.

Not only was this division less clear-cut than might initially appear to be the case; it cannot be assumed to have been the result of extraneous pressures, in particular the decision of whether to affiliate to the Third International, alone. In fact it has been argued that some such split between the various ideological currents within European socialism was more or less inevitable without this pressure. In Italy not only had the PSI been moving to the left before 1914 but at the party conference in September 1918, at which the maximalists commanded something like 70 per cent of the votes, there was already talk of expelling Turati and his faction from the party. Furthermore, Gramsci and some of the younger radicals in the Italian Socialist Party were becoming disillusioned with the caution of the official leadership and Serrati's failure to back the councils' movement in early 1920. This dissatisfaction was further heightened by the second wave of factory occupations in September; and thus the final decision at Leghorn in 1921 to affiliate to the Third International can only be understood against the background of earlier ideological struggles and divisions.[48] The same can be said of France. As we have already seen, the debates at Tours in December 1920 were most confused; and again there is evidence that some members of the SFIO wished for the removal of the right-wing

Renaudel and his faction from the ranks of the party independently of pressure from Moscow.[49] Moreover, the failure of the electoral strategy of French socialism in 1918, when the most right-wing Chamber of Deputies was elected since 1871, and the subsequent defeat of the CGT's general strike in 1920 further pushed French socialists into the search for an alternative to reformist and anarcho-syndicalist strategies. In Germany again the innumerable splits that occurred within the socialist camp were the product of deep-rooted ideological divisions and various domestic pressures. From 1918 the USPD was moving rapidly to the left and before its Halle Congress of 1920 conflict between the left and the right of the party was already producing schisms at a local level.[50] The interventions of Moscow, therefore, although obviously important, are perhaps best regarded as crystallising and hardening previous divisions.

The origins of the split between Social Democratic and Communist politics within the European working class cannot simply be reduced to a set of ideological divisions, whether of long or short ancestry. It is also possible to locate an economic and social origin of division; and again it is one that goes back to the pre-war years. We have seen that on the eve of the First World War the overwhelming majority of the organised working class was recruited from the relatively skilled sections of the work-force and that most workers engaged in no organised protest before that date. Just before the war, however, new strains were beginning to develop as a result of the growth of mass industries and the emergence of a semi-skilled work-force. There is a good deal of evidence to suggest that this division corresponds to a certain extent to the subsequent split between Communist and Social Democratic support. In France the workers who flocked to the ranks of the PCF in the elections of 1936 and who provided the mass basis of the great strike wave and factory occupations of that year came from the new mass industries, sometimes in new industrial regions; whilst the SFIO gained new recruits from some sections of the southern peasantry and from the white-collar salariat, the PCF established its hold in the large industrial conurbations.[51] In Italy the centres of radicalism were the huge engineering plants of Milan and Turin; and similar plants in St Petersburg, Budapest and Vienna provided the hard core of revolutionaries.[52] For Germany it has been established that the revolutionary movement and subsequently the KPD recruited support disproportionately from new industrial centres that had expanded rapidly during the war and which lacked SPD traditions, such as parts of the Western Ruhr and the giant chemical plant of Leuna.[53] There is further evidence that in later years the KPD began to recruit far more heavily from less skilled workers and above all from the unemployed.[54] Of course, this division between a new work-force in the new industries and an older labour aristocracy overlapped with and was reinforced by age differences. There is an overwhelming consensus that the radical movements and Communist parties of inter-war Europe drew far more of their support from the young than did the Social Democratic parties.[55]

Significantly this new and radical working class seems to have proved far more volatile in its industrial and political behaviour than the old aristocrats of labour. It could be mobilised with great speed but equally deserted the ranks of organised protest just as rapidly. In France the rapid mobilisation of thousands of new trade unionists and their involvement in strike waves between 1917 and 1920 was followed by an equally rapid demobilisation: after the failure of the 1920 general strike the membership of the CGT fell from 2 million to 600,000 within a few months.[56] In Germany the most ultra-leftist organisations of the Ruhr which recruited from a new and inexperienced labour force tended to lose members at a faster rate than their more cautious rivals; whilst by 1921 many radical workers had deserted the barricades for good throughout the Weimar Republic.[57] In Italy the wave of proletarian factory seizures and insurrections had already blown itself out before the Fascist offensive and thus constituted little obstacle to it.[58] Even in less troubled British waters an analogous development can be detected: the TUC, which had gained up to 8 million members by 1920, lost 2.5 million of these in the next two years. The failure of the 1926 British general strike saw a further drop in membership.[59] The massive influx of new members into the ranks of organised protest in the inter-war years, therefore, not only produced a more radical work-force in some places but a much more volatile one.

In discussing the different social bases of Communist and Social Democratic parties in this period, it is not really appropriate to discuss the case of Spain: there the Spanish Communist Party only really became significant in the course of the Civil War after 1936, when it effectively controlled arms supplies to the Republican forces. However, it is worth noting that the more significant division between anarcho-syndicalists and socialists in Spain can be related not only to ideological differences but also to differences in the social composition of the two movements. The anarchist CNT found its urban support amongst the depressed and small-scale textile plants of Catalonia, often from workers reared in areas of rural anarchism; whilst the Spanish Socialist Party was based upon the large-scale heavy industrial plants of the northern Basque provinces. Significantly, when the Socialist Party first began to recruit from the landless proletariat of rural Andalusia and Extremadura, its nature was transformed into a far more radical and far less disciplined organisation.[60]

Thus the division of the European labour movement into two camps between the great wars was partly a consequence of pressure from successful Russian revolutionaries, partly the result of earlier and deep-seated ideological antagonisms and partly an outcome of the changing structures of industry in this period. To a certain extent the radicalism of certain sections of the working class and their disillusionment with the traditional representatives of labour can also be attributed to a host of economic grievances. We have already seen that Continental inflation bit deeply into working-class living standards in the post-war period and led to strike waves in France, Italy and Germany.[61] Unemployment constituted another huge problem: there was serious structural unemployment in most European states throughout the 1920s and 1930s, but this was nothing compared to the havoc of the great depression, which left 3 million without jobs in Britain and a staggering 7 million jobless in Weimar Germany. Such unemployment certainly fuelled radicalism, providing the KPD with most of its membership and some support for the British Communist Party.[62]

Here, however, some caution must be exercised: once again the ranks of the radical were not composed primarily of the most impoverished. Engineering workers and miners, for example, stood fairly close to the top of the proletarian wages scale and to some extent their industrial militancy in the immediate post-war years was a consequence of their strong bargaining power in a short-lived boom in heavy industry. Furthermore, the areas of Germany which experienced the greatest labour insurrections in this period – the Ruhr, Saxony, Hamburg and Berlin – enjoyed above-average wage levels.[63] Thus it was not low wages as such so much as the erosion of living standards through inflation which constitutes part of the explanation of industrial militancy between 1918 and 1923.

Caution about the relationship between living standards and political radicalism needs to be exercised for yet another reason: in some countries similar deprivations did not produce a mass Communist movement. It is true that British workers escaped the ravages of Continental inflation and even enjoyed rising real wages in the immediate post-war boom;[64] however, the massive unemployment of the 1930s brought only limited support to the relatively small Communist Party. Equally, the structural industrial changes discussed above – deskilling, the emergence of a mass semi-skilled work-force – occurred as much in Britain as elsewhere but did not result in a fundamental political division in the ranks of labour. Hence, although economic and social developments are important for an understanding of the emergence of Communism, they certainly do not constitute a sufficient explanation of this phenomenon. Austria can also be used as a controlling case: for there too the Communist Party remained relatively insignificant and the Social Democratic Party remained united. This is all the more remarkable in the Austrian case, as the country experienced rampant inflation, massive food shortages and high structural unemployment in the wake of the First World War.[65]

In the case of Britain several relevant factors which help to explain the failure of Communism to become a mass movement can be identified. One such is the relative absence of a radical working-class political tradition *before* the war: as we have seen, the divisions that occurred in Continental Europe were built at least in part upon earlier ideological conflicts. Furthermore, there developed in Britain a relatively successful system of collective bargaining, including national wage agreements, with little outside intervention from the state.[66] Social welfare policies to some extent also cushioned the working class against the impact of unemployment.[67] Perhaps most important of all, the British state remained immune to extreme right-wing politics. The absence not only of a mass Fascist movement in Britain but also of an old elite of soldiers, bureaucrats and judges of the kind that still wielded considerable power in some parts of Europe meant that British labour was not subjected to some of those pressures which radicalised Continental labour. Certainly in Germany one of the major causes of working-class insurrection was the repressive activities of the Freikorps.[68]

These things may serve to explain the absence of rampant Communism in Britain after 1918. They are not so efficacious in explaining how the Austrian Social Democratic Party (SPÖ) remained united and managed to retain the loyalty of most of Austrian labour: for in the First Austrian Republic a reactionary old elite and a mass Fascist movement developed on the one hand, and the SPÖ had both a Marxist tradition and a history of pre-war ideological controversies on the other. However, it is true that the SPÖ as a whole tended to be rather to the left of German Social Democracy and did not possess such a sizeable right-wing faction. In consequence there was not the same pressure on the radical left to break away from the parent organisation. This was especially so in the context of the revolution of 1918, when the leadership of the SPÖ did not form an alliance with sections of the army to combat leftist insurrection as the SPD did in Germany, but rather allowed the formation of a Volkswehr, of a people's army recruited predominantly from armed workers.[69] Herein, it seems to me, lies the real explanation of the development of mass Communist movements: it happened where the old institutions of labour behaved in such a way as to lose the confidence of their membership. In Britain many of the wage gains of the post-war period were won by the old trade union organisations, which thus retained their legitimacy for most of the working class. Conversely, the German worker found himself confronted with inflation after the war. When he went on strike as a result, he in turn found himself in opposition to his official trade unions, which, in close alliance with a Social Democratic government, were primarily interested in the regeneration of the German economy. Not surprisingly, he often became alienated from both the SPD and the Free Trade Union leadership; and this alienation turned to anger, insurrection and desertion of Social Democracy when an SPD government sent reactionary Freikorps to deal with, for example, striking miners.[70] In Italy the failure of the PSI to give a lead to the factory occupations of 1920 led to a similar disillusionment;[71] whilst we have already seen that electoral defeat and the failure of a general strike in France in 1920 led some workers to seek a new strategy.[72]

The division of the European labour movement into Social Democratic and Communist camps was thus the consequence of a combination of ideological, economic and social factors. It also sprang from the decisions taken by the leaders of the old institutions of labour. What cannot be doubted is that this division was to prove fatal to the prospects of socialist revolution in most of Europe after 1918.

Revolutionary Success and Failure

In a sense it is hardly legitimate to pass judgement on the European labour movement of the inter-war period in terms of *revolutionary* success or failure; this, not only because Russia was the only country to experience that rare world-historical event, proletarian revolution, but also because many sections of the European working class showed no desire for revolution, either because they thought it too risky or simply because they were not interested and did not believe in the socialist millennium. Furthermore, significant gains were made for the European working class between 1918 and 1939 in certain areas. Unemployment benefits were introduced in Britain, Austria and Germany. The November revolution of 1918 in this last country also saw the formal, albeit grudging, recognition of trade unions by the major organisation of industrialists and the implementation of an eight-hour day, though this was to prove of short duration and the ultimate destruction of the organised labour movement by the Nazis after 1933 rendered all null and void.[73] Similarly in Austria before the triumph of reaction in 1934, great strides were made in the provision of social welfare benefits and municipal housing;[74] whilst the Matignon agreements of 1936 in the France of the Popular Front government won for the working class a forty-hour week, at least temporarily, and paid holidays for the first time.[75]

Bearing these gains in mind, it still remains true that the original programmes of the SFIO, the PSI, the SPD, the SPÖ and the PSOE, let alone of the Communist parties, remained unfulfilled in inter-war Europe: for all these parties subscribed, at least in theory, to the socialisation of the means of production, the destruction of capitalism, by whatever means — this of course was the issue on which they disagreed most violently — and the creation of an egalitarian society. Only in Russia was the old economic order destroyed root and branch. Only there did the proletariat succeed in implementing socialist revolution; although it is only fair to add that what passed as socialism in Russia hardly fulfilled the aspirations of many European socialists. Why was this the case?

One explanation for the success enjoyed by Russian revolutionaries and denied to the socialists of the rest of Europe is that provided by the Bolsheviks themselves and by subsequent Soviet and East German historiography. In Russia the revolution succeeded because of the existence of the Bolshevik party, because a party of committed revolutionaries purged of reformist and centrist elements and with tight central direction had been in existence for some time, from 1903 to be precise. Conversely, the failure of leftists to seize total power in Germany and Austria in the revolutions of 1918 and in Italy in the factory occupations and land seizures of the *biennio rosso* (1919/20) is ascribed to the absence of such a party 'of the new type'.[76] It may well be the case that the existence of a tightly disciplined organisation of dedicated revolutionaries facilitates or is even essential for the actual physical seizure of power, as happened in Russia in October 1917. Certainly the confused complexion of the various socialist parties in Italy and Germany and the role of reformists within their ranks explains a great deal about the absence of clear-sighted leadership for radical groups of workers in those countries. However, such an explanation of revolutionary success or failure is far too one-dimensional.

What requires investigation is not only the organisational structures of the European working class but rather the situations within which they operated: for there was a vast difference between Russian circumstances and those that prevailed in other countries.

First of all, it is possible to argue that the specific economic and political situation of Russia in 1917 would have produced a second revolution with or without the Bolsheviks. The Russian proletariat experienced appalling material distress as a result of the war and the ending of that distress therefore entailed the ending of the war. But the Provisional government, which had come into existence as a result of the February revolution, wished to continue the war. Hence the rectification of the material grievances of the Russian working class entailed the removal of the Provisional government. It therefore did not require Lenin's April Theses, which declared the possibility of going beyond the bourgeois revolution in Russia immediately, for the workers of Moscow and Petrograd to demand further political change. There was in the very situation an inbuilt stimulus to the radicalisation of the masses, as is testified by the fact that even Menshevik party members carried placards bearing apparently Bolshevik demands in the July rising of 1917, which itself happened almost in spite of the Bolsheviks.[77] To repeat: this is not to say that the existence of the Bolshevik party was irrelevant to the actual seizure of power. Nor is it to deny that the Bolsheviks successfully recognised the mood of the masses in their slogans of 'land, peace and bread'. What it does mean, however, is that the policies of the Provisional government and the continued prosecution of the war by the Russian authorities created an explosive situation which the Bolsheviks then exploited, admittedly with a high degree of astuteness.

In other European countries the situation was different. The democratic governments which were constituted in the wake of the Austrian and German revolutions of 1918 were committed to the rapid conclusion of peace and indeed achieved this end. Hence one major stimulant to radical activity that had been present in Russia was no longer relevant in Central Europe, let alone in victorious England, France and Italy. However, there were yet more important differences between Russia and the rest of Europe which gave the revolutionary sections of the working class in the latter far less room for manoeuvre, in particular differences of social structure and political cohesion.

In the first place, few European countries witnessed the total disintegration of the old state apparatus in the wake of the First World War. Whereas divisions within the Tsarist ruling class and above all the dissolution of the Russian Army formed the backcloth to Lenin's success, the armies and police forces of the victorious Entente powers remained intact and could be relied upon to deal with proletarian insurrection, as they did in Italy, often in alliance with the Fascists, or even industrial militancy, as they did in France in 1920. Obviously the same cannot be said of Austria and Germany, where workers' and soldiers' councils were able to seize power in November 1918 and the old armies had effectively ceased to exist, at least for a time. However, developments in these two countries highlight the crucial difference between the Russian situation and that in most other European states: here the proletariat confonted powerful oppositional and counter-revolutionary groups.

For a variety of historical reasons – dependence upon foreign capital and the close connections between the state and industrial growth – the Russia of 1917 did not possess a numerous and powerful industrial bourgeoisie which could be relied upon either to form the social basis for liberal democracy or fund the counter-revolution.[78] Thus there existed a relatively polarised social structure, in which a parasitic landed elite confronted an alienated peasantry and proletariat. Even the bourgeois intelligentsia, subjected to generations of repression and intellectual stimulus from the revolutionary ideas of the West, identified with the latter rather than the former.[79] In the context of a destroyed army and the absence of intermediate social strata, therefore, the Russian proletariat had a much freer hand than its Western counterpart; as long, that is, as it could act together with or at least without opposition from the peasantry. Herein lay the second crucial difference between Russia and the countries to her west: in 1917 the Russian peasantry was revolutionary, not in the sense of subscribing to the tenets of socialism, but at least in terms of its demand for rights of land ownership and resistance to those governments which refused to recognise its entitlement thereto. Thus Lenin's adoption of the Social Revolutionary slogan of land to the peasantry at least bought temporary quiescence if not actual support from the peasantry, whilst the threat that the White armies might return the land to its former aristocratic owners in the Russian civil war further served to paper over the growing rift between peasant and proletarian aspirations, enabling the Bolsheviks to further consolidate their tenuous control over the country.

In the rest of Europe things were very different. First, Britain, France, Germany and Italy possessed a numerous and powerful middle class. In some places, in the last three countries, in fact, industrialists could be relied upon not only to support but sometimes to finance the existing authorities, and even, on occasion, violent counter-revolution.[80] Furthermore, a revolutionary proletariat would have had to confront in any attempt at social revolution not only an industrial elite but significant hostile contingents of white-collar workers, small shopkeepers, independent artisans and *landowning* peasants. What is more, some of these groups had already been mobilised by counter-revolutionary organisations before the First World War, as in Germany, whilst others were under the sway of Catholic populist politics, as in post-war Italy.[81] It is true that few socialist parties had adopted adequate policies to mobilise the peasantry; but then it is difficult to see how they could have represented proletarian interests and remained true to their original principles on the one hand, and have mobilised peasant support from those who had already been granted their title to land by the old order on the other. Where socialist parties did make headway in rural areas it was either with wage labourers, as in parts of northern Italy and Weimar Germany, or amongst sharecroppers, as in Italy and France. Those independent, landowning peasants who also joined the left were certainly the exception rather than the rule and tended to suffer from special problems, especially the vicissitudes of the demand for wine.[82] In fact in the counter-revolutionary Freikorps, which repressed working-class insurrections in the Ruhr, and in the Italian Fascist movement, which finally defeated Italian socialism in the early 1920s, it was precisely peasant farmers and the urban and rural middle class who played a leading role.[83] Thus radical labour remained isolated from and opposed by numerous social groups in inter-war Europe. The degree of this isolation is perhaps indicated by the ability of the Freikorps to recruit no fewer than something in the order of 400,000 men in a very short space of time;[84] and by the fact that most European states possessed a large agricultural population in this period.[85] There was no love lost between Italian factory workers and peasants during the First World War, when each group believed it was being exploited by the other;[86] in Austria requisition raids by Social Democrats into the countryside for food and similar developments in Hungary in the course of the 1919 Revolution also alienated large sections of the agricultural population and further isolated industrial labour.[87]

None of this is meant to say that proletarian revolution has to be ruled impossible on the mechanical grounds of large numerical opposition: it might be argued that, as happened in Russia in October 1917, a proletarian minority can seize power in favourable circumstances.

However, it does mean that any attempt at socialist revolution would have been likely to lead to a civil war. Indeed, this was precisely an argument that the cautious leadership of the SPD employed to justify its refusal to engage in full-scale socialist revolution in 1918. Furthermore, the problem was not simply that proletarian insurrection might lead to civil war but also that there was a fair chance of defeat in any such encounter, to say the least. This seems to me to be the lesson that must be drawn from the Austrian civil war of 1934. In that conflict an organised, disciplined and *united* labour movement − even the Catholic trade unions fought on the side of the left − was obliterated by the combined forces of Fascist paramilitary organisations, recruiting from the peasantry and the urban middle class, and the institutions of the state, the army and the police.[88] Thus, even if European labour had been united behind a revolutionary banner and had possessed organisations of the Bolshevik kind outside Russia, it is still quite clear that any attempt at socialist revolution on its part would have met with fairly mighty obstacles.

However, it is also true that this labour movement was far from united, as we have seen. Most obviously it was divided into Social Democratic and Communist wings; but this was far from the whole story. Even on the radical left a further set of divisions tended to occur. In Germany, for example, the radical left comprised not only the KPD, itself divided into various factions and vacillating in its policies, but also the KAPD, which split from it in 1919/20 and was even more insurrectionary in its mentality, various anarcho-syndicalist groups in the Ruhr and also the USPD, only part of which joined with the until then embryonic KPD, also in 1920.[89] Under such circumstances it is hardly surprising that no concerted revolutionary leadership with clarity of intentions emerged. In Italy the PSI initially included reformists and revolutionaries; but when the Italian Communist Party was founded at Leghorn in 1921 it too was outflanked on the left by Bordiga and his followers.[90] The Hungarian revolution was likewise impaled on the divisions between Social Democrats and Communists.[91]

The absence of clear-sighted and united revolutionary leadership meant that the radical sections of the European working class would hardly have had their aspirations fulfilled in favourable circumstances. The counter-revolutionary or at least apathetic and cautious behaviour of the Social Democrats of some European nations left them without a chance. In Italy the leadership of the PSI refused to concert the factory occupations of 1920 into a more general working-class seizure of power.[92] Most famously of all, the German Social Democratic leadership actively allied with the German High Command and the old bureaucracy in the suppression of left-wing insurrections throughout 1919 and 1920. It even sanctioned the destruction of non-radical workers' councils and suppressed movements for *democratic* reform, which demanded the removal of the old officer corps and monarchist sympathisers in the civil service.[93] Clearly, therefore, we need to explain such behaviour on the part of the leaders of parties which were in theory committed to the introduction of a socialist order.

The explanation of caution provided by the SPD itself went something like this: in conditions of chaos at the end of the war immediate socialisation of the means of production is not possible, for it will lead to even greater economic deprivation. Therefore, for the moment our priority must be the regeneration of the German economy. Furthermore, socialisation might bring allied intervention and the confiscation of socialised enterprises. We also require the co-operation of the old institutions of state to maintain law and order, guarantee that food supplies reach their destination and demobilise the army. Thus the expertise of former civil servants and the discipline of army officers is essential to our aims. Finally, we cannot encourage civil war and the massive bloodshed that would ensue.

Some of these points cannot be dismissed lightly. Concern at the deplorable privations of everyday life in Germany at the end of the war and the desire to avoid bloodshed can hardly be condemned out of hand. The possibility of Allied intervention was not fantasy: after all, the Western capitalist powers did intervene in the Russian civil war in far less favourable circumstances subsequently. However, it is also significant that the SPD failed to use non-radical councils in place of anti-democratic bureaucrats, whereas the maintenance of law and order and demobilisation took place perfectly happily under the auspices of the newly formed councils. Thus there was something more to the ominous alliance between Ebert, leader of the SPD, and General Groener, spokesman of the High Command. That this was so is further revealed by the fact that the SPD repressed left-wing working-class insurrections and even encouraged the murder of Luxemburg and Liebknecht without a bad conscience. The real explanation of the behaviour of the official leadership of German Social Democracy lies in some of the developments before and during the war which have already been described. The SPD had built up a massive organisational empire before the war. What it was doing in the post-war years was defending that empire, and the organisation of its close allies, the Free Trade Unions, against competition from the radical left and from the councils' movement. In a sense the SPD was playing the same game as the German General Staff, namely that of self-preservation, in the course of the German Revolution. It is also true, however, that the reformists within the ranks of German Social Democracy, whose role was greatly strengthened by developments in the war and especially by the secession of more radical elements in the USPD in 1917, saw the achievement of parliamentary democracy rather than proletarian dictatorship as their main objective. Unfortunately the unsavoury allies they chose against the forces of the supposedly anti-democratic left were to be precisely those who helped to undermine Weimar democracy.

The counter-revolutionary behaviour of the SPD in 1918 and the following five years and the caution of Italian Social Democrats does raise another crucial point, however. Perhaps their policies corresponded to the wishes of their constituents and in a sense, therefore, the failure of revolutionary initiatives in non-Russian Europé reflected the non-revolutionary nature of the European working class. It has certainly been argued that this was the case in Germany; and it is not difficult to find evidence to support this contention. Most of the revolutionaries in Germany in November 1918 simply demanded peace and democratic reform. The national congress of workers' and soldiers' councils held in Berlin in mid-December 1918 voted for the election of a national assembly, 'bourgeois democracy', rather than the radical formula of 'all power to the soviets'; and the SPD won a large majority over the competing socialist parties in the Reichstag elections of January 1919. However, those election results were almost reversed in the following year, massive campaigns for socialisation developed in the Ruhr and in Saxony, several parts of Germany experienced working-class insurrections, the USPD dominated proletarian areas of the large industrial towns and subsequently the KPD won no fewer than 3 million votes in the elections of 1924.[94] In Italy the land seizures and factory occupations were not directed by the central institutions of labour but again reflected a substantial radical sentiment amongst certain sections of Italian labour.[95] I am not saying that the 'working class' in inter-war Europe was uniformly revolutionary. The important point is that significant sections of it *were* dissatisfied with the caution and moderation of Social Democracy.

This, however, raises another point which helps to explain the failure of the revolutionary left outside Russia: there were divisions not just between the different political factions of labour representatives but also at the root of the movement, between employed and unemployed workers, between the skilled and the unskilled, and even between different occupations. Thus skilled engineering workers in Britain failed to mobilise their less skilled colleagues in the movement for worker' control during the war;[96] whilst radical activities in the Ruhr in 1920 were restricted to miners and metalworkers.[97] In this latter case it is also possible to argue that 'radicalism' was far from uniform in its structure. Around Remscheid and Solingen in the southern Ruhr, in an area with long socialist traditions and dominated by a single union, the DMV, radicalism assumed a disciplined appearance in which workers responded to the directions of their leaders, who in the main came from the USPD. In the western Ruhr, which had experienced the most spectacular development in the war years, on the other hand, an undisciplined radicalism which found expression in anarcho-syndicalism and other ultra-leftist movements held sway, a radicalism, furthermore, which seemed out of the control of any particular political movement and which disappeared as quickly as it had originated.[98] Herein lay yet another problem for the prospects of proletarian revolution: the very volatility of the new work-force.[99] The European working class was not only divided in its economic interests and political aspirations, however; it was also divided geographically. Unlike Russia, the centres of industrial power in Germany and Italy were not located at the *political* centre. Events in Milan and Turin left large parts of Italy unaffected, including the capital city. In Germany there were proletarian insurrections in Berlin, as in the Ruhr, Saxony and Hamburg. But these took place largely in isolation from one another and at separate points in time.[100]

Even in countries where a radical labour force did exist, as in Italy and Germany, the absence of united and clear-sighted leadership, divisions both amongst the leadership and the base of the organised labour movement, and above all the strength of the opposition forces made successful socialist revolution unlikely. Paradoxically, the very success of Lenin and his Bolsheviks in Russia may have contributed to the prospects of failure as well. It is certainly true that the events in Russia encouraged many socialists and inspired some workers; but the forces of reaction also learnt lessons and in some ways learnt them better than their enemies. In particular, fear of Bolshevism served as a rallying cry for the European bourgeoisie and an ideological bludgeon with which to beat off the threat of socialism and the supposed barbarism *à la Russe* which would come in its wake. There remains one case, however, in which the forces of revolution and reaction were more nearly balanced in the inter-war period and in which socialist revolution was arguably possible: Spain. In Spain there existed an insurrectionary working class in the anarchist enclave of Catalonia, especially in Barcelona and Saragossa, which conducted extreme egalitarian experiments during the Civil War of 1936-9. In addition, the Socialist Party, which had been predominantly, though far from exclusively, reformist before 1914, possessed insurrectionary mining support around Oviedo in the Asturias and moved rapidly to the left in the 1930s in the context of a muted depression, the policies of right-wing governments between 1934 and 1936 and an influx of new and wild elements in the same period. The political left was then united by the anti-republican *coup* staged by the generals, including Franco, in 1936. What made the revolutionary forces so much more potent in Spain than other parts of Europe, however, was not simply the insurrectionary habits of its industrial population, but the existence of a large, deprived and revolutionary rural proletariat who worked the latifundia of Andalusia and Extremadura, and peasant tenants with grievances against their landlords in other parts of Spain.[101] Hence the start of the Civil War saw the two sides line up fairly well matched.

Even here, however, socialist revolutionaries met defeat at the combined hands of clerical conservatives, right-wing army officers and Fascists. Their defeat can again be attributed in part to the internal division of the left, which saw Trotskyites, anarchists and left-wing socialists engage in bloody conflict with right-wing socialists and Communists (of which more anon) in May 1937 in Barcelona. It was also the result of the aid supplied to the anti-republican forces by Fascist Italy and Nazi Germany and the fact that Franco commanded the only disciplined and battle-hardened professional units in the war, namely his Moroccan regiment.[102]

For these various reasons, above all the strength of counter-revolutionary forces and the internal disunity of the revolutionary left, as well as the existence of a significant non-revolutionary labour force in most countries, the years between the two great wars spelt distress and disappointment for those committed to the realisation of the socialist ideal. But in some countries, and even industrial countries, far worse was to happen: Fascism seized power and destroyed the organised labour movement in Italy and Germany, in countries with large and at least partly radical labour movements. How could this happen?

Fascism and European Labour

Three questions immediately suggest themselves under this heading:

the extent to which Italian Fascists and German Nazis succeeded in recruiting support from the industrial working class, why the organised labour movement failed to prevent the seizure of power by Mussolini and Hitler and what happened to labour protest under the Fascist regimes.

In popular mythology and even in some historical works it is possible to encounter the contention that the electoral triumphs of Nazism owed something to the German working class and especially to the unemployed.[103] After all, Hitler's party was called the National *Socialist* Party, attacked 'parasitical' finance capitalism and big business and claimed to believe in the dignity of labour. In the new *Volksgemein-schaft* (national community) the divisions between classes were to disappear. In Italy Mussolini had stood on the left of the socialist movement before the war and voiced anti-capitalist slogans. In France one of the many Fascist sects, the Parti Populaire Français, was founded by Jacques Doriot, a former member of the PCF; and even in Britain, where few gave the Fascists much of a chance, Sir Oswald Mosley had begun his political career as a Labour MP. The realities of political support, however, give a very different picture. It is true that some of Mussolini's early support came from former anarcho-syndicalists, disillusioned with the caution of organised socialism; however, as De Ambris stated, such people had deserted the ranks of a Fascist movement they now considered 'bourgeois' by 1921. Mussolini became increasingly dependent upon the rural reaction of landowners and urban middle-class support, whilst the industrial proletariat con-tinued to cast its votes for socialism or Communism.[104] In Britain Mosley's attempts to recruit support from the former ranks of the Labour Party came to nothing; and as he was obliged to look to other social groups for support, so his message became more reactionary.[105] In France Doriot's faction was the only Fascist group with any degree of working-class support; and it was minute.[106]

If one wants to find working-class Fascists, then post-war Germany would seem to be the obvious place to look: for here the Fascist movement generated a degree of electoral support and party member-ship which outstripped that of all other states, with the possible exception of Austria, by a spectacular margin.[107] It is possible to locate a signifi-cant percentage of industrial working-class members within the SA before Hitler became Chancellor in January 1933, most of whom had some degree of skill and had experienced some unemployment.[108] There were also some industrial areas which provided significant electoral support for the Nazis: this was the case in Brunswick, in some mining communities in the Ruhr and above all in the textile town of Chemnitz-Zwickau.[109] Having said this, however, it would be most misleading to take these cases as typical of working-class attitudes towards the Nazis. In the case of all three areas one may be dealing with workers who had participated in a variety of radical or Communist activities at an earlier date — all three areas witnessed significant leftist activity between 1918 and 1924 — but had become disillusioned by the betrayal of union and party functionaries and perpetual defeat. This is speculation; but it suggests that this proletarian support for Nazism had little to do with a belief in the more petty bourgeois aspects of Nazi ideology. This inference is supported by an analysis of SA attitudes: for the relatively high percentage of industrial workers in its ranks — much higher than in the Nazi party as a whole — there corresponded to strong anti-capitalist feelings and less emphasis on the anti-socialist aspects of the party's more general message.[110]

What must be stressed above all, however, is that these working-class Fascists were in no way typical of the Nazi movement nor of the German proletariat; it is only if one adopts the rather unhelpful definition of 'working class' adopted by Kele, which includes artisans and white-collar workers together with industrial manual workers, that one can conclude that the National Socialists did attract working-class support.[111] In actual fact Nazi electoral propaganda, which had initially been directed at the factory workers of Germany's large industrial towns, proved unsuccessful in precisely this area and, noting that its limited successes were coming from Protestant rural areas, switched the direction of its attack.[112] Psephological analysis reveals first of all that the Nazis gained their support primarily from previous non-voters and from the middle-class parties, which collapsed in the wake of its electoral triumphs in the early 1930s. The parties of labour, the KPD and the SPD, maintained their *combined* percentage of the vote (at around 30 per cent) throughout the last days of Weimar, as did the Catholic Centre Party. In addition, the centres of Nazi electoral strength were Protestant rural areas and small provincial towns, rather that the large industrial conurbations. Even the contention that the unemployed factory working class turned to the policies of Hitler for salvation cannot be sustained: unemployment was concentrated in industrial towns with populations of over 100,000, whilst it was precisely in such places that the Nazis were disproportionately unsuccessful in their electoral campaigns.[113] All of this suggests that when the SPD lost votes in the two Reichstag elections of 1932, the first occasions on which its electoral hold over its traditional constituency was dented, those votes went to the Communists rather than the National Socialists. Indeed, it was precisely at this time that the size of the KPD vote exploded.[114] It would appear from such analysis, therefore, that the electoral triumphs of Hitler were primarily dependent upon the support of the Protestant middle class; and this would further explain why Hitler was never able to gain more than 38 per cent of the total vote in any free Reichstag election before he became Chancellor. The industrial working class in the main remained immune to National Socialist propaganda, an impression reinforced by its disproportionately small representation in the party membership.[115]

That the factory proletariat was not taken in by Hitler and his cronies is hardly surprising. A diet of anti-socialist slogans could hardly be expected to appeal to workers schooled in socialist traditions; whilst the Nazi idealisation and idolatry of the peasant farmer and small businessman hardly corresponded to their perceptions. What talk of a corporate Fascist state meant for the industrial worker could already be gleaned from Mussolini's Italy. Perhaps as important as these things, however, was the fact that the traditional political parties of labour had sunk deep roots in the working-class areas of Germany. They were not just political parties for which one voted at election time but whole societies with their own clubs and pubs. It was precisely this which made it so difficult for the Nazis to make headway in industrial communities: their success was achieved through groups without such a strong tradition of political and social mobilisation.[116] (This would also explain their lack of success in recruiting German Catholics.)

The German Nazis and the Italian Fascists, therefore, did not owe their victories to active working-class support in the main. But this also raises the question of why a labour movement which was not taken in by promises of the corporate state and the *Volksgemeinschaft* should fail to resist the Fascist onslaught and ultimately be destroyed by it. In Italy, of course, Mussolini came to power with the backing of significant sections of the old order, backing from generals, members of the royal family and some sections of heavy industry. The power of Italian socialism had blown itself out in the wake of the ultimately abortive land seizures and factory occupations of the *biennio rosso* and was being torn apart by internal squabbles. Fascist armed gangs, the *squadristi*, controlled the streets under the benign gaze of an inactive constabulary.[117] In Germany, however, the failure to resist Hitler became a problem of much greater dimensions: for here the republican paramilitary groups outnumbered the Nazi SA by a factor of something like six to one in 1932 and it is known that some of this rank and file were prepared to risk their lives and fight the Nazis at that time.[118]

Many explanations can be given for the tragic failure of German labour in the face of Nazism, though it should be recorded that many workers did fight the Nazis in the streets − and did pretty well at it − before 1933. The most common explanation points to the fratricidal conflict between the SPD and the KPD, both of which seemed to spend more time attacking one another than the Nazi menace, and the blame for this short-sightedness of such fatal proportions is usually laid at the door of the Communists, with some justification. It is true that the KPD did its utmost to undermine Weimar democracy and that there were occasions on which its members allied with the Nazis, as in the Berlin transport workers' strike of August 1932. Furthermore, the KPD did reserve most of its venom for the Social Democrats, whom it described convolutedly as 'social Fascists'. That the KPD adopted such an attitude was at least in part the consequence of directions from Moscow. In 1927 the Chinese Communist Party was obliterated in a misguided alliance with that other supposedly 'progressive' organisation, the Kuo Min Tang. As a result Stalin and some of his colleagues drew the understandable conclusion that collaboration with other forces was dangerous. The onset of the world economic depression in 1929 and a left turn in Russian domestic politics associated with the drive against the kulaks further strengthened the line of independence. Indeed, the official Comintern (Third International) line now ran that the collapse of capitalism was at hand and proletarian revolution the order of the day. In consequence Fascism could be but a short-lived and abortive attempt on the part of monopoly capitalism to prop up the existing order. Another consequence of this line of reasoning − or perhaps unreason − was that the only thing which could now prevent triumphant socialist revolution was the action of ostensible leaders of the working class who misdirected it away from the impending upheaval. Thus Social Democracy became 'social fascism' because it offered capitalism its only chance of survival. Clearly such a line of argument and such false perceptions of Fascism did not help the German proletariat in its struggle against the growing Nazi threat. However, it should first of all be pointed out that the origins of the antagonism between the SPD and the KPD cannot be placed entirely on the shoulders of misguided Communists taking instructions from Moscow. The KPD knew, after all, that it was an SPD government that had organised the defeat of the revolutionary left in the aftermath of the First World War and that it had done so with enormous bloodshed.

Such wounds could not so easily be healed; and this especially so because SPD police chiefs in Berlin and other German industrial cities were still banning KPD demonstrations in the late 1920s and early 1930s. The most famous example of this was the ban which the Social Democrat Zörgiebel placed on the Communist May Day demonstration of 1929 in Berlin. In the event the demonstration took place and massive bloodshed ensued.[119] It was also asking rather a lot of the KPD to expect it to fight to defend the Weimar Republic tooth and nail when the radical left had suffered so much at its hands and it had done so little for the unemployed. Conversely, few members of the SPD were keen on forming a liaison with what they regarded as the Communist rabble.

(As an epilogue to the Comintern's 'social Fascism' line of the early 1930s, it should perhaps be pointed out that the disaster of 1933 in Germany, political changes within Russia and the need to find allies against the prospect of war with the Fascist barbarian combined to bring about a decisive shift in policy towards the 'popular front' strategy, i.e. collaboration with the socialists, as was implemented by the Communist parties in France and Spain in 1936.[120] Paradoxically, it can be argued that the over-cautious politics of the PCF and the Spanish Communist Party, rather than their revolutionary adventurism, then served to brake more radical actions on the part of the French and Spanish proletariat and in fact defused genuine revolutionary potential.[121])

To return to the internecine warfare between Social Democrats and KPD members in late Weimar Germany, it therefore cannot be claimed that this sorry state of affairs was exclusively the fault of the Communists. Indeed, it was the Communists who bore the brunt of most of the street fighting against the Brownshirts.[122] Furthermore, the SPD leadership was no more clear about what it should do in the crisis of the early 1930s than the Communists. Some SPD members shared the tragic deception that Nazism was a short-lived phenomenon which could not survive internal conflicts of interest between monopoly capitalism and lower-middle-class aspirations.[123] What is certainly true is that the executive of the SPD failed to give leadership to its rank and file not only in 1933, when Hitler became Reichskanzler, but also in the previous year when the Social Democratic Prussian state government was unconstitutionally dissolved by the national government of von Papen. The reasons for this inaction were various. In the first place, many of those at the head of the party had inherited something of the party's old fatalistic and evolutionary view of history, a kind of castrated Marxism embodied in Karl Kautsky, who was still an SPD member at this late date. Thus they had little idea of the possibility of changing the course of history, let alone knowing how to do it.[124] They had also imbibed a strongly constitutionalist position through having been the principal founders and defenders of democratic Weimar. Thus extraparliamentary action was almost unthinkable, especially as Hitler became Chancellor via a perfectly constitutional, albeit rather dirty, road. What is almost certainly true is that the leaders of the SPD were terrified by the prospect of a bloody civil war; and this fear was perfectly rational when one considers that the paramilitary republican forces were poorly armed, that they would probably have had to confront not only the SA and the SS but also the regular police and army in any conflict; and in the light of what happened in Austria in the following year.[125]

However, it was not only its own fears and indecision which tied the hands of German Social Democracy: in a sense the decision had been pre-empted for it by the Confederation of the Affiliated Free Trade Unions, the ADGB,. The trade union movement was on its knees as a result of the depression: it experienced a loss of membership, erosion of funds and by 1932 half its total membership were unemployed. Out of such weakness stemmed the readiness to enter into negotiations with virtually any politician and even with the likes of the political General Schleicher, who was involved in a whole series of government intrigues in 1932/3.[126] The ADGB had always been cautious and none too keen on involvement in what it regarded as rash political adventures; hence its support for some kind of anti-Nazi unconstitutional action would have been unlikely in the most favourable of circumstance. In 1933 such support was utterly improbable.

The weakness of organised unionism in late Weimar Germany leads us into what is perhaps the most important yet least studied explanation of labour's failure, namely the impact of the depression itself. The massive increase in the number of the unemployed and in particular the fact that 50 per cent of organised trade unionists were without jobs obviously nullified the possibility of strike action, especially as those groups hit especially badly by the depression, metalworkers and building workers, were amongst the traditionally most militant sections of the labour force.[127] Furthermore, the very reason why the German Communist Party was obliged to transfer so much of its activity from the factory to the neighbourhood in this period was its weakness in the former, caused by the fact that over 80 per cent of its membership were jobless.[128] Moreover, the problem was not simply that the unemployed could by definition not strike but also that the huge reservoir of those desperate to get jobs discouraged those still in employment from strike action as well, for such action became too risky with the possibility of easy replacement. This point raises yet another crucial issue: in a sense the great depression further exacerbated divisions within the labour movement at its very base. In the short term, at least, the employed and the unemployed had conflicting interests, as was pointed out in a brilliant essay by the Austro-Marxist, Max Adler, at this very time.[129] Furthermore, this conflict of interest explains some of the bitter hostility which characterised the relationship between the KPD and the SPD: it is not without significance that the KPD gained its greatest support at precisely the time that it espoused the 'social Fascism' thesis. Once again the origins of the internal divisions of labour had social as well as ideological roots. The politics of the KPD mirrored the anger and despair of the unemployed, an anger directed not simply at the employer but also at the Weimar Republic and the traditional institutions of labour which had proved themselves worthless in the crisis.

If we turn to the relationship between the working class and Fascism in power things become rather more complicated. Unfortunately I am not in possession of any detailed information on the activities of Italian labour under Mussolini between 1922 and 1939, although the well known difficulty the Fascists experienced in imposing their will on local communities, the scale of partisan activity and the subsequent re-emergence of strong socialist and Communist parties suggests that labour retained its independent attitudes. In Germany a wealth of detailed investigation has shown the popular view of a quiescent labour movement in Nazi times to be mythical.[130] In the first place the omnipresent surveillance and the terroristic apparatus of the Nazi state made it more or less impossible for overt opposition to be expressed on any significant scale; and thus a surface calm should not necessarily be taken to indicate tacit acceptance of the regime. Furthermore, the fact that political parties and trade unions had been dissolved made it all the more difficult for the isolated individual to protest. Equally, the scale of unemployment in the early thirties gave the National Socialist regime a further weapon to control dissent. Yet in spite of all of these obstacles, there is considerable evidence of proletarian disaffection which shows that workers did not swallow the myth of the classless *Volksgemeinschaft*. As Ian Kershaw's study of labour in Bavaria during the Third Reich has shown, workers continued to recognise that they did not receive adequate remuneration and complained about it; in fact, there were strikes on some of the *Autobahnen* in 1935.[131] Even more importantly, the economic upturn of 1936 and the return of something resembling full employment generated a host of industrial disputes, in which workers sometimes handed in their notices *collectively* to bring pressure to bear on employers, an alternative form of action to the strike when this last was illegal. They also managed to circumvent government restrictions on labour mobility. As before, therefore, labour was prepared to use its strong market situation to improve its lot; and this was even true of some Nazi Party members. By 1938 the government was so worried about industrial discipline that the labour law was criminalised — absenteeism and the like became an offence against the laws of the Reich — and work-education camps were established outside many German industrial towns. Most spectacularly of all, the advent of war caused Hitler to introduce legislation providing for a longer working day, lower wages and the abolition of holidays; but even in the context of war these measures caused great resentment amongst the working population and were met with serious disruption of production. In fact the seriousness of the situation was such that the government was forced to withdraw the measures and change its economic policies within twelve weeks. Top civil servants spoke of 'passive resistance'.[132]

In the factories, therefore, the Nazis did not succeed in abolishing the realities of the class conflict, at least at the economistic level. That this should be so is hardly surprising: for the Third Reich did *not* become the *Volksgemeinschaft* of mythical imagination. Social mobility remained as restricted as ever, with the exception of some functionaries within the Nazi Party itself, wealth differentials increased and capital became ever more concentrated in fewer and fewer hands. Krupp became ever wealthier; whilst legislation attempted to prevent the strike action which might have guaranteed a more equitable distribution of the national product.[133]

In addition to shop-floor protest, of course, the Third Reich did witness clandestine organisational activity on the part of the SPD and the KPD and significantly both organisations survived the persecution of 1933 to 1945.[134] Thus even the fear and the misery of the Third Reich failed to break the backbone of the German working class.

Notes

1.   Gordon Phillips, 'Industrialisation and Social Protest in Inter-war Britain', unpublished MS.; Antoine Prost, *La CGT à l'Époque du Front Populaire* (Paris,

1964), p. 37; Gerald Brenan, *The Spanish Labyrinth* (Cambridge, 1962), Chs. 8 and 10; Martin Blinkhorn, 'Industrialisation and Social Protest in Italy', unpublished MS.; Gerhard Braunthal, *Socialist Labour and Politics in Weimar Germany* (New York, 1978), p. 88.

2. Dick Geary, 'Radicalism and the German Worker: Metalworkers and Revolution 1914-1923' in Richard J. Evans (ed.), *Society and Politics in Wilhelmine Germany* (London, 1978), p. 273f.; Gerald D. Feldman, 'Socio-economic Structures in the Industrial Sector and Revolutionary Potentialities, 1917-22' in Charles L. Bertrand (ed.), *Revolutionary Situations in Europe, 1917-1922: Germany, Italy, Austria-Hungary* (Montreal, 1977), p. 161.

3. There are innumerable studies of the Russian revolutions of 1917. Some are: E.H. Carr, *The Bolshevik Revolution 1917-1923* (London, 1966); Lionel Kochan, *Russia in Revolution* (London, 1970); Marcel Liebman, *The Russian Revolution* (London, 1970); Marc Férro, *Révolution de 1917*, 2 vols. (Paris, 1967-80); J.M.L. Keep, *The Russian Revolution* (Westfield, 1976); Leon Trotsky, *The History of the Russian Revolution* (trans. Max Eastman) (London, 1967).

4. Feldman, 'Socio-economic Structures', p. 163; Jürgen Kyczynski, *Die Geschichte der Lage der Arbeiter unter dem Kapitalismus*, vol. 4, *Darstellung der Lage der Arbeiter in Deutschland von 1900 bis 1917/18* (Berlin, 1967), p. 350; R.H. Dumke, 'Trends in Income Distribution in Germany', unpublished MS. delivered to the third meeting of the SSRC/DFG Forum on German Economic and Social History at the University of Liverpool, May 1980, Graph 5; Hans-Ulrich Ludewig, *Arbeiterbewegung und Aufstand* (Husum, 1978), p. 51.

5. See below, p. 155.

6. Edouard Dolléans, *Histoire du Mouvement Ouvrier*, vol. 2, *1871-1936* (Paris, 1946), pp. 298-333; Edward Shorter and Charles Tilly, *Strikes in France 1830-1968* (Cambridge, 1974), p. 123; Alfred Sauvy, *Histoire Economique de la France entre les deux Guerres*, vol. 1, *1918-1931* (Paris, 1967), p. 99; Claude Fohlen, *La France de l'Entre-Deux-Guerres* (Paris, 1966), p. 35f.; Jacques Chastenet, *Histoire de la Troisième République*, vol. 5, *Les Anées d'Illusion 1918-1931* (Paris, 1960), p. 67; J. Lhomme, 'Le pouvoir d'achat de l'ouvrier français au cours d'un siècle, 1840-1940' in *Mouvement Social* (June 1968), p. 52f.

7. Blinkhorn, 'Italy'; John M. Cammett, *Antonio Gramsci and the Origins of Italian Communism* (Stanford, 1967); P. Spriano, *L'occupazione della Fabbriche* (Turin, 1964).

8. Karl-Theodor Stiller, *Gewerkschaftspolitik und Bewegungen in der Arbeiterschaft (1914 bis 1920)* (Offenbach, 1977), p. 23. For a detailed analysis of labour conditions see also Gerald Feldman, *Army, Industry and Labour in Germany, 1914-1918* (Princeton, NJ, 1966) and J. Kocka, *Klassengesellschaft im Krieg* (Göttingen, 1973).

9. Henry Pelling, *A History of British Trade Unionism* (London, 1966), pp. 151ff.

10. Annie Kriegel, *Aux Origines du Communisme Français* (Paris, 1964), Ch. 6.

11. See note 122 to Ch. 3 above.

12. Martin Blinkhorn, 'Industrialisation and Social Protest in Spain', unpublished MS.

13. Blinkhorn, 'Italy'; M. Degl'Innocenti, 'La guerra libica, la crisi del riformismo e la vittoria degli intransigenti', *Studi storici*, no. 3 (1972), pp. 502-6.

14. Blinkhorn, 'Italy'; Adrian Lyttleton, 'Revolution and Counter-revolution in Italy, 1918-1922' in Bertrand (ed.), *Revolutionary Situations*, p. 64f.; Paolo Spriano, *Storia del Partito Communista Italiano* (Turin, 1967), vol. 1.

15. Feldman, 'Socio-economic Structures', p. 160f.; Peter von Oertzen, *Betriebsräte in der Novemberrevolution* (Düsseldorf, 1963), p. 273f.; Barrington Moore Jr., *Injustice. The Social Bases of Obedience and Revolt* (White Plains, NY, 1978); David W. Morgan, *The Socialist Left and the German Revolution* (Ithaca,

NY, 1975), p. 72.
16.   See note 144 to Ch. 3.
17.   Ibid.
18.   Ibid.
19.   See note 68 to Ch. 3.
20.   Feldman, *Army, passim*; Susanne Miller, *Burgfrieden und Klassenhampf* (Düsseldorf, 1974), *passim*; Geary, 'Radicalism', pp. 280ff. Such developments were not exclusive to Germany. Similar tendencies can be detected in Italy and Austria: Feldman, 'Socio-economic Structures', p. 161.
21.   Ibid.
22.   Feldman, 'Socio-economic Structures', p. 161f. Also ibid., p. 165f., and Richard Comfort, *Revolutionary Hamburg* (Stanford, Cal., 1966), Ch. 7.
23.   Pelling, *British Trade Unionism*, pp. 151-6; James Hinton, *The First Shop Stewards' Movement* (London, 1973), *passim*.
24.   Kriegel, *Origines*, Ch. 6.
25.   Feldman, *Army*, pp. 104 and 113.
26.   On the polarisation of German society in the course of the First World War see Kocka, *Krieg, passim*.
27.   Sebastian Haffner, *Die verratene Revolution* (Frankfurt am Main, 1971), p. 119f.
28.   Leopold Haimson, 'The Problem of Social Stability in Urban Russia, 1905-1917' in Clive Emsley (ed.), *Conflict and Stability in Europe* (London, 1979), pp. 247ff.
29.   Lyttleton, 'Revolution and Counter-revolution', p. 64f.
30.   George Dangerfield, *The Strange Death of Liberal England* (London, 1966).
31.   Feldman, 'Socio-economic Structures'.
32.   Phillips, 'Inter-war Britain'; Pelling, *British Trade Unionism*, Ch. 10. Eve Rosenhaft, 'Social History of the German Communist Party, 1919-1933', unpublished paper; Richard N. Hunt, *German Social Democracy 1918-1933* (Chicago, 1970), pp. 89-138; Ossip K. Flechtheim, *Die KPD in der Weimarer Republik* (Frankfurt am Main, 1971), pp. 241 and 318-22.
33.   Rosenhaft, 'German Communist Party'; James Wickham, 'Working Class Movement and Working Class Life', unpublished MS.
34.   In Germany, for example, 2 million were jobless in early 1926.
35.   See above, pp. 123ff.
36.   Feldman, 'Socio-economic Structures', p. 164.
37.   See above, pp. 123ff.
38.   See note 144 to Ch. 2 above.
39.   This is the central argument of Carl E. Schorske, *German Social Democracy 1905-1917* (Cambridge, Mass., 1955).
40.   Albert S. Lindemann, *The 'Red Years'* (Berkeley, 1974), p. 24.
41.   Ibid., p. 6f.; David Stafford, *From Anarchism to Reformism. Paul Brousse* (London, 1971), *passim*; Claude Willard, *Socialisme et Communisme Français* (Paris, 1967), pp. 51-73.
42.   The Russian party, of course, had split into Bolshevik and Menshevik wings as early as 1903 over the question of the breadth of party membership, with Lenin desiring stricter terms of entry.
43.   For the struggles within the various socialist parties on the question of affiliation to the Third International see note 68 to Ch. 3.
44.   For a description of Moscow's relations with the other Communist parties see E.H. Carr, *The Interregnum 1923-1924, Socialism in One Country 1924-1926, Foundations of a Planned Economy, 1926-1929* (London, 1954-76), *passim*; Isaac Deutscher, *Trotsky* (London, 1954-63), vols. 2 and 3, *passim*; Richard Lowenthal, *The Bolshevisation of the Spartacist League* (London, 1960);

Hermann Weber, *Die Wandlung des deutschen Kommunismus* (Frankfurt am Main, 1969); Werner T. Angress, *Stillborn Revolution. The Communist Bid for Power in Germany, 1921-1923* (Princeton, NJ, 1963).

45.   Kriegel, *Origines*; Lindemann, *'Red Years'*, p. 270f.; Dolléans, *Mouvement Ouvrier*, vol. 3, *De 1921 à nos jours* (Paris, 1953); Jacques Droz, *Le Socialisme Démocratique 1864-1960* (Paris, 1966), p. 233f.; Ronald Tiersky, *French Communism, 1920-1972* (Columbia, 1976), pp. 23-36.

46.   Morgan, *Socialist Left*; Robert F. Wheeler, *USPD und Internationale* (Frankfurt am Main, 1975); Weber, *Wandlung*; Flechtheim, *KPD*.

47.   Geary, 'Radicalism', pp. 270-3.

48.   Lindemann, *'Red Years'*, pp. 24, 54 and 117.

49.   Ibid., p. 293.

50.   Ibid., p. 251; Wheeler, *USPD*.

51.   Droz, *Socialisme Démocratique*, p. 233f.; Shorter and Tilly, *Strikes*, pp. 132-6; Prost, *CGT*, pp. 66-73.

52.   Degl'Innocenti, 'La guerra libica', pp. 502-6; Spriano, *L'occupazione*; Feldman, 'Socio-economic Structures', p. 165f.

53.   Hunt, *German Social Democracy*, pp. 93-130; Flechtheim, *KPD*, p. 63f. and 241; Weber, *Die Wandlung*, vol. 2, pp. 26-34.

54.   Rosenhaft, 'Communist Party'; Wickham, 'Workers' Movement'.

55.   Geary, 'Radicalism', p. 277; Robert F. Wheeler, 'Zur sozialen Struktur der Arbeiterbewegung am Anfang der Weimarer Republik' in Hans Mommsen, Dietmar Petzina and Bernd Weisbrod (eds.), *Industrielles System und politische Entwicklung in der Weimarer Republik* (Düsseldorf, 1974), p. 182f.; Lindemann, *'Red Years'*, pp. 253, 262f. and 270.

56.   Mayone Ruth Clark, *A History of the French Labour Movement* (Berkeley, 1930), pp. 85ff.; Kriegel, *Origines*, pp. 359-521.

57.   Braunthal, *Socialist Labour*, p. 88; Flechtheim, *KPD*, p. 70; Angress, *Stillborn Revolution*, p. 72f.; Denis Authier and Jean Barrot, *La Gauche Communiste en Allemagne 1918-1921* (Paris, 1976), pp. 121 and 164.

58.   Lyttleton, 'Revolution and Counter-revolution', pp. 69ff.

59.   Pelling, *British Trade Unionism*, pp. 180 and 188.

60.   See above, p. 80.

61.   See above, p. 145.

62.   See above, p. 145.

63.   Ludewig, *Arbeiterbewegung*, pp. 53ff.

64.   Pelling, *British Trade Unionism*, p. 161; Phillips, 'Inter-war Britain'.

65.   Feldman, 'Socio-economic Structures', p. 162f.

66.   Phillips, 'Inter-war Britain'; Frank Wilkinson, 'Collective Bargaining in the Steel Industry in the 1920s' in Asa Briggs and John Saville, *Essays in Labour History 1918-1939* (London, 1977).

67.   Phillips, 'Inter-war Britain'; Alan Deacon, 'Concession and Coercion: The Politics of Unemployment Insurance in the Twenties' in Briggs and Saville, *Essays in Labour History 1918-1939*, p. 9.

68.   Ludewig, *Arbeiterbewegung, passim*.

69.   F.L. Carsten, *Revolution in Central Europe 1918-1919* (London, 1972), Chs. 3 and 4.

70.   George Eliasberg, *Der Ruhrkrieg von 1920* (Bonn, 1974), *passim*.

71.   Lindemann, *'Red Years'*, p. 117.

72.   See above, p. 151.

73.   Feldman, *Army*, pp. 523-31.

74.   David Caute, *The Left in Europe since 1789* (London, 1966), p. 197. Even more sweeping measures were introduced in Sweden.

75.   Alfred Cobban, *History of Modern France*, vol. 3, *1871-1962* (London, 1965), p. 152f.

76. A classic demonstration of this line of argument can be found in the East German account of events in the German Revolution of 1918/19: see the articles in *Zeitschrift für Geschichtswissenschaft*, 1968 and 1969.

77. See above, pp. 49f.

78. Trotsky, *Russian Revolution*, vol. 1, Ch. 1.

79. Kochan, *Revolution in Russia*, p. 18f.

80. As, for example, in the case of Italy: Lyttleton, 'Revolution and Counter-revolution', p. 71.

81. Hans-Jürgen Puhle, *Agrarische Interessenpolitik und Preussischer Conservatismus im Wilhelmischen Reich* (Hanover, 1966); Lyttleton, 'Revolution and Counter-revolution', p. 69.

82. See above, pp. 95f.

83. R.G.L. Waite, *Vanguard of Nazism. The Free Corps Movement in Post War Germany 1918-1923* (Cambridge, Mass., 1952); Lyttleton, 'Revolution and Counter-revolution', pp. 68-73.

84. Robert F. Wheeler, ' "Ex oriente' lux?" The Soviet Example and the German Revolution, 1917-1923' in Bertrand (ed.), *Revolutionary Situations*, p. 46.

85. G. Ranki, 'Structural Crisis in Agriculture in Postwar Years' in Bertrand (ed.), *Revolutionary Situations*, pp. 105-14.

86. Lyttleton, 'Revolution and Counter-revolution', p. 66.

87. Francis Carsten, 'Revolutionary Situations in Europe, 1917-1920' in Bertrand (ed.), *Revolutionary Situations*, p. 30.

88. Hans Hautmann and Rudolf Kropf, *Die österreichische Arbeiterbewegung vom Vomärz bis 1945* (Linz, 1974), pp. 162ff.

89. Authier and Barrot, *Gauche Communiste*; Flechtheim, *KPD*; Hans-Manfred Bock, *Syndikalismus und Linkskommunismus von 1918-1923* (Meisenheim an Glan, 1969); Gottfried Mergner, *Arbeiterbewegung und Intelligenz* (Starnberg, 1973).

90. Lindemann, *'Red Years'*, p. 274.

91. Rudolf L. Tökés, *Bela Kun and the Hungarian Soviet Republic* (London, 1967).

92. Spriano, *L'occupazione, passim*; Cammett, *Gramsci, passim*.

93. Haffner, in *Verratene Revolution*, takes this as his central theme. See also Eliasberg, *Ruhrkrieg, passim*.

94. For a discussion of the nature of the German Revolution see Geary, 'Radicalism'.

95. Cammett, *Gramsci*, Chs. 4 and 5.

96. Hinton, *Shop Stewards' Movement, passim*.

97. Ludewig, *Arbeiterbewegung, passim*; Eliasberg, *Ruhrkrieg, passim*.

98. Eliasberg, *Ruhrkrieg*, pp. 3 and 79; Erhard Lucas, *Arbeiterradikalismus: Zwei Formen von Radikalismus in der deutschen Arbeiterbewegung* (Frankfurt am Main, 1976).

99. See above, p. 79

100. Lyttleton, 'Revolution and Counter-revolution', p. 66; Ludewig, *Arbeiterbewegung*, p. 43f.

101. Brenan, *Spanish Labyrinth*, Ch. 6.

102. For descriptions of the Spanish Civil War see Brenan, *Spanish Labyrinth*; Gabriel Jackson, *The Spanish Republic and the Civil War 1931-1939* (Princeton, NJ, 1965); Hugh Thomas, *The Spanish Civil War* (London, 1961); Stanley G. Payne, *The Spanish Revolution* (London, 1970); Burnett Bolloten, *The Grand Camouflage. The Spanish Civil War and Revolution* (London, 1968).

103. Max H. Kele, *Nazis and Workers* (North Carolina, 1972).

104. On the social bases of Fascist support see G. Germani, 'Fascism and Class' in S.J. Woolf (ed.), *The Nature of Fascism* (London, 1968), pp. 65-96; also

various articles in S.J. Woolf (ed.), *European Fascism* (London, 1968) and S.M. Lipset, *Political Man* (London, 1964), Ch. 5. For Italy see Lyttleton, 'Revolution and Counter-revolution'; A. Lyttleton (ed.), *Italian Fascism* (London, 1973); P. Corner, *Fascism in Ferrara* (London, 1975).

105.   R. Skidelsky, 'Great Britain', in Woolf, *European Fascism*, Ch. 11.

106.   G. Warner, 'France' in Woolf, *European Fascism*, p. 268f.

107.   The literature on German Nazism is enormous. Amongst the works are W.S. Allen, *The Nazi Seizure of Power* (London, 1966); K.D. Bracher, W. Sauer and G. Schulz, *Die Nationalsozialistische Machtergreifung* (Cologne, 1962); M. Broszat, *Der Nationalsozialismus* (Stuttgart, 1960); R. Heberle, *Landbevölkerung und Nationalsozialismus* (Stuttgart, 1962); Alan Bullock, *Hitler* (London, 1962); D. Orlow, *History of the Nazi Party*, 2 vols. (London, 1969-73). For Austria see F.L. Carsten, *Austrian Fascism* (London, 1979).

108.   Conan Fischer, 'The SA's Rank and File Membership in the early 1930s', unpublished MS.; Conan Fischer, 'The Occupational Background of the SA's Rank and File Membership during the Depression Years, 1929 to mid-1934' in P.D. Stachura (ed.), *The Shaping of the Nazi State* (London, 1978).

109.   For analyses of the social composition of the Nazi Party see Lipset, *Political Man*, Ch. 5; L.D. Stokes, 'The Social Composition of the Nazi Party in Eutin, 1925-1932', *International Review of Social History*, vol. XXIII (1978), Part 1. For a more general discussion of the relationship between Nazis and workers see Kele's misleading account *Nazis and Workers* but above all Tim Mason, *Arbeiterklasse und Volksgemeinschaft* (Opladen, 1975).

110.   Fischer, 'The SA's Rank and File'.

111.   Kele, *Nazis and Workers*.

112.   Heberle, *Landbevölkerung*.

113.   See note 109 above.

114.   In the elections of November 1932 to the Reichstag the KPD amassed no fewer than 5,980,000 votes, compared to under 3 million in 1924 and 3.25 million in 1928.

115.   Harold Lasswell and Daniel Lerner, *World Revolutionary Elites* (Cambridge, Mass., 1965), Ch. 5; also note 109 above.

116.   A.K. Organski, 'Fascism and Modernization' and J. Solé-Tura, 'The Political "Instrumentality" of Fascism', both in Woolf, *Nature of Fascism*.

117.   See note 104 above.

118.   Erich Matthias, 'Social Democracy and the Power in the State' in Theodor Eschenburg *et al.* (eds.), *The Road to Dictatorship. Germany 1918-33* (trans. L. Wilson) (London, 1970), pp. 57-74.

119.   Ossip K. Flechtheim, 'The Role of the Communist Party' in ibid., pp. 93-110; Eve Rosenhaft, 'The German Communists and Paramilitary Violence 1929-1933', Cambridge PhD thesis, 1979; Flechtheim, *KPD*, p. 253f.; Friedrich-Wilhelm Witt, *Die Hamburger Sozialdemokratie in der Weimarer Republik* (Hanover, 1971), pp. 73 and 117f.

120.   For the French Front Populaire see Prost, *CGT*; Daniel Guérin, *Front Populaire. Révolution Manquée* (Paris, 1970); Tiersky, *French Communism*, pp. 54-58; Daniel R. Brower, *The New Jacobins* (Ithaca, NY, 1968); Nathaniel Green, *Crisis and Decline. The French Socialist Party in the Popular Front Era* (Ithaca, NY, 1968). For Spain, see Brenan, *Spanish Labyrinth*, Ch. 13.

121.   So argues the *gauchiste* Guèrin, *Front Populaire* for France, whilst Bolloten, *Grand Camouflage* constitutes a blistering indictment of the role of the Spanish Communist Party.

122.   Rosenhaft, 'Paramilitary Violence', *passim*.

123.   See, for example, the late writings of Karl Kautsky, who could still believe this in 1934: Karl Kautsky, *Grenzen der Gewalt* (Karlsbad, 1934).

124.   R.J. Geary, 'Karl Kautsky and the Development of Marxism', Cambridge PhD thesis, 1971, Ch. 13.
125.   Matthias, 'Social Democracy'.
126.   Braunthal, *Socialist Labour*, pp. 70-4. For a more positive assessment of German trade unions in the depression, especially as regards their attempts to formulate a new economic strategy, see Sydney Pollard, 'The Trade Unions in the Depression 1929-1933' in Mommsen, Petzina and Weisbrod, *Industrielles System*, pp. 237-69.
127.   Rosenhaft, 'Social History'.
128.   Ibid. and Rosenhaft, 'Paramilitary Violence', p. 68.
129.   Max Adler, 'Wandlung der Arbeiterklasse?', *Der Kampf*, vol. XXVI (1933), pp. 367-82.
130.   Mason, *Arbeiterklasse*; Tim Mason, 'The Workers' Opposition in the Third Reich', unpublished MS. For the idea that workers did swallow Nazi propaganda see David Schoenbaum, *Hitler's Social Revolution* (London, 1967), Ch. 3.
131.   Ian Kershaw, 'The Working Class in Bavaria in the Third Reich', unpublished MS. delivered to the second session of the SSSRC Modern German Social History Research group, University of East Anglia, January 1979.
132.   Mason, 'Workers' Opposition'.
133.   On the unchanging nature of German social structure under the Nazis see Franz Neumann, *Behemoth* (New York, 1963).
134.   Kurt Klotzbach, *Gegen den Nationalsozialismus. Widerstand und Verfolgung in Dortmund 1930-1945* (Hanover, 1969); Hans-Josef Steinberg, *Widerstand und Verfolgung in Essen 1933-1945* (Hanover, 1969).

5 CONCLUSION

We have come a long way from the educational societies of London artisans in the early nineteenth century to the defeat of anarchists and Communists in Italy, Germany and Spain between the two world wars. Until 1914 the organised labour movement of Europe was composed overwhelmingly of skilled workers, some with limited horizons and some of a more generous vision. Shortly before that date, however, and increasingly thereafter, labour protest assumed massive dimensions and came to embrace very different kinds of workers in huge factories and new industries. This gain also had its drawbacks: semi-skilled and unskilled workers were to prove highly volatile in their behaviour and often antagonistic to the old institutions of labour, which, even where they had possessed revolutionary ambitions, also adopted a more serene aspect. Such divisions and their concretisation in different political factions proved a major factor in labour's almost universal inability to create the socialist society, to which at least some sections of the European working class aspired, and an even more dangerous liability in the face of Fascism.

Division and diversity were not exclusive to the inter-war period. As we have seen, in fact, they were central to the working-class experience from 1800 to 1939. There were differences between national labour movements and differences within them, differences between skilled and unskilled workers, between workers of different occupations, between anarchists and socialists, between Social Democrats and Communists, revolutionaries and reformists. Such divisions had multiple causes: divergent economic interests, different ideological perspectives, the differing attitudes of the state and the employers in different places. In fact these last factors assume perhaps an additional and crucial importance: more often than not the shape of labour protest was determined by the role of those outside the movement. Repression stimulated working-class radicalism; whilst political relaxation and structures of free collective bargaining encouraged reformism. Once again, however, this revolutionary/reformist dichotomy is too simple and too misleading. The same workers could be reformist at one moment and radical very soon thereafter, as the upheavals at the end of the First World War show. Workers could change their attitudes in the light of success or defeat; or even as they grew older and gained new responsibilities. Thus the search for a universal structure of working-class opinion and action in all places and at all times may conceal more than it reveals. What is quite clear, however, is that working-class protest cannot be explained in any direct and simplistic way by reference to poverty and misery in themselves. Expectations played a crucial role, as did the actual ability to do something about one's problems: this was precisely why it was not the most impoverished who ever formed the backbone of labour protest in this whole period.

Outside Russia labour nowhere succeeded in realising the dreams of socialism; whilst even there the exigencies of economic growth in a primarily peasant society entailed sacrifices of a huge order and saw the destruction of independent labour institutions by the Bolshevik party. Indeed, for some the bureaucratic structures of the Stalinist state, its exploitation of labour as a commodity and its domination of society through a terroristic apparatus gave witness of either a *deformed* socialist revolution or even 'state capitalism'. In advanced industrial Europe revolutionary socialism had nothing to record but failure. But it must be stressed that this is only part of a much more complicated truth. For the strikes of working men, their organisation into political parties and trade unions and even their insurrections in some countries at the end of the First World War did lead to massive changes in state policy, by no means all of which were repressive. In many places employers recognised the necessity of some form of machinery of negotiation with their employees, although there was still widespread resistance to this in Continental Europe before 1939. In most European countries working-class action brought about an improvement in living standards and a shorter working day. In some countries council housing came to be provided and various social welfare reforms introduced to mitigate the hardships of accident, sickness and unemployment. Perhaps the most famous example of this took place in Sweden in the 1930s, where a homogeneous socialist government introduced a national health service, maternity benefits, increased pensions and a shorter working week.

This is not meant to say that the original dream of social equality had been recognised, nor that the structures of capitalist exploitation had been overthrown. Workers still had to sell their labour power to employers, who still possessed the rights of hiring and firing, and were still subject to the vicissitudes of the business cycle. Nowhere was working-class existence secure and free from worry before the Second World War. But the origins of the welfare state, perhaps our most important legacy from this period, were a testament to the struggles of ordinary workers. What the destruction of the unions and parties of labour meant can be judged from the horrors of the Fascist state.

BIBLIOGRAPHICAL NOTES*

There are innumerable histories of the development of socialist theories in Europe, some of which have stood the test of time rather well. This is particularly so of the work of G.D.H. Cole (*History of Socialist Thought*, several vols., London, 1956) and of the more recent writings of the late George Lichtheim (*Marxism. A Historical and Critical Study*, London, 1964; *The Origins of Socialism*, London, 1968; and *A Short History of Socialism*, London, 1970). Sadly there is no international study of European labour protest of the same calibre, though there are several works on the formal international organisations of the socialist movement, such as the Second and Third Internationals. See, for example, James Joll's *The Second International* (London, 1955) and Julius Braunthal's *History of the International* (London, 1967). An exception is the stimulating work of Charles, Louise and Richard Tilly, *The Rebellious Century* (London, 1975), which attempts to locate the sources of popular protest, especially of the violent variety, between 1830 and 1930, using a mass of statistical data. What the book does demonstrate is the inadequacy of models of protest based on poverty and uprooting, as do a plethora of articles by the same individuals (see notes) and the massive study of French strikes by Charles Tilly and Edward Shorter: *Strikes in France 1830-1968* (Cambridge, 1974). Through the multi-variable analysis of patterns of violence and strike action the Tillys also reject those explanations which tend to omit politics and stress the economistic motivation of working-class action. This brings them into conflict with another American historian, whose combined output has made a major contribution to European history: Peter Stearns (*European Society in Upheaval*, London, 1967; *The Revolutions of 1848*, London, 1974; *Revolutionary Syndicalism and French Labour*, New Brunswick, 1971; *Lives of Labour. Work in a Maturing Industrial Society*, London, 1975). His work, especially the last title, is

* Readers wishing for a more comprehensive bibliography should consult the chapter footnotes.

182

rare in its attempt to understand labour protest 'from below', as it were, in several different countries and is invariably stimulating, if not convincing. The stress on the limited horizons of labour has come under attack, as we have seen. Even more problematic is Stearns' commitment to a form of modernisation theory, a belief in labour's gradual and rational adjustment to the new industrial order. But to have any attempt to deal with labour across national boundaries is valuable, especially where the emphasis does not fall exclusively on formal organisations.

There is one other historian whose attempts to answer complex historical and moral questions have led him into work on the grandest scale: Barrington Moore Jr. His *Injustice. The Social Bases of Obedience and Revolt* (White Plains, NY, 1978) embraces historical, anthropological and psychological investigation to explain why certain groups of people sometimes revolt against oppressive circumstance. It is breathtaking in both its ambition and achievements, although of necessity it becomes more problematic, the more it focuses on particular historical issues. The account of German industrial and political militancy which occurs in *Injustice*, for example, is relatively weak on shop-floor problems. However, this perhaps highlights the difficulty of keeping abreast of the massive international output of detailed monographic works on European labour history. The easiest way to do this and certainly the most profitable is to consult a number of journals which regularly devote space to articles on European labour history, in particular *Archiv für Sozialgeschichte, Geschichte und Gesellschaft, Annales, Mouvement Social, International Review of Social History, Journal of Social History, Past and Present, Social History* and the *European Studies Review*.

Obviously one is much better served by the literature when one turns to the study of national labour and socialist movements. However, in the case of most European countries the majority of work has concerned itself with the institutions of labour (parties and trade unions) rather than the grass roots of protest. Thus there is no shortage of works on the German Social Democratic Party (Carl E. Schorske, *German Social Democracy*, Cambridge, Mass., 1955; Guenther Roth, *Social Democrats in Imperial Germany*, Totowa, NJ, 1963; Dieter Groh, *Negative Integration und revolutionärer Attentismus*, Frankfurt am Main, 1973) or the KPD (Ossip K. Flechtheim, *Die KPD in der Weimarer Republik*, Frankfurt am Main, 1971; Hermann Weber, *Die Wandlung des deutschen Kommunismus*, Frankfurt am Main, 1969). Nor of the PCI (Paolo Spriano, *Storia del Partito Communista Italiano*, Turin, 1967), nor of the PCF (Annie Kriegel, *Aux Origines du Communisme Français*, Paris, 1964; Robert Wohl, *French Communism in the Making*, Stanford, 1966;

Ronald Tiersky, *French Communism, 1920-1972*, Columbia, 1976). The Russian socialist movement has received similar treatment in, for example, Alan Wildman's *The Making of a Workers' Revolution. Russian Social Democracy, 1891-1903* (Chicago, 1967), Franco Venturi, *Roots of Revolution. A History of the Populist and Socialist Movements in Nineteenth Century Russia* (London, 1960) and J.L.H. Keep, *The Rise of Social Democracy in Russia* (Oxford, 1966). Britain too possesses an even more massive literature on the history of the Labour Party (Henry Pelling, *Origins of the Labour Party*, Oxford, 1965) and on trade unions (Henry Pelling, *History of British Trade Unionism*, London, 1966; A.E. Musson, *British Trades Unions, 1800-1875*, London, 1972). Trade unions are fairly well served in France (Georges Lefranc, *Histoire du Mouvement Syndical Français*, Paris, 1937; Paul Louis, *Le Mouvement Syndical en France*, Paris, 1947; Jean Reynaud, *Les Syndicats en France*, Paris, 1963), as they are too in Germany (H. Varain, *Freie Gewerkschaften, Sozialdemokratie und Staat*, Düsseldorf, 1956).

Although some of these works are more or less exclusively concerned with the formal organisations of labour and the policies of leadership, the better amongst them do attempt to give some account of the rank and file and problems of social composition. Few do this to the same extent, however, as Claude Willard's magnificent study of the French Guesdistes (*Les Guesdistes*, Paris, 1965), which engages in a systematic analysis of the regional and social composition of support for that movement. There are also, of course, many works which approach certain aspects of working-class history through biographies of its leading figures. Although such an approach has obvious limitations, the better works of this genre often provide a great deal of insight into the workings of the labour movement and socialist parties. See, for example, J.P. Nettl, *Rosa Luxemburg* (Oxford, 1966), Harvey Goldberg, *The Life of Jean Jaurès* (Madison, Wis., 1962), C. Tsuzuki, *H.M. Hyndman and British Socialism* (Oxford, 1961), Isaac Deutscher, *Trotsky*, 3 vols. (London, 1959-67), Adam B. Ulam, *Lenin and the Bolsheviks* (London, 1969) and Israel Getzler, *Martov* (Melbourne, 1967).

There have been several attempts to write national histories of labour movements incorporating both political and trade union organisations. Amongst the most useful are David Kynaston, *King Labour* (London, 1976), Hedwig Wachenheim, *Geschichte der deutschen Arbeiterbewegung* (Cologne, 1967), Helga Grebing, *The History of the German Labour Movement* (London, 1969), Dieter Fricke, *Zur Organisation und Tätigkeit der deutschen Arbeiterbewegung* (Leipzig, 1962), Edouard Dolléans, *Histoire du Mouvement Ouvrier*, 3 vols. (Paris, 1936-47),

Bernard Moss, *The Origins of the French Labour Movement* (Berkeley, 1976), Guiliano Procacci, *La lotta di classe in Italia agli inizi del secolo xx* (Rome, 1972) and Gerald Brenan, *The Spanish Labyrinth* (Cambridge, 1962). In some cases, as in the books of Moss and Procacci, for example, these do involve extensive investigation of the grass roots of labour protest. However, at the level of the grass roots it is the literature on the British labour movement which has by far the most to offer, including E.P. Thompson's unrivalled *The Making of the English Working Class* (London, 1978), Malcolm Thomis, *The Town Labourer and the Industrial Revolution* (London, 1974), John Foster, *Class Conflict in the Industrial Revolution* (London, 1974) and the seminal essays of Eric Hobsbawm in *Labouring Men* (London, 1964). These last are important both in their general conclusions and in an approach which often focuses on specific sections of the work-force to understand labour organisation and protest.

There can be no doubt that some of the most fruitful historical research has stemmed from such an analysis of specific occupational groups and their organisations, though Continental scholarship has a long way to go to catch up. For Britain see, in addition to Hobsbawm, R. Page Arnot, *South Wales Miners* (London, 1967), James B. Jefferys, *The Story of the Engineers* (London, 1946), H.A. Turner, *Trade Union Growth, Structure and Policy: a Comparative Study of the Cotton Unions* (London, 1962). In France such an approach has dealt very successfully with glass workers (Joan Wallach Scott, *The Glassworkers of Carmaux*, Cambridge, Mass., 1974) and in Germany Ruhr miners have been the subject of an exhaustive investigation (Klaus Tenfelde, *Sozialgeschichte der Bergarbeiterschaft an der Ruhr im 19. Jahrhundert*, Bonn-Bad Godesberg, 1977). Other occupational studies include R. Trempé, *Les Mineurs de Carmaux* (Paris, 1971), Fritz Opel, *Der Deutsche Metallarbeiterverband* (Hanover, 1962), D. Geary, 'Radicalism and the German Worker: Metalworkers and Revolution' in R.J. Evans (ed.) *Society and Politics in Wilhelmine Germany* (London, 1978), George Sayers Bain, *The Growth of White-Collar Unionism* (Oxford, 1972), Robert J. Bezucha, 'The *Canuts* of Lyons' in Clive Emsley (ed.) *Conflict and Stability in Europe* (London, 1979), Jürgen Kocka, *Unternehmerverwaltung und Angestelltenschaft* (Stuttgart, 1969), Christopher H. Johnson, 'Economic Change and Artisan Discontent: the Tailor's History, 1800-1848' in Roger Price (ed.), *Revolution and Reaction. 1848 and the Second French Republic* (London, 1975).

As well as occupational studies, investigations of specific towns or regions have also made an enormous contribution to our understanding of the world of labour, especially as far as the British 'labour aristocracy' is concerned. In this context see Geoff Crossick's elegant study of Kentish London (*An Artisan Elite in Victorian Society: Kentish London, 1840-1880*, London, 1978), Iowerth Prothero on *Artisans and Politics in Early Nineteenth-century London* (London, 1979) and R.Q. Gray, *The Labour Aristocracy in Victorian Edinburgh* (Oxford, 1976). For other regional studies see D. Vasseur, *Les Débuts du Mouvement Ouvrier dans la Région de Belfort-Montbehard* (Paris, 1967), William Sewell, 'Social Change and the Rise of Working-class Politics in Nineteenth Century Marseilles' in *Past and Present* (1974), William M. Reddy, 'The Textile Trade and the Language of the Crowd at Rouen 1752-1871' in *Past and Present* (1977), Lawrence Schofer, *The Formation of a Modern Labour Force. Upper Silesia, 1865-1914* (Berkeley, 1975), Jürgen Tampke, *The Ruhr and Revolution* (London, 1979), Jürgen Reulecke, *Arbeiter an Rhein und Ruhr* (Wuppertal, 1974), Tony Judt, *Socialism in Provence, 1871-1914* (Cambridge, 1979) and Sydney Pollard, *A History of Labour in Sheffield* (Liverpool, 1959).

It is even possible to focus on not only the region or the occupation but the specific factory, as in the study of an engineering plant by Heilwig Schomerus (*Die Arbeiter der Maschinenfabrik Esslingen*, Stuttgart, 1977) or of a textile factory by Peter Borscheid (*Textilarbeitershaft in der Industrialisierung*, Stuttgart, 1978). Such studies provide a wealth of detail on occupational problems, income and other areas of daily existence for the worker which often run counter to more general statements. However, in these two works there is little attempt to link such discoveries to the development of labour protest and working-class consciousness. Such cannot be said of Rudolf Vetterli's brilliant investigation of the Georg Fischer concern at Schaffhausen in Switzerland, which concerns itself explicitly with the connections between occupational structure and industrial militancy within a single factory (*Industriearbeit, Arbeiterbewusstsein und gewerkschaftliche Organisation*, Göttingen, 1978).

Finally, in talking about the detailed analysis of labour protest at a local level, mention must be made of David Crew's *Town in the Ruhr. A Social History of Bochum, 1860-1914* (New York, 1979); for this book not only deals with labour protest in a way which is both detailed and sophisticated, but also locates it within the overall social structure of the town and thus is better able to comprehend the dynamics of social conflict and social change.

Not surprisingly, there is a vast literature devoted to the more spectacular episodes in European labour protest, as in the case of the

Spanish Civil War (see note 102 to Ch. 4), the German Revolution (note 122 to Ch. 3) and especially the Russian Revolution (note 3 to Ch. 4). In the last case most of the literature has been concerned with the activities and policies of the Bolshevik party and its leaders, although Marc Férro's *La Révolution de 1917*, 2 vols. (Paris, 1967-80) and J.M.L. Keep's *The Russian Revolution: a Study in Mass Mobilization* (Westfield, 1976) make some attempts to understand the nature and causes of grass-roots labour protest in revolutionary Russia. Other important episodes to have attracted significant attention are the British shop stewards' movement for workers' control at the end of the First World War (James Hinton, *The First Shop Stewards' Movement*, London, 1973), the occupation of factories in northern Italy in 1920 (Paolo Spriano, *L'occupazione della fabbriche*, Turin, 1964) and the civil war in the Ruhr in 1920 (George Eliasberg, *Der Ruhrkrieg*, Hanover, 1974). A major contribution to this last subject and to our understanding of working-class radicalism in general appears in Erhard Lucas, *Arbeiterradikalismus: Zwei Formen von Radikalismus in der deutschen Arbeiterbewegung* (Frankfurt am Main, 1976). This attempt to analyse different kinds of militancy deploys a wide range of investigative techniques and concerns itself not only with the role of political parties and trade unions, but occupational structure, residential patterns and the age and sex composition of urban populations. It is amongst the most convincing works on labour protest to have appeared so far.

INDEX